Histories and Historicities in Amazonia

Histories
and
Historicities
in
Amazonia

Edited by

NEIL L. WHITEHEAD

University of Nebraska Press

Lincoln and London

Library of Congress Cataloging-in-Publication Data
Histories and historicities in Amazonia / edited
by Neil L. Whitehead.
p. cm.
"Derives from a special session of the American
Society for Ethnohistory that was part of a series
of plenary sessions on global and local histories"
– Introd.
Includes bibliographical references and index.
ISBN 0-8032-4805-9 (cloth : alkaline paper) –
ISBN 0-8032-9817-x (paperback : alkaline paper)
1. Indians of South America – Amazon River Wa-
tershed – Historiography. 2. Indian cartography
– Amazon River Watershed. 3. Indigenous peoples
– Ecology – Amazon River Watershed. 4. Ethno-
history – Amazon River Watershed. 5. Oral tradition
– Amazon River Watershed. 6. Amazon River
Watershed – Colonization. I. Whitehead, Neil L.
F2519.1.A6 H57 2003 981'.100498—dc21 2002032241

Contents

INTRODUCTION

Neil L. Whitehead

This volume derives from a special session of the American Society for Ethnohistory that was part of a series of plenary sessions on global and local histories.[1] The results of that exchange of ideas are very much present in this volume, especially with regard to issues of globalization and modernity. At the same time, the papers collected here, two of which were not presented at that session, reflect the burgeoning of new scholarship on "history and historicity" in Amazonia.[2]

AMAZONIA IN EXTERNAL HISTORIOGRAPHIES

Amazonia is something of a last frontier for the study of history – the epitome of a place where we may yet find "people without history" – not least because the challenges of the tropical Amazon environment appear to have provided little opportunity for the elaboration of culture and society beyond the mere "tribal" level. This impression is further strengthened by superficial comparison with other regions of the Americas, and Amazonia is thus pictured as socially and culturally marginal, especially when compared to the better-known imperial worlds of Mexico and Peru.

This marginal historical status for Amazonia is no less true within the national histories of those countries that share the parts of the Amazonia region. For example, the recent special issue of the *Hispanic American Historical Review* (80:4) on "Brazilian Beginnings," issued in November 2000, actually contains no papers on Amazonia at all. In fact *Amazonia* is a relatively recent intellectual construct and so is quite literally still "being discovered." As such it has "no history" but exists in an eternal present of "first contacts" and "marvelous discovery." However, this lack of cultural significance and historical depth was an assumption even before the modern era, and historical writings about Amazonia from the 17th and 18th centuries are largely cast in terms of travelogues, ethnological inventories, tales of heroic evangelical redemption, or natural histories of the fauna and flora, in which the Natives figure only as an especially exotic form of savage, wildlife.

Moreover, when one contemplates the source materials that are fundamental to the writing of Amazonian histories, their titles alone often proclaim this absence and erasure of an internal indigenous history and the prevalence of external travel, discovery, evangelism, and natural description. For example, Claude d'Abbeville's *Histoire* (1614) is of the Capuchin missions, not of the people of Maragnan; Cristobal d'Acuna's "New Discovery" (1859) is of the river, not of its people; Samuel Fritz's *Journal* (1922) is of his travels and labors, while Ralegh's *Discoverie* (1997) is of Guiana, not the Guayanos, and so forth. This is not to suggest that the texts themselves ignore the Native population, only that they are largely the backdrop for the history of something else.

Certainly the idea of history, especially *ethnohistory* understood as history that principally refers to cultural others, was itself evolving in the European mind at this time, but the notion that the history of the indigenous people of Amazonia was either uninteresting or unknowable was able to take hold and continues to influence the idea of Amazonia in historical writing to the present day. Amazonian ethnohistory was uninteresting because there appeared to be few indications that the mighty states and empires that were encountered in the Andes had ever existed in Amazonia – there were no stone buildings and monuments, and the region seemed relatively sparsely populated to the commentators of the 17th and 18th centuries. At the same time the sheer scale and variety of the Amazonian environment, and its potential for development and wealth extraction, occluded interest in the customs and habits of what was seen as an indigenous population fated for extinction under the divine judgment of disease and the temporal chastisement of conquest.

It is only in the last decade or so that this view has been directly challenged, and we can now say that large-scale sociopolitical organization was present in Amazonia and that Amazonian cultures are of a deep antiquity. This occlusion of radical historical process in the colonial era results from the way in which the image of Amazonia as a wild and largely uninhabited zone of pristine nature, which emerged from 17th- and 18th-century European writings, actually reflected fundamental changes that had already occurred among those ancient Amerindian polities in the 16th century. In short, the hundred years between the first descent of the Amazon by Francisco de Orellana and the first ascent of the river by Pedro Texeira, in order to establish Portuguese control, was one of rapid and lasting change, as is evident when we compare the descriptions from those two journeys and their aftermath.

However, subsequent historical and ethnological accounts have tended to project the scene of disconnected and small-scale village polities that Texeira and his successors mostly encountered, right back to the 16th century and into the archaeological past. As a result, archaeological evidence of past complexity, historical accounts from the 16th century, and the lingering cultural forms encountered ethnographically were seen as being either unique or idiosyncratic – a remnant of some external influence from the Andes, or simply the wild imaginings of the tropically fevered brains of mal-educated *conquistadores*.

Undoubtedly the myth cycle of the Amazons, the often unsuccessful hunt for precious metals, and the problematic nature of early European writing on other cultures all contributed to this misperception. However, it is as much the challenge to our cultural preconceptions, offended by the thought of vigorous civilization growing in the steamy biomass of the jungle, as the actual evidence itself that has proved perhaps the key factor in producing past ideas of Amazonia and its peoples.

However, even if it is accepted that ethnohistory in Amazonia may be more interesting than had been assumed, there still lingers the notion that it may nonetheless be practically unknowable. The argument here is that the sources that we might use for the construction of Amazonian ethnohistories are so few and unsatisfactory that we might as well act as if the past were a given – a cyclical and perpetual repetition of fundamental social-cultural forms whose structures, rather than dynamics, are the only viable option for anthropological study. Certainly this kind of functionalist argument was made about many, if not all, "tribal" societies by most ethnographers until quite recently, but this fails to take into account two important considerations.

First, this neglects to consider that working with incomplete as well as socially and culturally biased materials is the condition of historiography for many other times and regions, including Europe itself. This has not inhibited, nor should it inhibit, the study of history and the attempt to develop more sophisticated interpretative strategies – for the simple reason that history has to be created; it does not wait to be discovered – it is a moral, not natural, discourse. Second, the argument does not consider that even if there is a critical cultural difference between Europeans and Amazonians, this difference does not render invalid the attempt to read others through the witings of their conquerors, though it does pose complex issues of hermeneutical approach. It is not enough to say simply that cultural bias in European writing on non-Europeans needs to be factored out, accounted for, or otherwise made overt – for this leaves us only with hollow texts and empty documents. Therefore, going along with this critical appreciation of the culturally dependent nature of historical and ethnographic representation, we must also consider Native social and cultural practices, particularly as expressed in Native discourse. In doing so we can immediately see that Amazon warriors, ferocious cannibals, and even El Dorado himself appear to be less the pure result of European cultural projection and as much an element in existing Native cosmologies and mythologies. The presence of analogous symbolic and discursive motifs in both Amazonian and non-Amazonian thought makes interpretation more difficult but simultaneously provides the hermeneutic strategy by which such histories may be written – for they are histories of the mutual, mimetic, and entangled relations of Amazonians and non-Amazonians over the last five hundred years. In this way Native cultural practice is itself an equally necessary and viable context for the interpretation and analysis of European texts (see Whitehead 1997).

Similarly, the question of the forms and limits that our knowledge of others may take cannot be assessed adequately by the critique of a few key colonial texts alone. We must at least address the full range of textual production that took place during European colonial expansion, for without this more tedious and lengthy exercise it becomes quite impossible to say what the relationship of European description to Native cultural practice may have been. This also means that the study of the kinds of textual production of the 17th and 18th centuries, referred to above, has to be complimented by study of the letters and reports produced by individual missionaries and colonial officials. In consequence, and again inhibiting a proper development of historical anthropology is the fact that this entails the kind of commitment to archival and literary analysis that many anthropologists and graduate students do not wish to undertake – not least because it tends to preclude ethnographic research, which is both challenging and time-consuming in different ways. By the same token, if ethnography can no longer be historically naive, then *ethnohistory* must also practice the ethnography of historical consciousness.

In general, anthropology has by now accepted that historical time and the meaning of the past are topics integral to the credible ethnographic study of other cultures and societies. This implies not just the study of textual or artifact sources but also the investigation of the social and cultural patterns and attitudes that give rise to those indigenous histories and history making. So, in this volume, we are not concerned with making arguments for the relevance of history that seems undeniable; rather, we are particularly interested in the investigation of the cultural schema and subjective attitudes that make the past meaningful, that is, to *historicities*. This distinction between history and historicity is also important to ethnographic and historiographical practices since a lack of appreciation of its significance has important consequences for how we do ethnography and the theoretical ambitions of anthropology more widely. *Historicity* thus encompasses *historiography*, which is the culturally particular methodology of how the past may be written or otherwise expressed.

By *history* is meant those culturally constructed texts, visual and aural representations, verbal narratives, and oral and somatic performances that are the discrete tales that make specific *histories*. History is not then a shorthand or cipher for "time," but the creation of time itself. By *historicities* is meant the cultural proclivities that lead to certain kinds of historical consciousness within which such histories are meaningful. For example, the coming of missionaries or other contacts with national society are invariably narrated within Amazonian histories, but the social role and cultural meaning of that narration is not uniform – it reflects both the historical experiences of a given group and the cultural significance of recalling the past. Thus multiple histories may occur from multiple historicities, but our record of histories has expanded much farther than our understanding of the historicities that create them, and this disjuncture in our understanding has produced a rather defective framework of analysis in anthropology.

This is shown by the way in which a general recognition of the relevance of the past to the present does not in itself automatically produce better understanding. In Amazonian anthropology in particular we need to synthesize certain kinds of conceptual opposition that (rightly or wrongly) have bedeviled our thinking, particularly the widely misunderstood distinction, originated by Lévi-Strauss, between "hot" and "cold" societies, but also the idea that history and time are equivalents, or that culture can suppress or render irrelevant the action of historical conditions. Given that the culture concept is so primary in anthropology, it is not surprising that the question should continually arise as to which is determinate – history or culture. But in asking such a question we have another example of those oppositions that seem to demand, and permit, an answer but in fact are only methods of categorizing the processes of human change and expression that we are trying to conceptualize. A view of history, one's historicity, and the stories (histories) that result are obviously culturally dependent, but culture itself is a historical product, so that even the denial of a given history results from cultural processes that are shaped through that denial. The means by which history may be denied or obliterated is, of course, a vitally important part of the study of others' historicities (see Cormier, in this volume; Oakdale 2001; Taylor 1993), but that it occurs is not proof of the irrelevance of history as a cultural or ethnographic fact – as Sahlins forcefully insists, the point of a historical anthropology is "not merely to know how events are ordered by culture, but how, in that process, the culture is reordered" (1981:8). The point here is that historicity itself is historical, as is the rest of culture.

Recent attempts to recover the relevance of the work of Lévi-Strauss argue that his treatment of myth is, in fact, deeply historical. Although Gow (2001:15) rightly criticizes some of the misplaced critiques of Lévi-Strauss's work, the notion that "myths obliterate time" or "give the illusion of timelessness" and "appearance of stability" is a very limited and inaccurate assessment of how "myth" really plays into a people's historicity. The peoples discussed in this volume are certainly not the victims of some "illusion" or evanescent "appearance" in their thinking about the past. The point so often missed by the conflation of "history" and "myth" in this way is that there is substantive cultural divergence over the nature of cause, time, and action in human affairs that entails the interpretation of that cultural difference, not its reduction to the dyadic formulas of structural linguistics. Current work in Amazonia (Taussig 1987, 1997; Vidal and Whitehead, in press; Wright 1998) and Africa (Comaroff and Comaroff 1993, 1998; Geschiere 1997) on the "modernity of witchcraft" or the emergence of "occult political economies" illustrates the absolute historicity of myth, ritual, and symbol in the dynamic contexts of modernity as well as colonialism. In any case, such arguments simply overstate the epistemological and ritual uniformity with which oral performance – the historical occasion for myth – is enacted and understood.

This was clearly demonstrated by Basso's (1995) discussion of Kalapalo historicity and has been underlined by other ethnographies of discursive practice, such as Graham's (1995) account of ideas of immortality among the Xavante or Hendricks's (1993) presentation of Shuar autobiography. Moreover, the notion of performance, so critical to appreciating the active manipulation of myth narratives in historical time, is not accessible to analysis in Lévi-Straussian style since, given the intellectual roots of structuralism in Saussurean linguistics, the formal properties of signs (semiosis) are conflated with their actual cultural usage (poesis), which is a matter of ethnographical and historical investigation.

It may be useful to organize our ethnographies of history and historicity in a way that provides a typology, but that typology refers to our ethnographies, not the historical practice of others. The varieties of Amazonian historicity, therefore, are a good starting point for a general discussion of these issues, and we might expect there to emerge, in view of the shared historical circumstances of colonial and neocolonial conquest, a basis for cross-cultural comparison of both Amazonian historicities and Western forms of history making.

In this light, the dark and vicious history of conquest becomes the very basis for understanding the historicity of others, for it is a shared history that has produced many mutual representations and that has made both cannibal savages and vampiric colonials prevalent and mimetic forms of representation. At the same time, the case studies in this collection show that such an interpenetration of historical representations across cultures also results in the production of white shamans and Native revolutionaries, suggesting that the processes of history making are inclusionary as well as exclusionary. The following case studies give substance to these more general and abstract ideas and suggest ways in which we can further explore and develop them.

Perhaps most clearly of all, the landscape emerges as a highly significant category for the sense of history and the construction of those histories. The first three chapters in particular consider that concept in relation to indigenous ideas of space, time, and their cartography. This is beautifully demonstrated in the chapter by Silvia M. Vidal, which is part of an impressive research program with the Arawakan groups of northwestern Amazonia. Vidal shows us that not only may geographic knowledge be encoded in a variety of ways but that such knowledge is a ritual form that directly influences the pattern of history and history making.

The "religion of Kuwaí" thus guides both understandings of history and how that history is written into and read from the landscape. Through time this has meant that such knowledge also has served as a vehicle for resisting colonial intrusion and for shaping land claims in the present. In short, colonial cartographies of indigenous space and identity are countered by Arawakan cartographies of their landscapes and the knowledge of their connection to far distant groups. This, as Vidal indicates, may be considered part of a general reevaluation of indigenous cartography and spatial conceptions, as well as an aspect of understanding the cultural nature of landscapes.

Other chapters in this volume likewise reflect that process of intellectual innovation, but they do so with a particular interest in how those landscapes affect historical sensibilities, or historicities. The chapter by Whitehead outlines a number of ways in which Patamuna landscapes contribute to and constitute their forms of historical consciousness. Trees, battle sites, caves, legendary creatures and spirits, petroglyphs, and ecological contrasts are all marshaled to create narratives of Patamuna emplacement in the Guyana highlands and to provide the correct rules for engagement with the landscape and its nonhuman occupants. Historical narratives also point to prophetic acts as the past is continually remade through the divination of the future, and the unseen world is made manifest through the sites and traces of its invisible actors, be that the abode of spirits or the marks of the ancestors inscribed in petroglyphs.

In turn, the chapter by Berta E. Pérez shows us the importance of landscape in the construction of both historical narrative and a historical sensibility but also as an intellectual and physical site for the contestation of political and economic power, just as the chapter by Nádia Farage casts issues of political struggle and economic advantage in terms of external contacts as much as internal social logics. This is not simply a matter of the possession of, or use-rights over, a geographical location, but a complex inclusion of spatial relationships, significant sites, and a continually re-created narrative of those relationships. This theme is also taken up by Domingo A. Medina, who clearly shows us that a legal title to land is not sufficient to ensure cultural survival, since how that landscape is used and how that landscape may be changed by the activities of others need to be recognized as factors that contribute to the way in which a sense of place produces a sense of identity, both ethnically and individually. As Pérez demonstrates, shared landscapes, where landscapes are understood as culturally produced interpretations of and rules for activity in environments, are a critical basis for ethnogenesis itself. Indeed, given the prevalence of theories of ethnic identity that cite their own emplacement in the landscape as the source of authenticity and continuity, it may be said that landscape has a particularly significant role to play in the creation and continuation of specific identities.

Given that landscape is constituted by memory as much as by ecological uses, then the question of how and who may be said to "own," "control," or "dominate" a landscape is not limited to use-rights in that environment. This can be seen by the way in which European cartographies anchor themselves in the landscape by reference to landmarks, sites, and features that are significant in Native cosmology and history. These features are a *genius loci*, the spirit of the place, which is then exorcized or used to legitimate external cartographies. In this way Western mapping becomes a means of historical disempowerment as it remakes aboriginal emplacement in the landscape by transculturating key symbols and physical contexts (see Burnett 2000).

Pérez also shows that there is a critical interpenetration of historicities across cultural contexts. In this way both the content and the form of history making do not occur without regard to the external world; rather, it is a mediation of that external world and the actions of others that appear as disjunctural within a given historical tradition. It has been amply demonstrated by recent work stemming from approaches based in discourse analysis and verbal art that a process of mimesis is fundamental to picturing processes of cultural contact, but such mimesis in the virtual world of representations does not adequately address the wider processes of social and cultural change in the actual world of history. Historical processes of change, articulated socially in the "tribal zone" (Ferguson and Whitehead 1999) and depicted discursively in a "contact zone" (Pratt 1992) of representational production, are also revealed in the episodic, transitory, and particular nature of sociocultural contact. Historical analysis thus explodes both the concepts of culture and society by reference to disjunctural and punctuated historical events that are the tokens of sociocultural change through time. This explosion of society and culture is experienced by the colonized as a need, and by the colonizer as a demand, for identity. The basis for sociocultural integrity and continuity is thereby persistently challenged by colonial and neocolonial appropriation of land, resources, and intellectual property.

This is clearly demonstrated in the paper by Domingo A. Medina, who, as well as showing us significant changes in the forms of Ye'kuana cartography, also addresses the responses of the Ye'kuana to encroachment by the Venezuelan state intent on development of their region. The production of maps and the textual transmission of traditional knowledge are both innovations for the Ye'kuana, but they are a well-judged response to attempts to exploit the Amazon region. Earlier histories by the Ye'kuana show no less an engagement with the external world, but their oral form suggests a more episodic encounter with the national state. The change from oral to textual forms of historiographical representation by the Ye'kuana thus signals an important disjuncture in historicity occasioned by the new challenge of globalized market forces and a predatory nation-state. If the Ye'kuana are to have any significant input into these processes, or if they are to divert them, they must therefore achieve the status of an ethnologically known and politically relevant "people" or "ethnic group" – in short, they must become a known feature in that "global ethnoscape" (Appadurai 1997) that is central to the political vista of the global economy.

In this way globalization, present in the drive by the Venezuelan state to produce commodities and raw materials from its Amazonian possessions for the world markets, requires an increasingly intense production of "histories," not just "identities" or claims to ethnic recognition, since it is histories that legitimate identities through a narration of their sources of authenticity and relative permanence. This was seen all too clearly in the vicious production of "Serb," "Croat," and "Kosovar" in the Balkans. Consequently, our ethnography of historicity cannot take that historicity as a cultural isolate – historicity is designed to mediate the disjunctural and so perforce is attuned to engagement with that which is understood as external.

The chapter by Nádia Farage also recognizes this feature of Native history and historicity and carefully lays out the background in Guyanese national society to the progressive transculturation of both the Wapishana and their colonial patrons, the Melville family. This mutual transculturation continued to the point that they became joint actors in a moment of armed rebellion and disassociation from the Guyanese state. Indeed, this moment is particularly revealing for the way that it shows how national borders, especially when weakly defined, can be a major factor in the constitution of historical consciousness involving this cultural convergence of histories and historicities. Just as we have had to learn the hard lesson as to the permeable and dynamic nature of *culture*, so we must in turn accept that the same is the case for histories and historicities. In Farage's chapter we see that the intrusion of external actors not only affects the Wapishana sense of history but also suggests a radical departure in their discursive practice. By having ethnographic access to the historical experience of an Amazonian society, Farage therefore can show how Western historicity causes profound misinterpretations of indigenous social practice and cultural performance. However, this is not the end of the story, for she also correctly suggests that this by no means precludes Native historicities that incorporate whites as meaningful cultural agents. As a corollary of this, she is also able to suggest that historical knowing is part of wider epistemology, requiring both a more subtle reading of indigenous historicity and also a clear appreciation of the epistemological origins of our own.

Issues of the cultural ways of knowing others are very much taken up in the chapter by Mary Riley, who expands our appreciation of how indigenous historicity may be quite directly linked to representation *for* others as well as *of* others. Riley explores Makushi representations of the past in the present and how they occur in cultural performances produced for Amerindian and non-Amerindian audiences alike. Riley also details the nature of Makushi historicity in the context of contemporary Guyana and gives us a wider sense of how representations of Amerindian identity are crucial to legal and political arguments for keeping Amerindians as a distinct legal ethnic group under the present Guyanese Constitution. The "cultural performances" she discusses, particularly those for public festivals, are carried out in accordance with these specific historicities, re-presenting and re-designing Guyanese Amerindian identity for non-Amerindian Guyanese as well as for an international audience that is interested in indigenous cultural preservation, environmental and biodiversity conservation, intellectual property, and human rights issues. Riley also reviews the contribution of cultural performances to the growing Amerindian (indigenous) rights movement in Guyana over the past decade.

Loretta Cormier continues and develops this theme of historicity as a means for recapturing and reinventing the meaning of the past, itself an effective form of political action in the present. Cormier argues that understanding that historical representation is a selective process and that cultural meanings are embedded in not only the events and personalities of a history but also in the process itself of remembering the past, its historicity. Cormier goes on to state that it is not only the content of the encounter with the historical other that should be understood, but also the form of that encounter. The Guajá people of eastern Amazonia thus "encounter the past" through the somatic experiences of dreaming and ritual visitation of the past, not the textual experience of reading. The Guajá past is viewed as an alternative spiritual realm, existing simultaneously with the present. Historical consciousness is therefore present in the landscape and revealed through the actions of spirit beings. It is also continually present in Guajá cultural practice or "ways of being," which through their enactment both perform and create the historical past. In this manner Guajá historicity is able to ritually transform the past and so can serve to change the meanings of acculturation and adaptation to national society in the present. This becomes a potent means to preserve a dynamic cultural identity that can respond and adapt to changing historical circumstance.

The chapters by Rafael Gassón and by Franz Scaramelli and Kay Tarble remind us that historicity is not limited to the horizon of events that are being actively circulated in narrative but, as part of the landscape, may appear to us as archaeological in nature. The archaeology of history is particularly important for the study of cultures that have left little if any textual evidence and again highlights the importance of being able to "read" a culturally made landscape as an alternative to the reading of documents and textual accounts. The landscape is like a text, but the tools with which its meaning becomes apparent have to include the methodologies of archaeology as much as cultural anthropology. The palimpsest that is left by the physical imprint of others' lives may be recovered through careful excavation, but its meaning can be appreciated only if such evidence is read in conjunction with ethnological and ethnographic materials (see also Whitehead 1997). These authors unfold for us a dynamic in the history of Orinocan groups that is not part of overt memory but that nonetheless substantively underpins the historical creation and continuity of sociality and difference. Gassón quite rightly makes the general point that there is a pressing intellectual need to integrate the data of archaeology with a critical interpretation of the documentary records and oral narratives. He shows us how earlier forms of historicity, expressed in genealogical idioms, were a key part of the performance of historical knowledge and meaning in the context of feasting. This construction of community through commensality then has its ultimate ritual expression in the physical consumption of chiefly bodies. To get at this rich and suggestive analysis, Gassón also uses the ethnographic record, reminding us that the past can be present without this implying a denial of "coevalness" (Fabian 1983).

Scaramelli and Tarble most elegantly take us into the later colonial period to show us how that complex of feasting, and its intimate connection to both the formation of identity and society, were consciously manipulated by colonial actors. The trade and exchange of *caña* (cane rum) is shown through the archaeological presence and prevalence of European ceramic forms in old village sites. Trading in *caña* by Venezuelan criollos and the missionary suppression of indigenous "fiestas" are part of the ethnohistorical information that Scaramelli and Tarble use to show us the processes by which these ceramic distributions were created. This process precisely illustrates the interpenetration of histories and the ways in which new aspects of material cultures were transformed according to extant ideas of commensality, but it also shows us how the circulation of new commodities fundamentally changed Native sociality. The colonial transformation of the Orinoco was not merely a matter of conquest and conversion but also the slow and formidable process of transculturation.

Taken together, then, these essays demonstrate the way in which ethnographic approaches to history and history making can reveal not just the important features of indigenous historicity but also the need for a better approach to the interpretation of ethnographic materials. The essays collected here clearly show that historicity is not an adjunct to cultural sensibility and practices but rather is constitutive of them. This means that ethnographic practice must be historicized, both as an aspect of the relation between the colonizer and indigene and as a dynamic factor in the development of indigenous historicity; the one is often mutually productive of the other. The ethnological categories of fifty years ago can therefore become the materials for an indigenous reimagining of themselves and the past, just as the presence of ethnographers becomes the occasion and means by which forms of indigenous historicity may be represented and expressed to the outside world. This interrelation between the ethnographer and the indigenous production of history is not, therefore, necessarily one of a contamination by the ethnographer of the historical vision of the indigene but is actually the precondition of its production in a form that is effective for its purposes – self-presentation on the stage of a global modernity. It is for these reasons that although we may encounter a mimetic production of historical representations, it is the transculturation of persons though such discursive and mimetic forms that makes historical change necessarily appear episodic, transitory, particular, and, therefore, disjunctural in the lives of actual individuals. For these reasons, too, attention to historicity forces the simultaneous contemplation of both the social and the cultural, and as a result it is properly anthropological in a way that the ethnology produced by an unhistoricized ethnography could never be. This is perhaps a subversive conclusion, but the evidence of the materials collected here certainly bears out that conclusion and suggests a new style of ethnographic engagement that better suits the world as it has come to be.

NOTES

1. Thanks are due to Marshall Sahlins for initiating and organizing those sessions and to the Wenner-Gren Foundation for funding the participation of colleagues from outside the United States. Thanks are also due to Manuela Carneiro da Cunha for co-organizing the Amazonia session.

2. The term *Amazonia* is used here as an ethnological category rather than a geographical one and so also makes reference to the peoples of the Orinoco drainage basin, which itself is connected to the Amazon drainage via the Casiquiare and those north-flowing rivers that empty into the Atlantic Ocean between the Orinoco and Amazon Rivers.

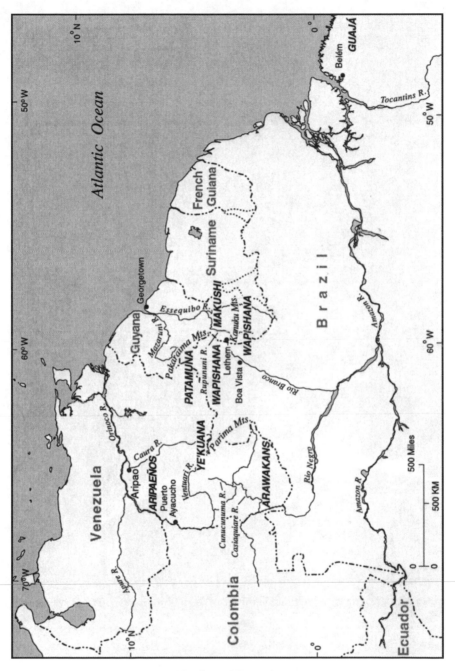

Northern Amazonia

Histories and Historicities in Amazonia

Landscape and Cartography

1

From Keeping It Oral to Writing to Mapping

The Kuyujani Legacy and the De'kuana Self-Demarcation Project

DOMINGO A. MEDINA

There is no question that what we call *globalization* is ultimately nothing more than an accelerated expansion of a process of world integration at different scales. This process is largely determined by a world order mainly shaped by Western ideology (beliefs, values, and lifestyles) and an economic system that originated in the political-economic relations of colonialism (Smith, Burke, and Ward 2000). Such an order is being constructed by overt and covert impositions on nations and localities, partly driven by technological advancement in telecommunications but also by economic models of development. This process may be observed in the integration of peripheral localities within particular cultural and social organizations into a homogenizing global structure and culture controlled by cores of political and economic power (e.g., multilateral financial institutions and corporations) by means of unequal socioeconomic relations.

The above paragraph, which might appear to be a formulation deriving from some contrived conspiracy theory, is nonetheless a reality for many peripheral populations, and specifically for indigenous peoples in many parts of the world. For these people, globalization represents a continuation and intensification of the process of colonization, which threatens their cultural survival and their possibilities for self-determination (i.e., control of their culture, history, land, knowledge, and future). Indeed, state-promoted globalization – in the form of "development" and "national defense" – has generated serious human rights issues and political/ecological conflicts resulting from social change and environmental degradation (Johnston 1994; Painter and Durham 1995) – conflicts that are also observed in the imposition of Western models of environmental conservation. Scholars, mainly anthropologists, geogra-

3

phers, and historians, have been concerned with the past and present linkages, interactions, and outcomes between global forces and localities. They have focused on the question of how Native or non-Western ethnic groups experience and interpret those forces, including the different forms of cultural responses they adopt (e.g., myth, oral history, or political activism).

For many indigenous groups the response to globalization comes in the forms of *adoption, resistance,* and *negotiation* with the dominant political-economic system in which they are immersed; any of these responses will always generate impacts, mostly detrimental, for these groups. This is not to say that these are the only forms of indigenous responses to globalization. Indeed, the issue is more complex when we consider the different levels of analysis from the local dynamics to the global context. Yet, the responses certainly fall within a continuum from total adoption to total resistance and along the continuum levels of negotiation that imply an interplay between keeping cultural control and social and cultural changes to articulate with the capital economic system and ideology.[1] Adoption – that is, the embrace of the Western system – is observed in Native groups whose political and historical processes have eroded their cultural basis, diminishing the capacity of the community to respond to the inevitable transformations of global pressures. By contrast, resistance in terms of migration, disobedience, hostility, or social movements grounded on strong traditional structures of social organization has proven somewhat effective against political-economic interests and internal conflicts caused by social change.

Finally, negotiation implies a proactive development by indigenous people of new cultural strategies to maintain cultural continuity vis-à-vis globalization that may or may not imply cultural changes. This essay describes such a case in the self-demarcation process of ancestral lands of the Ye'kuana people. It describes a social-religious and political movement of indigenous resistance and negotiation oriented toward securing lands rights and cultural survival, in which the power of myth and history is consciously used as a source of strength and guidance.

The Ye'kuana in Venezuela have had a long political struggle in securing land rights to protect their people and environment during a long history of neglected land recognition and the effects of the expansion of state and private promoted development schemes in Amazonas state. These schemes have come in the form of new official policies of land use and conservation strategies, illegal gold mining, and uncontrolled

4

tourism development (Arvelo-Jiménez and Conn 1995). Such history has brought internal fission, instability, and cultural and social changes that have threatened the Ye'kuana environmental resource relations and cultural sustainability. Since 1993 the Ye'kuana in the upper Orinoco have found new ways to empower their political agenda by engaging in a process of self-demarcation of their ancestral lands (approximately 22,300 square kilometers) reconstructed and grounded in their history and myth. This process is crystallizing a movement geared toward a pan-ethnic political cohesiveness that started in the 1970s but that lacked at the time a collective coordination beyond the autonomy of each Ye'kuana community. In this way the Ye'kuana have become the principal agents of change through a process that has allowed them to uphold political power by fostering social unity and strengthening their social and political institutions. In this way, they secure cultural control in the face of severe threats and pressure from outside regional and national interests. This essay describes this process, whose ultimate implications are yet to fully unfold.

I first provide a brief ethnographic and historical description of the Ye'kuana and subsequently underline their conception of their universe and landscape. This serves as a backdrop and context to the Ye'kuana-mapping project. Second, I describe the self-demarcation project, which is a result of the mobilization of De'kuana leaders and an analysis done by the De'kuana of their situation with respect to the Venezuelan state and society showing a consolidation of an emerging ethnic and historical consciousness. In addition, I focus on the legacy of the cultural hero Kuyujani, who is the mythical, religious, and historical base that oriented the project. Finally I provide a preliminary analysis of the self-demarcation as both a political strategy and a cultural response, and I draw some parallels with the Kayapó of central Brazil.

ETHNOGRAPHIC AND HISTORICAL SYNTHESIS OF THE YE'KUANA

The Ye'kuana (also known in the literature as Maquiritare) are mainly a Cariban-speaking group native to the lowland tropical forest in Venezuela. They inhabit an extensive region from the north bank of the upper Orinoco River to the upper regions of the Caura and Ventuari Rivers (see Figure 1.1).

Fig. 1.1. The Ye'kuana settlement area (Department of Anthropology
at the Venezuelan Institute of Scientific Research)

This region comprises large river systems, rapids, waterfalls, savannas, rainforests, and mountains with an altitudinal gradient from 27 to 2,900 meters above sea level. Politically the Ye'kuana communities are found in the states of Amazonas (along the Ventuari, Cunucunuma, Padamo, Cuntinamo, and Orinoco Rivers) and Bolívar (along the upper Erebato, upper Caura, and mid Paragua Rivers) representing 6 percent and 5 percent of the indigenous population, respectively. Some small Ye'kuana groups are also found in the state of Apure and in Brazil. By 1992 the Ye'kuana population was about 4,472 people scattered among 59 communities (37 in Amazonas and 22 in Bolívar), 31 composed of Ye'kuana exclusively and the remaining communities made up of other ethnic groups as well (OCEI 1994). It is a population with an annual growth rate of 4.7 percent and a doubling time of 15 years (Mansutti 1993), as it recuperates from its demise during the rubber boom in the Amazonas.[2]

The Ye'kuana have been categorized into four groups, the Ye'kuana, De'kuana, Ihuruana, and Kunuana, defined not only by linguistic variation due to their geographical separation but also by the mytho-historic significance for the Ye'kuana (Guss 1989). Today only two terms are in use. The term *Ye'kuana* refers to the whole ethnic group but specifically to the people that inhabit the upper Caura and Ventuari region. The term *Ihuruana* refers to those "headwater people" living in the sacred and original land of *Ihuruña*, where the "authentic" Ye'kuana come from. This land corresponds to the headwaters of the upper Caura and Ventuari and of the Cunucunuma, Padamo, and Cuntinamo Rivers. Yet these people refer to themselves as De'kuana. Likewise those who settled down river along the Cunucunuma, Padamo, and Cuntinamo Rivers and headwaters of the Alto-Orinoco refer to themselves as De'kuana. They argue they are descendants of the "authentic" De'kuana who were created by Wanadi in De'kuanajödö in the third cycle of origin. They are the people who migrated down river from Kamasowoiche in Ihuruña, the original savanna from which the first Ye'kuana departed (Guss 1989). For Koch-Grünberg the Kunuana were the people of the Cunucunuma, Padamo, and Orinoco Rivers. Yet if this term was ever used, today it has lost its use.

This essay refers to the self-demarcation movement of the De'kuana, who reside in 15 villages in the upper Orinoco, and who in the 1992 census totaled 1,591 inhabitants, representing approximately 35.5 percent of the Ye'kuana population.[3] This group has a population density of 0.07 inhabitants per square kilometer, which is below the parameter for the Alto-Orinoco Biosphere Reserve. The density for the latter is 0.08 but

7

concentrated in 88,715 square kilometers (Perera, 1995). Compared to the total Ye'kuana population, the De'kuana have a greater growth rate of 9.5 percent per year and a doubling time of 7.3 years.

At the time of contact, the Ye'kuana already were settled in the lowland forests of Guayana, extensively exploiting interfluvial areas in rainforest zones. A model of Carib expansion that tries to bring together linguistic, archaeological, ethnological, and ethnohistorical evidence suggests that probably the Ye'kuana were dispersing along with other groups in the interior of the Venezuelan Amazon between 800 B.C. and A.D. 500, slowly pushing away Arawak groups who preceded them (Tarble 1985). This expansion was in a gradual and nonlinear mode due to scattered resources that required adaptive strategies such as small, dispersed settlements, decentralized political organization, and persuasive local leaders. Also, it required a subsistence economy based on cultivation of *yuca* and other roots and the practice of fishing, hunting, and gathering. Likewise, it included commercial activities and interethnic relations with neighboring groups (Coppens 1981; Tarble 1985; Wilbert 1972) within the "System of Orinoco Regional Interdependence" (Arvelo-Jiménez and Biord 1994).[4]

Traditionally the Ye'kuana have settled in relatively small villages organized in a communal round house (*ättä*), which in its early stages of formation holds a minimum of two extended families. In a mature stage, the house holds four extended families that can total between 60 to 80 people (Arvelo-Jiménez 1974). By 1992, of the 15 De'kuana villages, 7 villages displayed traditional patterns of settlement (16.8 percent of the population), especially the headwater villages. Four of these villages were in the formative stage and 3 in the mature stage. The other 8 villages (82.9 percent of the population) surpassed the traditional pattern (by containing more than 80 inhabitants) and are concentrated in large population centers along the mid and low sections of the rivers, where they have greater contact with the Venezuelan society and outsiders. In fact, the settlements along the Orinoco (Tama Tama and La Esmeralda) have the largest population growth rates of all the villages. This is due not only to De'kuana residents but also to the settlement of other ethnic groups and non-indigenous groups.

The social structure of the Ye'kuana is bilateral, with a tendency to keep an endogamous kin group and matrilocal residency (for a thorough analysis see Arvelo-Jiménez 1974).[5] Each extended family is an autonomous unit of production and consumption that at times of special occasions unites efforts with the rest of the families that compose a village. This is observed in activities such as the formation of a new village, the construction of a communal house, or the slashing of forest areas for *conucos*, or shifting cultivation plots (Morales and Arvelo-Jiménez 1981). The political structure of the Ye'kuana – which is still very much in place – is decentralized, with the power divided among elder members who represent each extended family and together form a *círculo de ancianos* (elders circle). This circle elects the maximum authority of the village, the *adaja*. The division of power impedes any monopoly of the *adaja* that could result in the emergence of a stratified centralized political power (Arvelo-Jiménez 1973; Morales and Arvelo-Jiménez 1981). A shared history and cosmology transmitted orally, a common language, matrimony alliances with members of different villages, mutual ritual services, and even commercial exchanges are key mechanisms that in the absence of a centralized government unite the Ye'kuana people and provide them with a sense of ethnic identity (Morales and Arvelo-Jiménez 1981).

BRIEF HISTORY: GLOBAL FORCES AND LOCAL RESPONSES

The Ye'kuana probably had their first outside contact in 1744 with the Spanish Jesuit Manuel Roman, who traveled up the Orinoco to confirm Indian enslavement by the Portuguese. Yet the first incursion into Ye'kuana territory was conducted by Francisco Fernández Bobadilla in 1759 as part of the frontier commission searching for the headwaters of the Orinoco where the Parimé lagoon and El Dorado were believed to be located (Civrieux 1992). Commercial relations with Spaniards followed in the mid-18th century but lasted only 17 years (1759–1776). The Spaniards offered protection against slave traders, both the Carib (Kariñas) allies of the Dutch and from the Portuguese in exchange for their alliance and such goods as *cacao* (Gonzalez del Campo 1984).[6] When the Spanish Crown wanted more military presence and colonization in the region to protect the frontier against the advancement of the Portuguese and the Dutch, friendly relations turned into forced resettlement, Franciscan mission activities, and maltreatment of the Ye'kuana population. The presence of the Spaniards ended when several Ye'kuana settlements and other indigenous groups united to destroy 19 military posts that connected La Esmeralda with the capital of Guayana, Angostura, and killed almost all the Spaniards (Tavera Acosta 1954; Civrieux 1992; Guss 1989).[7] The significance and impact of this contact is recorded in the Watunna, which recontextualizes these events and incorporates them

9

into the Ye'kuana narrative structure and cosmology.[8] In this way it explains the antagonistic behavior of the Iaranavi and the Fañuru, which is the result of the eternal conflict between Wanadi and Odosha (Guss 1986).[9] In the Watunna, the defeat over the Spaniards is attributed to the undoing of Mahaiwadi, a powerful shaman from the Arahame River protecting the tribe against the aggression of the Odoshankomo.[10] After this first experience, years followed of periodic contact and trade with European (as far as Demerara, Berbice, and the rest of Dutch Guiana) and criollo merchants and explorers within and outside Ye'kuana territory. This brought marked changes in the Ye'kuana lifestyle, settlement patterns, house construction, economy, religion, and political cohesiveness (Arvelo-Jiménez and Conn 1995).

Ye'kuana ethnohistory is marked by Ye'kuana-Sanema (Yanomami group) interethnic relations and by the period of the rubber boom. For more than a hundred years the Ye'kuana kept interethnic relations and conflict with Sanema groups who up to the early 20th century were pushing north and east from the south in the Sierra Parima on territory previously settled by the Ye'kuana. This forced the migration of Ye'kuana semi-permanent settlements northward, temporarily altering some of their habits and social organization to avoid open confrontation (Arvelo-Jiménez 1973). Yet by the 1930s, the pressure forced the affected Ye'kuana communities to unite forces under the leadership of the *capitán* Kalomera to carry on several attacks overriding the Sanema (also known as Guaharibos) with their military superiority (Gheerbrant 1952; Colchester 1997).

The rubber boom beginning in the mid-19th century marked a time of economic opportunities for some Ye'kuana who settled in mixed temporary villages to take advantage of the boom.[11] However, it was also a time of the exploitation of cheap indigenous labor (particularly Ye'kuana), introduction of new diseases, the demise of indigenous groups, and widespread sorcery (Arvelo-Jiménez 1973; Jiménez and Perozo 1994). This occurred especially between 1913 and 1921 when Tomas Funes took by force San Fernando de Atabapo and controlled the civil and military power of the territory as well as its resource extraction economy based on indigenous debt and patron relations and slave labor (Gómez-Picón 1953; Arvelo-Jiménez 1973; Bros et al. n.d.; Coppens 1981). Funes made many incursions and raids into the Ye'kuana territory looking for workers, killing many, and forcing resettlements and fragmentation of villages whose members searched for refuge in the hinterlands and outside of the traditional territory following the same defensive strategy as with the Yanomami (Arvelo-Jiménez 1973; Bros et al. n.d.; Barandiaran 1986).

Both Catholic and evangelic missions have been instrumental in generating acculturation processes among the Ye'kuana. The Catholic mission started operating in 1936 following the mission law that granted them the responsibility to reduce, civilize, and integrate indigenous people into the national life. The evangelical missionary activities of the New Tribe missions in Amazonas started in 1946. The New Tribe extended their activities to Ye'kuana, Piaroa, and Yanomami territory such as in Culebra (Belen) and Caño Platanal in 1947, San Juan de Manapiare in 1949, the Ventuari and Ocamo Rivers in 1950, and Akanaña in 1956 (Luzardo 1988). Catholic mission activities were stressed in 1959 in upper Erebato with the foundation of the mission town of Santa Maria de Erebato. Missionary evangelism brought divisions and fusion of settlements as well as migration down river and concentration in population centers, breaking the traditional settlement patterns. Furthermore, it brought different paces of acculturation while breaking the Ye'kuana political and social life and territory into political regions, influenced by ideas of Catholic modernity and by evangelical fundamentalism generating significant religious conflict between them (Arvelo-Jiménez and Conn 1995; Coppens 1981; Jiménez 1974).

Ethnic awareness was starting to emerge during this period, especially among the few bilingual Ye'kuana leaders who understood the political-economic interests of their lands. In 1969 the Ye'kuana territory in the Cacuri savanna in the region of the upper Ventuari River was invaded with major repercussions for the social life and political structure of the Ye'kuana society. This resulted in internal migrations and the formation of new settlements with heterogeneous sociopolitical structures (for a detailed analysis, see Arvelo-Jiménez and Conn 1995; Coppens 1981). In 1971 for the first time some Ye'kuana leaders mobilized in Caracas to denounce the illegal invasion of their territory and discuss the problem of land distribution for the indigenous communities. Since then there has been a clear intention among Ye'kuana leaders of becoming active agents in securing land titles and in controlling their development process. In the 1970s it became evident that the Ye'kuana had no place to hide nor to resettle and that they had to engage in a legal fight for their ancestral lands. At this time the Ye'kuana were still lacking an ethnic-wide political cohesiveness that could foster the process (Arvelo-Jiménez 1973).

The 1960 Agrarian Reform Law created many expectations but resulted only in the "peasant" classification of indigenous land fragmenting ethnic territories into small farming areas, and just provisional land titles were granted. By the 1970s the government launched CODESUR, a project for "the conquest of the south" of the country in an effort geared toward integrating the region with the rest of the country and to study its economic and development potential. Subsequently the Ye'kuana have also been affected by the conservation policies of the Venezuelan government. Between 1974 and 1978 the government set aside large extensions of land for parks and reserves in a questioned conservation policy (Arvelo-Jiménez 1982, 1989).[12] The Duida-Marahuaka National Park was created in 1978 overlapping the Ye'kuana territory.[13] However, it was not until 1993 that officials of the National Park Service visited the community of Culebra to inform and consult its members about the management plan and zoning.[14] The plan was already drafted without the Ye'kuana participation in the decision making, as if there were no human beings living and taking care of the land (Jiménez and Perozo 1994).[15] The creation of the park and its management plan proposes to delimit zones for the use of indigenous people (Zona Especial de Uso Tradicional Indígena) and settlement zones (Zona de Uso Poblacional Autóctono) (INPARQUES 1993). These zones fragment the Ye'kuana ancestral land and reduce the area of access to the land they are claiming. An extensive "primitive or wilderness zone" proposed for recreation, environmental education, and scientific research overlooks the existence of all the Ye'kuana communities in the eastern sector of their territory. This zoning, if imposed, will affect the Ye'kuana long-term sustainability and limit their capabilities to steward the land they have had access to and protected for generations. Similarly, in 1991 the Alto Orinoco-Casiquiare Biosphere Reserve was established also overlapping the Ye'kuana territory (including some communities that hold a small provisional land use title issued by the National Agrarian Institute) and incorporating the Duida-Marahuaka National Park within its boundaries.[16] Although the reserve was established with a more pro-indigenous view, both ABRAE (areas under special regimes of administration) are considered by the Ye'kuana to be "legal" invasions of their territory (Jiménez and Perozo 1994).

In 1993 the massacre of Yanomami by Brazilian *garimpeiros* in the village of Haximúon the border with Brazil made it clear to the Ye'kuana that reserves or parks such as the Yanomami park and the biosphere reserve are no guarantee for their sustainability (Albert 1994; Comissao

1993). Other perceived threats to the status of their territory are the illegal gold mining in the neighboring Yabarana National Park, government gold-mining concessions in the Imataca Forest Reserve in Bolívar State, and the creation of local government bureaucracies in Amazonas State.

The Ye'kuana were never dominated militarily and were always able to seek refuge in the hinterlands of their territory or migrate to other areas as a strategy against outsiders. However, other forms of domination have brought changes. Today the traditionally subsistence economy is very much in place between the Ye'kuana as well as being the basis of their social and political organization. Nonetheless the history of conflicting events since the emergence of the nation-state and leading to missionary evangelism, economic development schemes, conservation policies, and other expanding frontiers has resulted in the fragmentation and instability of the Ye'kuana people. Many Ye'kuana are now sedentary and concentrated in population centers exceeding traditional settlement patterns and depleting nearby resources in areas of already scarce resources. This coupled with acculturation processes, changing resource relations, dependency on outside services, and a steady integration into the market economy for outside resources is threatening the traditional lifestyle, the basic unit of reproduction of the Ye'kuana society, and their political autonomy that has allowed them to survive. All these changes have an explanation within the cosmology of the Ye'kuana people. Simeon Jimenez (1995), a De'kuana leader involved in fighting for the original rights of his people since the early 1970s, explains:

> My people the Ye'kuana believe that the social world is constantly changing and falls naturally into disorder and decomposition. Changes occur inevitably and steadily worsen everything, producing pain, anguish, and despair, but we never lose hope of renewal, for when chaos finally closes one of the cycles of change, it heralds the beginning of a time of renewed hope in a reborn world. So history is a result of the many cycles of life that arise, change, decompose, and destroy themselves only to be reborn. This belief was transmitted to us by our ancestors and reflects lessons learned through living so close to nature; it could be telling us that the peoples of Amazonia have always known that the world is changing and that each cycle demands answers consonant with the environmental conditions of the moment. (P. vii)

The Ye'kuana believe that they are living today in a third cycle of creation of the world that probably began about a thousand years ago. This world will imminently be destroyed only to see the emergence of a new cycle marked by the return of Wanadi through another *damodede* so to reunite Kahuña with the earth.[17] Again, these cycles are a result of the eternal power struggles between Wanadi and Odosha (Civrieux 1992; Guss 1986, 1989).

According to the Ye'kuana, the imminent destruction is reflected in the breakdown of true political leadership, the social instability of the Ye'kuana communities, and their changing environmental resource relations due to new ecological and economic conditions. Also, this destruction is reflected in the deterioration of the capacity of ethnic groups to complement interethnic relations and the advancement of the frontier of the dominant society, which is irrationally exploiting forest resources and pushing the Ye'kuana to marginal lands while bringing waves of new and old diseases into the region (Jiménez 1995). This frontier does not recognize boundaries nor understand the importance of the territorial base for indigenous people to fully develop their way of life. All this has accelerated the destruction of the forest resources and with them the Ye'kuana wisdom and knowledge (Jimenez 1995).

Despite the above situation, the Ye'kuana have been inspired by their history, religious beliefs, and myths in order to change the present situation and have control over their future (while waiting for the return of Wanadi in the fourth cycle of creation). This has set up a slow-paced but coherent reformist movement with an integrationist view, which has the objective of resolving their sociopolitical and socioeconomic problems. This is the basis of the needed ethnic-wide political cohesiveness that is being established through the self-demarcation project.

THE YE'KUANA UNDERSTANDING OF THEIR LANDSCAPE

Before describing the self-demarcation project it is important to discuss how the Ye'kuana conceive of their landscape. The landscape is socially and culturally constructed (Bender 1999). For indigenous societies it is central to the reconstruction of their ethnic space as it embeds the cosmology, myths, and history of the people as observed among the Andoque, Warekena, and Patamuna people (Espinosa Arango and Andoque 1999; Vidal and Whitehead, in this volume). Also, it is central to their sense of identity, feeling of belonging, and subsistence. This understanding comes from the study of spatial representations of indigenous people from architecture, crafts, celestial maps, and elicited maps and the inclusion of their spatial ideas into Western cartography (see Whitehead 1998 for a thorough analysis). In addition, it could be observed in the Native people's use of Western style cartography to represent their spatial ideas such as in the case of self-demarcation initiatives.

For the Ye'kuana there is no dissociation between nature and culture (Silva Monterrey 1997). The universe is structured by three overlapping parallel worlds: a superior world or heaven, an intermediary world or earth, and an inferior underground world (Barandiaran 1986).[18] The superior world has eight layers of increasing power and is where the cultural heroes such as Wanadi and the guardians and protectors of natural elements (i.e., water, fire, thunder) live. Life is eternal for its inhabitants and resembles earth in its features. Yet there are several suns, there are no clouds, rains or storms, and there are no nights. In addition, it is the world where you find the moon, stars, and constellations. The underground world, on the other hand, is composed of three planes: the underwater, the cave, and the damned worlds, each with particular features and powers.[19]

The intermediary world or earth is where humans, animals, and plants live. It is also where the active powers and the owners of both the living species and nonliving objects (i.e., mountains, water, and winds) coexist. This world goes through cycles of genesis and destruction and is where all the conflicting forces of good and evil mediate and influence humans and other beings. For instance, animals and plants that are socially organized have a counterpart or "owners" in an invisible supernatural world. Arvelo-Jiménez (1974) explains that in this world power between the forces is balanced. The Ye'kuana alter this balance when they hunt an animal or cut a tree. This can generate a reaction from the forces in the invisible world resulting in bad luck, illness, and even death. To avoid or mitigate this reaction, the Ye'kuana engage in ritual practices before utilizing resources such as when they open a new shifting cultivation area, gather material for a new house, and fish or hunt for food. On the earth, the Ye'kuana are engaged in a constant effort to counteract the negative supernatural forces. This requires the ability to practice rituals that follow cultural norms and that indicate instances of behavioral prohibitions.

The Ye'kuana notion of space and how they conceive the universe are represented through different means. The round communal house of the

Ye'kuana – the *ättä* – was first built by Attawanadi and models the universe, with its parts symbolizing the different divisions and linkages of the superior world and earth and creating a code of how the universe is understood and visualized (Arvelo-Jiménez 1974; Wilbert 1981). Likewise, elements of the cosmology have been worked into their body paintings and other arts and crafts (Guss 1989; Whitehead 1998).

The Ye'kuana's understanding of the universe mediates and regulates their relation with their environment (Silva Monterrey 1997). As discussed later, this understanding of the universe and the Ye'kuana's interaction with their environment have implications for the self-demarcation of their territory and probably for the decision to use Western cartography to map their ancestral lands.

THE SELF-DEMARCATION PROJECT

In 1993 after the tragedy of Haximúin the neighboring Yanomami territory, De'kuana leaders in Culebra asked themselves what would happen 10 to 15 years into the future and what they could do in the face of social instability, internal fragmentation, and outside pressure. Certainly the loss of their culture, ethnic identity, history, language, and territory was a matter for what Turner (1987) calls a conscious concern and concerted political actions (see Figure 1.2). The issue was how to build a concerted political action in the face of many obstacles such as the skepticism of a great part of the Ye'kuana population, who were in despair and tired of waiting (Jiménez and Perozo 1994).

The De'kuana realized that their self-demarcation project had to be grounded in the history of the village that is demarcating the land on which it acts because it is in the history of the village that the basis can be found to claim the land as theirs (Jiménez and Perozo 1994). The self-demarcation in this context is defined as an ethnic group initiative to delimit the boundaries of their ancestral land based on oral history and topograms.[20] This differs from demarcation processes of indigenous land driven by specifications of a government agency.

During the months of March, April, and May of 1993 community members from seven villages met in Culebra in the Cunucunuma to discuss the best way to protect their ancestral lands and agreed to delineate their boundaries and request its recognition by the government.[21] The meeting served to coordinate the self-demarcation of the land inspired by the legacy and mandate of *Kuyujani*. At this meeting the Ye'kuana

16

Fig. 1.2. Discussing and planning the self-demarcation of the De'kuana land in a meeting in Culebra (Otro Futuro Photographic Archives)

pointed out that they have already lost a great part of their sacred legacy, the land that *Kuyujani* demarcated and left to them for its protection. They argued that they needed to defend their territorial base, just as other religions respect and request that others respect their beliefs, churches, and places of worship (Jiménez and Perozo 1994). Furthermore, the Ye'kuana maintain: "There is no major transcendental basis other than the pacific, productive (quantity of cultigens produced for food for both indigenous and non-indigenous people), and conservationist occupation that we the Ye'kuana have made of the land that was left to us by Wanadi and Kuyujani for its custody. Now, since there is so much discussion about conservation and sustainable development, is when there is more reason for the Venezuelan state to remember our rights. Legally granting us the lands that we have occupied for centuries would be not only an act of justice but a warranty of sustainable development" (Jiménez and Perozo 1994:25; my translation).

The De'kuana decided to put in writing what was until then exclusively theirs through oral history. This marks a significant change from the time when the Ye'kuana preferred to keep their religious narratives and rituals in an oral format, restricting anybody from recording them as a way to protect them from losing their power (Guss 1986).[22] The writing of the

Kuyujani legacy became the basis for protecting the Ye'kuana culture and territorial base. In the book *Esperando a Kuyujani: Tierras, Leyes y Auto-demarcación*, the De'kuana explain where they come from, who their creator is, what their mission is in the land that their creator entrusted to them. The De'kuana felt obligated to reveal the most intimate details of their history because they were convinced that this history together with their land claims would legitimize their efforts. This became the "ethno-cultural basis of the De'kuana land claims." Jose Felix Turón, an elder historian, shaman, and *capitán* of Culebra, was responsible for writing the document while Simeón Jiménez, a De'kuana leader involved in fighting for their rights since the early 1970s, translated the sacred history into Spanish and provided a critical analysis of its content. At another meeting in Culebra the Ye'kuana approved the document, thus uniting for the first time the different religious factions and traditionalists in a common agenda, putting aside 30 years of religious discord, and focusing on the Ye'kuana identity and territory (Arvelo-Jiménez and Conn 1995).

THE KUYUJANI LEGACY: THE FIRST DEMARCATION OF THE YE'KUANA LAND

According to the Ye'kuana's origin, Wanadi (or Wanasedume) created the earth and made it inhabitable. Wanadi created the earth for the Ye'kuana to inhabit, to live on, to take care of, to feed themselves from, to enjoy its resources, and to die on. Wanadi said, "Take care of it, this is yours, do not destroy it" (Jiménez and Perozo 1994). Wanadi in his third visit or cycle of creation came down to earth from Kahuña in the form of a *damodede* called Attawanadi. Attawanadi created the first De'kuana from the mud of the sacred mountain De'kuanajüdü in the Ihuruña region. Attawanadi also is responsible for the creation of other people such as the Piaroa, the Macaw, the Yabarana, the Yanomami, and the Iaranavi, among others (Guss 1989). He gave land to this entire people so they could enjoy the land and live in harmony without conflict. Kuyujani carried on the mandate of demarcating the land for the Ye'kuana people,[23] as the oral history recalls:

> Kuyujani, leaving Ye'kuanajüdü to demarcate the land entrusted to us by Wanadi, was reached by Tunamö [flood] at Mount Anaicha, and to save his life and the lives of his people he had to find refuge in this mountain. Kuyujani initiated his journey from the Cuntinamo, where Ye'kuanajüdü is located. He continued down the Metacuni, down the Orinoco to Atabapo.

18

He passed Atures and the Cataniapo and reached its headwaters in Mount Anaicha. He later departed from here with his sisters Kaddesawa, Kuyunu, and Wadimena and the rest of his people and went toward Ye'kuanajüdü, crossing Mount Washadijüdü (Danto), the headwaters of the Ventuari, the Parima Sierra, and returned to Ye'kuanajüdü. It was a long walk, and once he returned, Kuyujani with all his people immersed into the innards of Mount Ye'kuana. He will return to live among us as he promised. This is our greatest prophecy. (P. 13; my translation)

The Iaranavi people broke the mandate – influenced by *Odosha* – by seeking to conquer and take over the Ye'kuana territory, thus altering the world order and bringing conflict and despair.

There are many versions of the Kuyujani legacy that vary somewhat according to the region within the De'kuana territory. In October 2000 the De'kuana mapping team had the opportunity to travel to Ihuruña, center of the Ye'kuana territory, the "headwater place," the place of origin of the De'kuana. Their purpose was not only to involve the communities in the mapping process but also to gather information about Kuyujani by interviewing the elders (perceived as authentic De'kuana) and taping their version. At this moment the story and legacy of Kuyujani is still being discussed among the De'kuana, and they are in the process of writing a version by consensus of the people involved in the demarcation. Yet this discussion has empowered the whole demarcation process, unifying the De'kuana people and legitimizing their claims.

The content of the Kuyujani legacy – as written so far – only underlines the route followed by Kuyujani and his people departing from Ye'kuanajödö, the mountain where Attawanadi formed the Ye'kuana in the third cycle of origin. The Kuyujani legacy does not create divergence given that he is an emissary of Wanadi the creator, and therefore the effect is to unite and consolidate the current generations of De'kuana. The journey of Kuyujani is full of symbols, stories, historical events, and religious meanings yet to be written. Yet the history is recorded or embedded in the landscape linking the De'kuana to their past, their myths, and their land. For many young De'kuana this is a process of discovery. Writing the Kuyujani legacy and mapping the territory help to transmit the legitimacy of their claims and reinforce the cultural boundaries of the De'kuana people, who continue their struggle for control of their culture and their land. It crystallizes the history, the language, and the space in a format that will allow future generations to continue revising, interpreting, analyzing, and rewriting their history.

THE SECOND SELF-DEMARCATION

Long before the De'kuana made the decision to map their territory for land rights claims, they had already shown their ability to produce a map of their territory. In a 1950 expedition to the upper Cunucunuma, geologist Marc de Civrieux sought the help of Dawásehúma – his local Kunuana guide – to draw a map of the poorly mapped territory, which was needed for scientific and geographical purposes (Civrieux 1957, 1959). Civrieux knew of indigenous geographical knowledge and the use of map sketches by indigenous groups in the Guyanas and Amazonas and was impressed by the instinctive understanding of indigenous mapmakers and the relative scales and accuracy of the maps. Dawásehúma provided much information in terms of toponymy and cartographic skills, enabling Civrieux to create an overview of the De'kuana territory that he named after Dawásehúma. The overview was used to check the discrepancies of former maps of sections of the territory such as those of Robert Schomburgk (1841) and Tate and Hitchcock (1930).

This knowledge and skills proved again to be useful for the self-demarcation of the De'kuana territory. Assisted by Otro Futuro – a Caracas-based nongovernmental organization (NGO) – and the Local Earth Observation Project (LEO) – a Canadian NGO – the De'kuana received funding from Canada's Assembly of First Nations (AFN), which was interested in mobilizing resources, to develop a methodology and help indigenous demarcation experiences. In 1994, a third meeting on self-demarcation took place in Culebra with 15 villages participating and with the assistance of Otro Futuro, LEO, and the AFN. The meeting focused on a discussion of the territorial base, which resulted in a hand-drawn map illustrating the principle features of the territory and its boundaries (see Figure 1.3). The map captured key features of ancestral territory such as mountains, major rivers and tributaries, settlements, and some sacred areas. On the map, essential features were targeted for demarcation (Jiménez and Perozo 1994).

Next the De'kuana discussed the methodology to follow, dividing internally the territory defined by each village to decentralize the demarcation effort (Jiménez and Perozo 1994). Human, financial, and material resources were assessed for the demarcation, and from here six teams were organized composed of 16 women and 16 men. The teams were to travel by foot to the selected features marked on the map, clearing trails connecting the villages to the perimeter points and then clearing circles

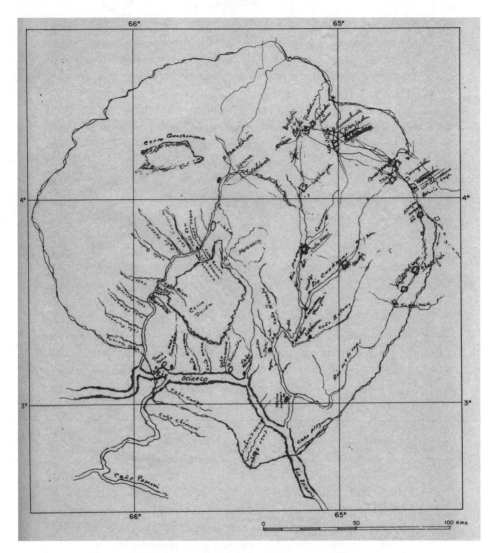

Fig. 1.3. De'kuana map of their land (Jimenez and Perozo 1994)

of 30 meters in diameter so Global Positioning System (GPS) points could be gathered. This task took two months to complete. It represents a supra village effort and involved internal mobilization and coordination of resources unparalleled in the recent history of the De'kuana. After this, LEO gathered the coordinates of each circle from a cessna 206 aircraft flying along the boundary territory. Later LEO developed a "technical map" (see Figure 1.4) from an official government base map (1:500,000 scale topographic map) and included the geo-referenced ground points that mark the boundary line of the Ye'kuana territory.

A third map is underway illustrating the Ye'kuana's resource base, land use, and cultural elements including the landmarks of Kuyujani's journey, sacred and historical sites. This third map has been a process of apprehending the Kuyujani legacy from their oral history, interpreting the mandate of Kuyujani, and then reading from the topograms and toponymy of their land to reconstruct their ethnic space. This has motivated the young leaders of the mapping team to learn the meaning of each feature of the landscape, interview the elders around the territory, corroborate information and different versions of the Kuyujani mandate, verify the chronology of events, and eventually reach a consensus to write a final version. It also is a process of mapping their environmental knowledge to demonstrate their capacity of land management (see Figure 1.5).

This process has created several spin-off effects resulting in local initiatives and development projects that address long-term community social, cultural, and economic needs (see Figure 1.6). One of these spin-offs is the De'kuana Atlas and Archive, which is a clear expression of cultural and political awareness similar to those efforts observed among the Shuar in the late 1970s. The Shuar were actively involved in helping collect their own myths and published their *Mitología Shuar* in both Shuar and Spanish with the hope that teaching the lore at home and in school would not only preserve their myths but also keep the vitality of their people (Bierhorst 1988). Another spin-off is a biodiversity conservation project to be funded by the Global Environmental Facility. For this the De'kuana have created a new organization to coordinate and manage the project. This organization, called Kuyujani Originario, is a supra village organization and comprises the 15 De'kuana communities. It is different from the traditional social and political organization but respects the political and economic autonomy of the traditional structures of each village. Finally, the demarcation project has inspired other Ye'kuana groups in the Caura region that have also demarcated their land supported by international

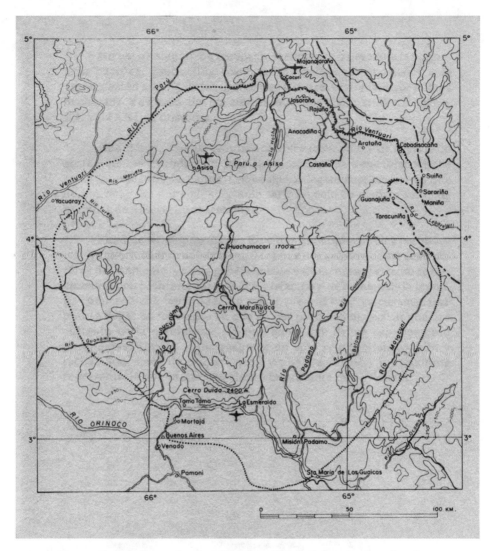

Fig. 1.4. Technical map developed by LEO of the De'kuana territory based on
the De'kuana information (From Jimenez and Perozo 1994)

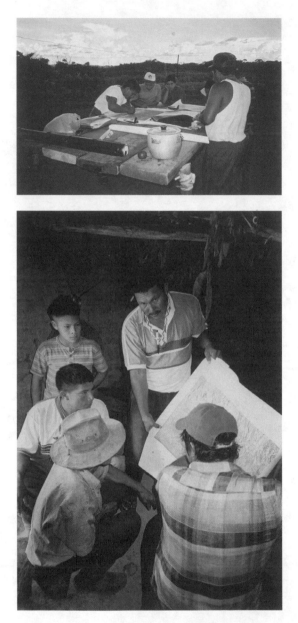

Fig. 1.5. (top of page) Mapping the east sector of the De'kuana territory in Adajameña in the sacred *Ihuruña* region (Photograph by Domingo Medina)

Fig. 1.6. (bottom) Members of the mapping team interviewing and consulting an elder leader in Konoiñamaña (Photograph by Domingo Medina) and national organizations such as the Rainforest Movement in England and the UNEG (University of Guayana) anthropology department at Ciudad Bolívar.

Ye'kuana oral history and ethnographic research have recorded conflicting events experienced by the Ye'kuana since first contact, including trade relations (e.g., cacao and rubber), missionary evangelization, interethnic relations and confrontation, interactions with explorers and researchers, and state-promoted development and conservation schemes. In each of these instances the Ye'kuana have responded through different behaviors or strategies such as retreating, fissioning of settlements, temporarily altering their social structure, organizing and uniting settlements in armed conflict, adopting Western ideology, keeping cultural elements in oral formats, and so on. The self-demarcation of their land, writing their legacy, and mapping their territory is the latest chapter in their long struggle for their original rights. The demarcation of the land can be considered the third historical instance recorded in which the Ye'kuana have mobilized resources and organized beyond the individual settlements to unite forces for resistance guided by a shaman or capitán.[24] The difference is that this last movement has not been through violent means but rather through a process that can be considered both an innovative political strategy and a creative cultural response.

Rather than just reacting or evading global pressure, the De'kuana are acting proactively by combining their mythical and historical consciousness with global resources (mapping technology and international funding) to build social unity and resist global threats. Mapping becomes a means to exercise cultural control using maps to represent their space, their historical and mythical linkages, and their knowledge and relation with their environment. The De'kuana expect land recognition and the inclusion for their information on official maps. Such an attempt will reflect, as Whitehead (1998) points out, a negotiation of power relationships whose results are yet to be seen and analyzed.

It can be said that the self-demarcation is a result of a process of cultural awareness and historical consciousness that started in the 1970s. This means that conditions were created that allowed for an awareness of their own society as a product of their own action in historical time and a realization that elements of the national society are subject to change by their own present or future actions (Turner 1987). In other words the De'kuana became active agents of their own history shaping their own future. This can partially explain why the De'kuana change from keeping their history and religious beliefs oral to writing down these beliefs to guide their cultural and political agenda and mapping their land. But why did the De'kuana decided to use Western cartographic technology to map their territory? For the De'kuana what is important is to be able to reconstruct their space legitimized by their oral history, not the material object of the map. Arvelo-Jiménez (2000) explains that the latter is important only because it is highly regarded by the dominant society and is a means to convey their message and for negotiation. An analysis consistent with De'kuana cosmology can be drawn from Magaña's (1993–1994) rationale on how indigenous peoples in the Guyanas interpret modes of expression such as the spoken words, silence, and the written words. Magaña argues that these forms of expression (e.g., silence, rituals, prayers, animal language skills, written words) are used by Native groups in the Guianas as a means of relating with other humans and with animals and plants within their socio-cosmological context. In different instances, these forms of expression are used to acquire or mimic characteristics of animals or to communicate and influence the supernatural world (e.g., owners of animals and plants, the god of the whites). Following this I hypothesize that if the De'kuana still conceive of their universe as discussed above, then having access to and mapping with Western standards is a mode of expression similar to ritual practices to communicate with owners of resources in the supernatural world and to be able to negotiate or avoid retaliation. It is a way to adopt the nature of the Iaranavi people and to be able to influence their power.

The Kuyujani legacy resembles somewhat a messianic movement. The De'kuana with whom I spoke do not know when Kuyujani will come or how they will know when he arrives. Likewise, they do not know what will he do or what would happen. What they know so far is that he is coming back or that he is already among them in spirit helping in the second demarcation. It is a shared and encouraging feeling of a better future. The Kuyujani prophecy probably will come true once the De'kuana receive their land titles. What is true is that the Kuyujani legacy and prophecy have triggered a stronger emerging collective awareness. It has catalyzed an ongoing resistance movement that was lacking an ethnic-wide political cohesiveness. The movement put the De'kuana as active agents mobilizing the forces of the Venezuelan state and society and a world system that has clear stakes in their territory. It is a resistance against a homogenizing assimilation into the national life, claiming their rights to control and make decisions regarding their culture, territory, and future.

Five years after the first meeting of the De'kuana in Culebra the movement is slowly gaining momentum. The new gain in social unity among the De'kuana shows their great resiliency and internal cultural consistency by sharing their history – now in new formats – to unite the Ye'kuana people and reinforce the ethnic identity and cultural boundaries. This coupled with the new Venezuelan constitution provides a light and gives strength to a movement of cultural control and land reclamation that is the basis for their cultural survival. The new constitution recognizes the original rights of indigenous people over their ancestral lands and warrants the rights of collective property (Bello 2000). Now the different indigenous peoples in Venezuela need to get organized and present their claims. The government has the responsibility of demarcating the land, and still there are no clear criteria of how to go about demarcating indigenous peoples' land. The Agrarian Reform Law experience shows the De'kuana that land recognition can be a long process with many political and economic interests creating obstacles to fulfilling the Kuyujani prophecy.

The self-demarcation project is not unique to the De'kuana. Other indigenous groups such as the Shuar and the Awa in Ecuador and the Amuesha people in Peru have developed their own experiences (Chirif Tirado, Garcia Hierro, and Chase Smith 1991). Indeed, there is no "one way" for demarcating indigenous land, as the process depends on the circumstances and historical context of the ethnic group, such as in Peru where the strategy was to claim small land areas and then unify them given the extent of the colonization of the land by outsiders.

What is unique to the De'kuana process is its emphasis on its oral history and mythology. The demarcation processes presented by Chirif et al. depart from the history of the territory as part of a diagnosis and strategy for defending the territory. However, the emphasis is on occupation of the territory, migrations and invasions, dispossession and lost resources, and actual conflicts (Chirif Tirado, Garcia Hierro, and Chase Smith 1991). Aside from this, an ethnohistorical base should be part of any self-demarcation process of ancestral lands because it empowers communities to work together beyond the land recognition.

Land titles are not enough to secure cultural survival. A case in point is the Kayapó people of central Brazil, with whom the De'kuana can draw many parallels to their situation and can foresee a possible scenario of their future. Although their kinship system is different, the De'kuana share similarities with the Kayapó such as in the size of the population and settlement distribution, social and autonomous political structure in place, historical political tension and rivalry between groups within the same ethnic group with differential contact influences and development experiences, and internal tensions between generations. The De'kuana more closely resemble the Western "Xingu" in that they live within a national park but do not have international support. The difference is that the Kayapó have land titles from living on reserves demarcated by the Brazilian government since the late 1980s and have had more direct impacts with the development frontier and expansion of the Brazilian society (Fisher 1994).

The Kayapó are known to be very successful politically, relying on their traditional social organization and autonomous political institutions that facilitate collective actions. In this way they have reproduced their own forms of resistance and have been able to adjust to the national society on their own terms (Turner 1995). In fact, the Kayapó in Gorotire went from being highly dependent on both the government indigenous protection service and missionaries in the 1960s to having within their community and reserve control over each institutional and technological element, which constituted dependency on the Brazilian society and culture in the 1980s (Turner 1991). This self-determination allowed Kayapó leaders to permit mining and logging concessions in their territory in a decision balancing between exercising their rights on their land and providing for basic needs given the cut in aid from the Brazilian government in 1990. Opinions were split along the lines of age structure and marital status in those communities that permitted both types of extraction. Young men viewed gold and timber as a source of income to satisfy their demand for Western commodities and lifestyles. Yet the gold and logging boom resulted in differential economic benefits for villagers and increasing environmental degradation in the form of mercury contamination, malaria, and deforestation of hunting and gathering areas (Turner 1995). It took a concerted effort of social and political forces in the villages to generate an internal revolt and force the expulsion of miners and loggers from the territory between 1994 and 1995. This required an alliance between young emerging protesters and elder traditional chiefs to force the young leaders controlling and benefiting from the concessions to change their policies. The alliance was forged along the traditional structures of political and ritual authority, showing an example of strong cultural continuity against global forces. From this experience the Kayapó are now experimenting with alternative environmentally sustainable sources of income in creating new associations at the village and intervillage levels and establishing new alliances and partnerships outside institutions and businesses (Turner 1995).

Both the De'kuana and the Kayapó cases are examples of what may represent the future for many indigenous groups who want to forge their future by maintaining traditional political and social structures and cultural continuity and developing innovative cultural responses to find a niche within the global context. Further analysis and study of this process can shed light onto how indigenous societies reassert themselves under contemporary conditions and how social, religious, and political movements emerge and why they take the form they do.

NOTES

1. I use the term *cultural* control as defined by Bonfil Batalla (1989). In this view, cultural control is a system through which an ethnic group has the social capacity to decide to act upon its cultural elements. Cultural elements are all the components of a culture that are necessary to develop every social action: maintain daily life, satisfy needs, define and resolve problems, formulate and try to fulfill aspirations. In the case of the Ye'kuana, cultural control is keeping the power of decision making regarding autonomous and appropriated cultural elements, as well as processes that will affect their lives.

2. The Ye'kuana represent only 1.4 percent of the indigenous population in Venezuela and rank as the ninth largest ethnic group out of 30 after the Wayuu, Warao, Pemón, Añu, Yanomami, Guahibo, Piaroa, Kariña, and Pumé.

3. The De'kuana reside in Akanaña, Culebra, Huachamakare, Jododuiña, Mawishiña, Wanaña, Konoiñamaña, Adajameña, Mejidedaña, Yanatuiña, Watamo, Tookishanamaña, Müdeshijaiña (Buena Vista), La Esmeralda, and Tamatama.

4. This system is defined as a complex regionwide web of interethnic relations that facilitated the integration of the ethnic groups in the system in a horizontal and differential manner through articulatory mechanisms such as trade, ritual services, interethnic marriage alliances, political agreements, warfare, etc. This was done without compromising the local political autonomy and cultural and linguistic diversity of the different groups within the system (Arvelo-Jiménez and Biord 1994).

5. Similar social structure has been observed among other Carib groups in Venezuela such as the Pemón (N. Thomas 1971; Urbina 1982, 1983–1984; Cousins 1991) and Kariña (Schwerin 1966). A hypothesis yet to be tested is whether the flexibility of the Ye'kuana social organization is one of the articulatory mechanisms that facilitated their functioning in the System of Orinoco Regional Interdependence.

6. During colonial times, the main market for the Venezuelan cacao was the Virreinato de Nueva España (Veracruz, Mexico) and not Spain. In exchange for cacao exports Venezuela received gold, and the cacao became a very important commodity in which the economy of Guayana developed to a point in the 17th century that facilitated the formation of a powerful economic social class (Fuentes-Figueroa Rodriguez n.d.). Commercial trade in Venezuela (both imports and exports) was monopolized by the Royal Guipuzcoana Company in the name of the Spanish Crown until 1778, when free trade was established in the colony (Moron 1970). Cacao was used not only for making chocolate but also as a monetary figure for transactions such as purchasing slaves for many small farmers. The production and trade of cacao was an important criterion for the establishment and support of population centers such as in the case of La Esmeralda in the Alto Orinoco, where the abundance of cacao in the rainforest was the center of the Guayana Governor Centurion's economic plan for developing the region and the country (Gonzalez del Campo 1984).

7. The destroyed posts were Ipurechapana, Quirabuena, Uatamao, Inabapo, Masibibiane, San Félix del Padamo, Carimena, Matape, Curapasape, Machapure, Uaramamunomo, Teripiaba, Sanamaparo, Periquita, Uaiquetame, Uenituari, Continamo, Yaurichapa, and Tupure (Tavera Acosta 1954). These posts were built with indigenous labor, mostly by the Ye'kuana, and plotting the location of these posts on a map indicates how the Spanish attempted to cut through Ye'kuana territory to accomplish their own political and economic plans.

8. The Watunna is the Ye'kuana mythical tradition, religion, and oral history of the origin and world cycles sung in ritual collective dances (Civrieux 1992).

9. According to the Watunna, the Iaranavi was a dressed, criollo white man, the owner of the iron. It was a good, wise, rich, and powerful creature who fell into the hands of demons. Wanadi was the son of the sun and creator and Odosha, who incarnated the negative forces of the universe (Civrieux 1992).

10. The Odoshankomo were the people of Odosha, demons and bad spirits (Civrieux 1992).

11. The exploitation of rubber in Venezuela that started in 1860 was promoted by the French entrepreneur Augusto Trouchon, who was strongly supported by a trade company in Paris. The exploitation of rubber in Venezuela was intensive until 1920 due to the demand for it during the First World War and then between 1942 and 1946 during the Second World War (Gómez-Picón 1953).

12. The amount of land allocated for national parks alone experienced an increase of almost 175 percent in 18 years (from 1976 to 1993), covering almost 15 percent of the national territory and representing 20 percent of all the protected areas in the country.

13. This park is located in the center of the Macizo Guayanés in the central part of Amazonas State, between the Iguapo, Padamo, and Cunucunuma Rivers, with an area of 2,100 square kilometers (between 500 and 2,800 meters above sea level). The Duida-Marahuaka massif (Roraima formation) are flat mountain-tops. The highest point in Cerro Duida reaches a height of 2,360 meters, and Cerro Marahuaka peaks at 2,800 meters elevation. The park area contains an extensive biodiversity of species of flora and fauna. The protection of the Cucununuma and Padamo River basins, which are tributaries of the Orinoco, is one of the objectives of the Duida-Marahuaka National Park.

14. Culebra and the communities of Akanaña and Huachamakare are leading the land claim process.

15. This reflects a government attitude toward indigenous peoples that has existed since the 1936 Ley de Tierras Baldías y Ejidos, which indicates that land without official ownership is considered public property and therefore owned by the federal government (Kuppe 1997).

16. Fifteen Ye'kuana communities are contained within the biosphere reserve. To correct the estimates made by Perera (1995), these communities represent 11.3 percent of the 132 ethnic communities in the reserve (Perera 1995).

17. A damodede is a spirit messenger or double that is conceived of as an *akato* (spirit) that can be controlled and directed, a power that only *huhai* (shaman) and Wanadi himself are capable of attaining. Kahuña represents heaven and the invisible world, a place of rest and eternal life (Civrieux 1992:178).

18. Arvelo-Jiménez's (1974) data show that the Ye'kuana conceive of the universe as having two parallel stages.

19. See Barandiaran (1986) for an extensive description of the worlds.

20. Santos-Granero (1998) defines topograms as elements of the landscape that have acquired their present configuration as a result of the past transformative activities of human or superhuman activities.

21. The villages that were represented were Culebra, Akanaña, La Esmeralda, Tookishanamaña, Watamo, Müdeshijaiña, and Huachamakare.

22. Magaña (1993–94) explains that for many indigenous tribes in the Guayanas, the act of writing and Europeans are closely associated with demoniac origins, therefore explaining why the Ye'kuana view the use of writing by Europeans as a means destined to take away their memories in order to destroy them. Indeed, writing was a source of power for the privileged. A shaman of Alto Ventuari interviewed by Barandiaran (1986) explains that both the Hañoro (Spaniards) and the Yaranavi (Venezuelan criollos) were favored people of

Wanadi. They were given paper on which to write instead of *cazabe* (manioc cakes) and a dog for hunting. With the paper, they were able to have access to iron, money, and horses, making them stronger than the Ye'kuana.

23. Kuyujani is a cultural hero. He was chief of Ye'kuanajüjü'ña in primordial times when there was no food and the Ye'kuana ate only mud. Kuyujani took over the responsibility for demarcating the land for the Ye'kuana following Wanadi's mandate. This reflected a higher local leadership figure appropriate for the traditional political social structure of the Ye'kuana that emerges in times of needs, conflict, or regional cohesiveness (Abel Perozo, personal communication, June 10, 2001).

24. The three instances of resistance were Mahaiwadi leadership against the Spanish in the late 18th century, Kalomera against the Sanema in the 1930s, and José Felix Turón with the demarcation.

2

The Arawak-Speaking Groups of Northwestern Amazonia

Amerindian Cartography as a Way of Preserving and Interpreting the Past

SILVIA M. VIDAL

The religion of Kúwai directly challenges two important European (Western) concepts of cultural tradition and knowledge, those of time (history) and of space/place (geography/cartography) (Vidal 2000a). The Arawakan peoples of northwestern Amazonia have used this religious system not only to confront colonial (European) and national (criollo) ways of constructing and interpreting the past, but to resist the imposition of European cartography upon their own ideas of spatial representations or their cosmographical, geographical, and geopolitical knowledge. Moreover, due to the Arawakan peoples' insertion in the colonial regime, since the very beginning of the European colonization of the Orinoco-Amazon region, this indigenous religious system has also influenced the European mapping of the Amazon and Orinoco basins.

Kúwai teachings and knowledge (or Kuwé Duwákalumi) have proved for the Arawakan peoples to be not only their shamanic or shamanistic way of constructing and interpreting myth, history, culture, and unequal socioeconomic hierarchies of power, but also their powerful model for constructing ethnic and political identities within colonial and national states. For the Warekena and other Arawak groups, Kuwé or Kúwai is not only the voice of the creation that opened up the world but is also a monstrous, primordial human being (Hill 1993:xvii), the master of all visible and invisible beings (Wright 1993) and capable of controlling the sky and the universe through his powerful knowledge.

From the 16th century, the European colonial powers began their search and explorations of their overseas territories, but it was not until the 18th century that they intensified their explorations and demarcations of their colonial possessions in the Orinoco-Amazon region.

These exploratory and expansive processes meant that European colonial states had to send civil and military explorers to different regions in order to elaborate maps and inventories of natural resources, to expel foreign intruders, and to use indigenous groups and territories as markers of the extension of their colonial sovereignties. During this century Amerindian cartography was slowly displaced by the official colonial cartography, and in this way the European space-territorial pattern was implanted. The new pattern divided indigenous South America into colonial states with European municipalities, villages, and parishes. This colonial cartography and pattern have been used since 1777 as a territorial and political model for the creation and delimitation of Latin American nation-states. In other words, to the indigenous population of lowland South America colonialism and postcolonialism represent the compulsive displacement and substitution of their cosmographical or spatio-geographical and geopolitical knowledge with their own interconnections for the European spatial distributions and hierarchies of power.

Papadakis (1998:150) points out that maps are important mechanisms for conceptualizing territoriality and also the primary tools of national symbolism to delimit what is an area of legitimate actions. Boyarin (1994:4) mentions the closed relationship between mapping, boundary setting, inclusion, and exclusion of places and peoples, and Gupta and Ferguson (1997:35) suggest that the "presumption that spaces are autonomous has enabled the power of topography successfully to conceal the topography of power." Along these lines, Mignolo (1995:222–223, 227) has stated that the move toward colonization and reconfiguration of space (European cartography) during the colonial process introduces a double perspective. On one hand, it produces the dissociation between a center determined ethnically and a center determined geometrically that complements the ethnic center. On the other hand, there is the assumption that the locus of observation (geometric center) does not disrupt or interfere with the locus of the enunciation (ethnic center). Mignolo (1995:223) also suggests that "the power of the center does not depend necessarily on the geometric rationalization but . . . [is] enacted around the power of the ethnic center."

Indigenous and Western geographical imagery and their confrontations are central to the understanding of the historical processes in building dominant global cartographies. For Shapiro (1997:ix) these confrontations produce the institutionalization of the dominant colonial or nation-state geographical imagery over the indigenous cartographic knowledge. This institutionalization includes the mapping of spatial and geographical contexts within which dominant powers and strong political decision makers calculated, selected, and gave meanings to spatial distribution and economic exploitation of colonized peoples. In addition, this process also ignores the important contribution of the colonized peoples to the European cartography of the Americas.

Mundy (1996) has shown interesting differences between European and Amerindian mapmakers of the Americas. The former employed two types of projections to represent space: the Euclidean or base of the map, wherein the distances between points in space are set out on a grid or similar graticule while their dimensions are reduced geometrically; and the Albertian or panoramic projection, representing space as if seen from a single viewpoint to single out architecture and other human-made constructions, thereby assigning these as the defining and constituting features of space. Amerindian mapmakers of Tenochtitlan reflect a long tradition of city maps from the pre-Columbian past. The Aztec map (the 16th-century Mendoza Codex) is better thought of as being a humanistic or social projection – that is, the physical space of the city has not been filtered through and reduced by an overlying graticule; rather, its structuring device is the human or social layout of the city. This means that they were rooted in a spatial understanding of the human world, where the spatial reality was defined and structured by social relationships (Mundy 1996: xii). This use of the social organization to structure the understanding and the representation of space was as common in ancient Mexico as the use of Euclidean geometries to define space was in Europe (Mundy 1996:xvi).

The Arawakan peoples also encode their sociopolitical relationships in their representations of space, but one of their most important shared characteristics is the process of inscribing their historical knowledge into the landscape (Hill 1993; Santos-Granero 1998; Vidal and Zucchi 2000; Vall de la Ville 1998; Vidal 2000a; Zucchi 2000). Santos-Granero (1998:140) demonstrates that by attributing a transcendental reality to particular elements of the landscape, the Yanesha, an Arawak group in Peru, transform these salient natural features into signs that recall past events. Among the Yanesha three different types of topograms can be distinguished according to the predominant means through which they have been infused with historical significance: personal reminiscences, collective oral traditions, and mythical narratives. "In spite of the importance of these three types of topograms as means of preserving historical information and memory, however, they turn into powerful mnemonic devices only when they become the subject of mythical narratives" (Santos-Granero 1998:141).

One of the ways through which the Arawakan groups of northwestern Amazonia construct, preserve, and interpret their histories and identities is the religion of Kúwai and its map of sacred places, which represents their traditional cartography. In this essay, I analyze the relationship between this cartography and the religion of Kúwai, and also the way through which the past is constructed and preserved. I also demonstrate that this cartography represents ancient and contemporary Amerindian geopolitical knowledge, which includes sociopolitical, religious, economic, cultural, and historical relations in the region between the Orinoco and Amazon Rivers. Although the essay refers to all the Arawakan peoples of northwestern Amazonia, my ethnographic data and analysis are mainly centered on the Warekena people (bésa inépe Walékhena) of the Itiniwini (San Miguel) River and middle Guainía basin (see Figures 2.1 and 2.2). However, this essay is also part of a wider re-evaluation of the forms and the meaning of indigenous cartography in lowland South America (Whitehead 1998; but also see Whitehead and Medina, both in this volume).

THE SOCIOPOLITICAL AND RELIGIOUS STRUCTURE OF CONTEMPORARY ARAWAK-SPEAKING GROUPS FROM NORTHWESTERN AMAZONIA

The Arawak-speaking groups of northwestern Amazonia share not only important aspects of their cultural and political histories but also a hierarchical sociopolitical structure, organized in several patrilineal, localized, and exogamic phratries. Each phratry consists of two or more patrilineal, localized, and exogamic sibs, ranked according to the birth order of the ancestral mythic brothers.

Hierarchy is the most important criterion to classify people and place them in a given status. It also influences intragroup and intergroup alliances and plays a key role in processes and mechanisms of ethnogenesis and social reproduction. Each phratry and sib are identified with a specific area within its group's territory in the northwestern Amazonia region. Localized phratries and sibs exercise political and economic control

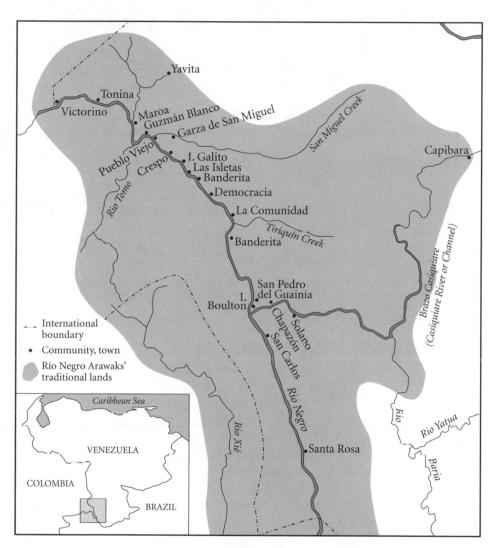

Fig. 2.1. The Rio Negro basin and Arawakan townships

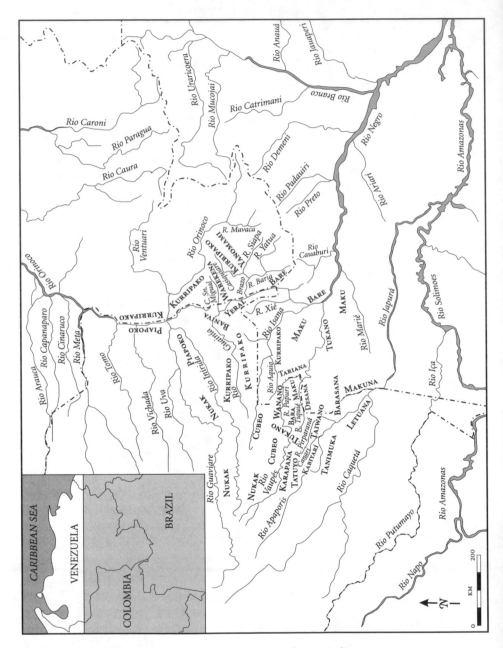

Fig. 2.2. Northwestern Amazonia and Amerindian groups

over rivers, sacred places, and natural resources of their territories. During the 17th and 18th centuries Arawaks and other peoples of northwestern Amazonia had well-defined territorial boundaries (Vidal 1993, 1999, 2000a, 2000b), and today they still practice this ideology of well-defined territorial boundaries among phratries and groups. However, this territorial control and these boundaries have been flexible enough to allow negotiations through economic bargaining and political alliances among phratries and groups.

Exogamy makes it possible for these groups and their subgroups to associate with each other and other societies. Arawakan-speaking groups practice a nonlinguistic exogamy and place all their in-laws in a single category ("the other"), allocating them ambivalent and contradictory meanings ("people", "nonpeople", "relative" or "brother-in-law," potential "ally" or "enemy," and so on) (Hill 1987:190–191; Vidal 1987, 1993, 1999). These cultural characteristics have influenced their forms of leadership, their control and expansion of alliances, and the emergence of interregional multiethnic sociopolitical formations.

The Arawakan cross-cousin marriage system is basically focused on the expansion of alliances in order to incorporate groups that are not their traditional affinal kindred (Vidal 1987, 1993, 1999). The marriage network has enormous potential for politico-regional alliances because at the regional level it includes in the category of "siblings" ("we/us") a larger number of social groups and segments. This system also implies the amplification of the alliance networks among affinal kin of diverse groups ("They/the others"). In turn, this system of regional exogamy relates and is based on their religious system (Kuwé, Kúwai, or Yuruparí) and in their beliefs on the origin of the world and the ancestors.

The religious system is divided into two or more mythical cycles. Each cycle, consisting in a corpus of narratives (stories, myths, chants, songs, prayers, advisories, etc.), ritual knowledge, puberty rites, male ritual societies, and festivals, comprises a wide variety of ideological-symbolic and practical codes that teach important knowledge related to Kúwai and the Trickster Creator (*Nápirríkuli* or *Nápiruli*). These codes have influenced and oriented indigenous peoples' strategies to face events and situations of their ritual and secular lives. For these Arawakan groups the origin of people is linked with a unique and special place that is shared by all groups. In this place, the first ancestors emerged in a hierarchical order from older to younger siblings, and from there they were dispersed throughout the Orinoco-Amazon region. This hierarchical emergence not only refers to each Arawakan phratry and sib but also to each non-Arawakan-speaking group of northwestern Amazonia.

Arawakan historical interpretation and mythical representation of the world, society, natural beings, and humankind is closely related to their system of ancient beliefs. Their mythic narratives and oral history constitute two complementary genres through which they can narrate and interpret their past and present processes of transformation.

ARAWAKAN CARTOGRAPHY AND THE RELIGION OF KÚWAI

The Warekena cartography is closely related to the religion of Kúwai and their ideas of the origin and development of the cosmos and people. Through the transmission of Kúwai teachings and knowledge from one generation to another, the Warekena people learn about the natural and supernatural forces, the processes of transformation and continuity represented by Kúwai's creative and destructive powers, and also the mythical journeys of Kúwai and Amaru. These processes of cosmogenesis and ethnogenesis are built on the connection of the cosmos and the earth through two important axes Mundo, or "navels" of the world. The first is located at Hipana in the Isana River, and the second one is placed at the Lémi Creek, in the Itiniwini basin. These two axes interconnect two complementary but different dimensions: (1) the macrocosmic or vertical dimension of space-time for social and cosmic transformation, which is related to the generational time, to processes of coming into being, and to social and hierarchical orders; and (2) the microcosmic or horizontal dimension of space-time for the opening or closing the sociogeographic world of riverine places, through movements between downstream regions and remote headwater areas. The creation of a sociogeographic space (social space) is closely related to the emplacement of people because in the Warekena cosmology and cultural or ethnic identity, the idea of person, place, and time is an integral and indivisible concept; this means a sense of belonging due to the connections with their ancestors and place of origin. Moreover, for most of the Arawakan peoples of the Negro River region, the intimate connections between place-naming and historical consciousness is based on Kúwai's mythical narratives, on the mythical journeys of Kúwai and Amaru, and their sacred rituals. Among the Arawakan peoples of the Negro and Orinoco Rivers, these connections have been used during and after their processes of migration and sociopolitical and religious change, such as famous millenarian movements of the 19th century.

THE ARAWAKAN TRADITION OF INSCRIBING HISTORY INTO THEIR LANDSCAPE

To the Arawakan peoples, Kúwai is the voice of the creation, which opened up the world. He is also the monstrous, primordial human being (Hill 1993:xvii), the master of all visible and invisible beings (Wright 1993), capable of controlling the sky and the universe through his powerful knowledge. He came to this world to teach people his sacred ritual powers. Men secretly learn the powers or Kúwai's teachings during initiation or puberty rites. Thus, Wright (1993:3, 9) calls it "the cult of the sacred flutes and trumpets . . . representing the first ancestors of the phratries."

Kúwai's cult is associated with a hierarchical political and religious organization, known as male ritual society, which represents the Kúwai and his troops and includes chiefs, masters (ritual specialists), warriors, shamans, and servants. The relationship between male ritual society and "Kúwai and his troop[s]" is based on the association that the Arawaks have established between their mythic or first ancestors (such as Kúwai, Nápiruli, Purúnamínali, and Dzúli) and their living elders. The religion of Kúwai is also a link with collective death and rebirth, world destruction and renewal. Jonathan Hill (1993:156) states that "the cult of Kúwai and of the ancestor spirits has continued to serve the Wakuénai [another Arawak group] as a power resource for negotiating interethnic relations along lower Guainía River in Venezuela."

The mytho-historical and ritual narratives of the Arawakan peoples of northwestern Amazonia can be divided into three cycles that outline complex processes of cosmogenesis and ethnogenesis. The first cycle begins at Hípana, an ancient community located on the Ayarí River, also the mythical place of the "beginning of the world." In this beginning (Miyaka) or genesis of the universe (and of the Milky Way and of the planet earth), the Unique Spiritual Being (only creative mind and thought) was the epicenter of a big emptiness (there was no place or space, nor time), and everything was in silence. This silence is known as Makuku (Rojas 1994). Then, Makuku with his thought began the creation of all life, separating time and space, and he also spoke to the universe. After speaking, he became Dukuku, and his speech, song, and voice

41

(as thunder) divided the universe between darkness and light and began the creation in six steps or stages. During each stage one of the child-spirit-creations spoke. During the fifth stage, Kúwai, the magnifier or enlarger of the firmament and voice of the world, was heard.

After the genesis of the universe (Miyaka), the earth and nine other heavens or planes were given to other spiritual and flesh-and-bones beings, for the continual evolution of life (Rojas 1994; see Figure 2.3). At this point, the creative actions, reactions, and interactions of Nápiruli, Amáruyawa (primordial woman), the first Kúwai, and a group of human-animal beings began. Nápiruli created the first world and was entrusted to eliminate all the dangerous animals and imperfections. This world was destroyed by a great flood from which only Nápiruli, Amáruyawa, and some human-animal beings survived.

The second cycle narrates the expansion of the miniature world until it reaches its actual size, with mountains, rivers, and forests; the central actors are Nápiruli, his three sons, Amáruyawa, the second Kúwai, Káli, some human-animal beings, and the first ancestors. This cycle explains the life and death of Kúwai. Kúwai taught agriculture (*kalítani*) and the sacred rituals of initiation to the first ancestors. At the end of the first ritual Kúwai performed for the first ancestors, Nápiruli "killed" him in a great fire, and Kúwai left the world and went to "heaven." From his ashes sprout the materials for making the sacred flutes and trumpets ("his voice") that today are played in initiation and other sacred rituals. Amáruyawa and other women stole the sacred instruments from the initiated men, and this act of Amáruyawa and her troop of women set off a long chase from the Ayarí and Isana Rivers to different places in the Orinoco, Negro, and Amazon basins, which again opened the world. The chase ended when Nápiruli and his men regained control over the Kúwai's instruments. For most Arawakan groups, the "death" of Kúwai and the chase of the women were two important historical moments that changed forever their culture and society. From that moment on the forefathers of contemporary Arawakan, Tukanoan, and Makuan groups gathered together to celebrate initiation rituals, which received the names of Kasimájada (in Baré) or Kasíjmakasi (in Warekena) and which are dedicated to the cult of Kúwai and the forefathers or first ancestors. In these initiations, the male ritual society (Kúwai, his troops), and the elders (men and women) reproduce (the time/space and the actions of the beginning) and transmit their history and important knowledge to new generations.

5	Kumatau	"heaven of purity"
4	Chiwichiwi	"heaven of the gulls"
3	Wayuri	"heaven of the vultures"
2	Mujida	"heaven of the stings"
1	Madejari	"heaven of green wasps"
	Hípai	"heaven of human beings"
1	Aapi	"heaven of the serpents or snakes"
2	Yupinai	"heaven of the enchanted beings"
3	Ewáda	"golden heaven"
4	Uwápili	"heaven of the women, root of the sky"

Fig. 2.3. Hípai (the earth) and the planes of the cosmos

The third cycle of narratives accounts for the relationships among peoples, between them and their ancestors, and between human beings and powerful spirits from other parts of the cosmos and also the connections among different regions of the cosmos. It narrates the human past of the mythic ancestors (Nápiruli, Amáruyawa), whose central characters are Purúnamínali ("giver of names"), Puméyawa, Kuámasi, and other real and mythic forefathers. This set of narratives mostly takes place in Arawakan ancestral lands and is also related to some of their economic, migratory, commercial, political, and shamanic activities.

To the Arawakan peoples, the earth, or Hípai, is a material and spiritual entity full of life and power that along with the other nine planes forms the cosmos. The planes are interconnected through special sacred places located in different sites of the Arawakan ancestral lands. The inner and outer space of the earth and the other nine planes are inhabited by a large number of beings that are docile or obedient to human beings (especially to shamans and ritual specialists). Hípai, spiritual and human beings, and the religion of Kúwai are also associated with a map of sacred routes and places, which can be considered as a symbolic structure that connects meaningful physical and spiritual locations of this world and the cosmos. The most complete elaboration of the use of spatial movements as metaphors for the social construction of history is given in male and female rituals (Hill 1993, 1996; Vidal 1993, 1999, 2000a, 2000b; Wright 1981, 1993).

This map of sacred routes and places is part of Kúwai's geographical, ecological, botanical, and zoological teachings and knowledge. For the Warekena, Kuwé Duwákalumi literally means "where Kuwé passed by" and includes not only mythical journeys with powerful naming processes of geographical places during shamanistic rituals or other religious festivals but also a complex network of routes that connect different regions of South America (Vidal 2000a). These terrestrial and aquatic routes comprise rivers, creeks, lakes, and sea, as well as roads, trails, and narrow paths through tropical forests and savannas. These terrestrial routes frequently link the headwaters of several river basins. Yet, it is the combination of land and water routes that gave in the past and still provides the Arawakan-speaking groups ways to develop resistance strategies. In other words, Kúwai routes represent the location of and the connection with (1) sacred places related to the creation of the world, the people, and the social order, and also to the performance of ceremonies of Kúwai's religion and shamanic rituals; (2) sacred and secular strategic resources (e.g., gold, silver, stones); and (3) peoples and places important for sociopolitical, migratory, and commercial purposes (see Figure 2.4).

In his interpretations of the Kúwai's journeys among the Arawakan Hohódene, Robin Wright (1993) concludes that these travels represent their notions of territoriality and collective identity as well as their sense of cumulative historical knowledge, which includes their experiences of contact, trading networks, and also wars with other ethnic groups. In short, the integration and relationship between the secret male societies and Kuwé teachings and knowledge constitute a model of their societies and of their geopolitical relations. During the 18th century, the integration and relationship between ritual male societies and Kuwé Duwákalumi conformed to the sociopolitical and religious basis for the regional leadership of powerful Arawakan chiefs and groups within multiethnic confederacies (Vidal 2000b).

For the Warekena and Baré people, the history of their ancestors can be divided into three important phases or periods that implied processes of unification/separation of different groups (i.e., fission-and-fusion processes) and of sociopolitical and religious transformation. The first of these processes, related to the first cycle of mythical narratives, took place in the Isana River, when the world was created.

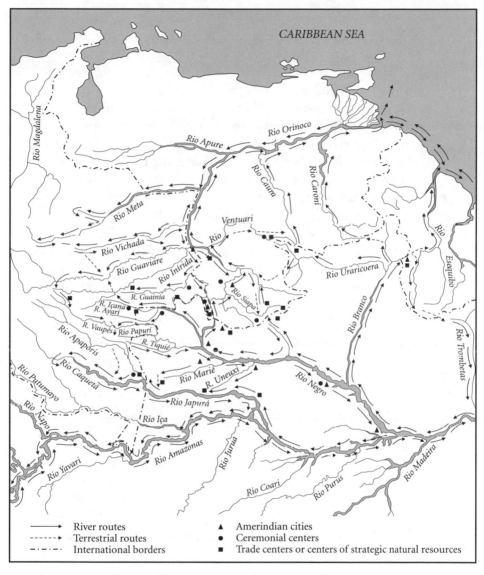

Fig. 2.4. Routes of Kuwaí and associated sacred and secular places

The second phase deals with the transformation of the initiation rituals and Kúwai cult into a religion, which includes the organization of warriors and secret male societies. It began during the time of the grandfathers Deré-deré (-náwi) and Benábena, when they established initiation rites for young girls. To begin with the sacred festival, they first traveled by Kúwai routes to different places inviting relatives, in-laws, and friends to the ritual, and all the people gathered at Maracoa (now known as San Fernando de Atabapo, in the upper Orinoco basin). Later, in Capihuara and in other places of the Casiquiare basin, the forefathers performed an important initiation rite for the daughters of the grandfather Siwali (an ancient "captain" of the Warekena). During this occasion many different peoples (ancestors of the Baré, Warekena, Baniva, and so on) attended the ceremony, which was performed by Dépenabe, the master of the rite, and Dzúli as the great shaman. After that, many groups related to the Warekena, Baré, Baniva, and their in-laws and allies began to celebrate male initiation ceremonies, and in that way, they gave rise to the religion of the Kúwai. Following the path opened by their mythical ancestors, Arawakan secret male societies, or Kuwé and his troops, continued traveling to the north, west, and east of the Amazon basin.

The third historical period began when the Kakáhau people murdered Puméyawa and her husband in the Aguachapita River, a tributary of the Casiquiare. Puméyawa saw their "Kuwé," and in doing this she broke the sacred laws of the religion of Kuwé. Before dying she gave birth to Kuámasi (or Kuámati, in Baré), who was raised and protected by the Inámalu and Inilíwiyu peoples. When Kuámasi grew older, he waged a war against the Kakáhau people, their allies, and their in-laws. He and his men killed the captain Ipíchipiméhli, and most of the Kakáhau people. The victory of Kuámasi generated a new process of sociopolitical reorganization, through which a new generation of groups or peoples began.

In these oral histories the names of some of the mythical and historical ancestors of the Warekena and Baré are intermingled, especially those of several shaman-warrior-chiefs of the 18th century, such as Cocui, Davipe, Cabi, Cayama, and Basimúnare, among others. During the 18th century, some of these powerful Arawakan leaders and their groups were impersonating Kúwai and his troops and were traveling, migrating, trading, and battling using the Kúwai sacred routes. It is also interesting to highlight that in these narratives the ancestors are portrayed as people who constructed and opened new roads, wrote messages and knowledge in the stones along rivers and waterfalls (petroglyphs), and traveled by the Kúwai routes.

ARAWAKAN CARTOGRAPHY AS A WAY OF PRESERVING AND INTERPRETING THE PAST

European Expansion and Colonial Cartography

European colonization of the Negro River and middle-upper Orinoco River basins began by the mid-17th century. Spanish, Portuguese, Dutch, French, and British colonial empires were competing among themselves and also with some of the leading Amerindian groups of local macro-polities in order to control the indigenous populations and the regional trade systems of the Orinoco and Amazon Rivers. By the end of the 17th century, Amerindian macro-polities of the Orinoco, Negro, and Amazon Rivers were disappearing or undergoing drastic sociopolitical transformations. These processes caused the mobilization and regrouping of the indigenous people and by the early 18th century gave rise to new sociopolitical formations that I have called "multiethnic confederacies" (Vidal 1993). From 1700 to 1770 there were at least 15 multiethnic confederacies led by Arawak-speaking groups of the Orinoco-Negro region (Vidal 1993, 1999). The European written records and the oral history of Arawak-speaking groups led to the conclusion that powerful chiefs or caciques and their followers of the multiethnic confederacies celebrated big ritual festivals related to the Kúwai religion. These festivals were held in sacred places at special men's houses and included whipping and fasting and such musical performances as dancing, singing, and the playing of trumpets, flutes, and drums. Besides their importance and their esoteric and religious value, the sacred places and the religious of Kúwai were also strategic for migrations, defense, and trade.

Between 1756 and 1760, both Spanish and Portuguese Crowns sent official expeditions to define their possessions in the upper Orinoco and upper Negro region. Military and civilian authorities tried to impose changes in the organization of their respective colonies, and the founding of new towns, cities, and fortresses began. Mission towns were transformed into secular villages under the control of imposed European or Amerindian authorities, and Europeans even prohibited indigenous leaders and peoples from moving freely within and between colonial territories (see Figure 2.5).

I. Imperial Level and Authorities

    Emperor/The Pope

    Council of the Indies
    Missionary Orders

II. Overseas Possessions or Supra-Regional Level

    Vice-Royalties
    (Viceroy)

    General Audience

III. Regional Level

    Capitaincies/governorship
    (General Capitain or Gobernor)

    Regional Audience

IV. Local Level

    Provinces and Cities
    (Head of Province and City)

    Municipal Council or Cabildo

    Property or Landowners (enconmenderos)
    and Missionary Authorities

    Indian Leaders (Caciques, Capitanes, and Curacas)

    Mission Towns/Indian Towns

    Indian Commoners (or encomendados)

    Free Indian Individuals (Christian and
    Spanish-speaking Indian)

    Indian Slaves

    Free Indian Groups or Gentiles
    (do not belong to the Empires)

Fig. 2.5. Colonial political authorities and territorial ordering

However, many Arawakan leaders and groups of the multiethnic confederacies were using their ancient cartographic knowledge (Kúwai routes and sacred places) as an alternative strategy to migrate from one colonial empire (i.e., Portuguese) to the other (i.e., Spanish) (Vidal 1993).

Spanish and Portuguese colonial political encroachment on indigenous peoples and lands gave rise to more socioeconomic and political changes. By the end of the 18th century, most of the village sites along major routes of colonial mobilization were virtually uninhabited, and several independent Arawakan groups of the upper Orinoco and Negro Rivers had been transformed into assimilated individuals, families, and groups with political autonomy (Vidal 1993). The evidence also demonstrates that there was a close relationship between the cult of Kúwai and the male ritual societies of powerful Arawakan shaman-chiefs who led different multiethnic confederacies. This political and religious strategy allowed the Warekena and other Arawakan ancient leaders to build political communities and new cultural identities within the colonial regime of the 18th century. The forefathers of the Warekena and other Arawakan groups used this strategy not only to participate in the trading network of Indian slaves and European goods (especially firearms, knives, and machetes) but also to evade or challenge the colonial dominion.

From 1798 to 1800, the indigenous population of northwestern Amazonia began to loose more of their economic and political autonomy due to the legal imposition of the debt peonage system (*endeude* in Spanish) as a mechanism of human exploitation and dominion. In this system, European and criollo traders advanced some European merchandise (such as food, clothes, tools) to Indians in exchange for tropical forest goods. Beginning around 1810, the Portuguese colonial power was transferred to Brazil, while the independence process of Venezuela was beginning. However, the enslavement of indigenous groups and the pressure over their political autonomy continued. By 1821 the independence processes from European colonial empires of Brazil and Venezuela were consolidated, and both countries were experiencing great changes in their territorial order and political economy. In the Orinoco-Negro region these processes were mainly centered in the extraction of tropical forest goods (e.g., the Rubber Boom), an incipient mining of gold and other precious metals and stones, and the exploitation or enslavement of indigenous individuals and groups. These processes led to a number of indigenous riots and rebellions in 1817–18 in Venezuela (Iribertegui 1987; Henríquez 1994) and in 1835–40 in Brazil and Venezuela

(Codazzi 1940; Weinstein 1983). The best example of this last event was the so-called Cabanagem that included indigenous groups, blacks, mestizos, and poor criollo populations of the Orinoco-Amazon region (Neto 1988; Reis 1974; Weinstein 1983). However, the most amazing indigenous strategy for survival and resistance to the postcolonial dominion was the emergence of important pan-indigenous messianic movements (Hill and Wright 1988; Wright and Hill 1986). These movements, led by Arawakan and Tukanoan shaman-chiefs, were strongly influenced by the religion of Kúwai and the Arawakan traditional cartography. They allowed the physical survival and sociopolitical continuity of the peoples of northwestern Amazonia.

Contemporary Warekena Cartography and the Mapping of Their Traditional Lands

The Warekena's cartography embraces a set of representations of the cosmos, the Amazon region's natural landscapes, and the local and regional sociogeography of their traditional territory. Their cosmography includes representations of the cosmological landscape, the celestial entities, and its human and animal analogies. Constellations are viewed as people or animals whose past and present actions influenced the transformations and the social and environmental conditions of this world. Part of this cosmography is also embedded in certain places along the San Miguel River, as for example in Kamúi Tápule (small creek of the sun), Alé-numá (the day door), Jiwémi Wadákakalumi (where Ursa Minor fell down), or the famous Mée and Tápu Creeks. These two creeks connect the San Miguel River to the Casiquiare channel and were opened by Mawáda (the water anaconda) and his wife, Mayúkelu. Mawáda also represents the constellation of the Pleiades.

The sociogeography of the Warekena's traditional territory and its surrounding areas is heavily influenced by two important aspects of this group's cultural characteristics: their sociopolitical structure of sibs and phratries, and the intimate connection between place-naming and historical consciousness, a trait that is shared by most of the Arawakan peoples of the Rio Negro region. This connection is based on the Kúwai's mythical narratives, the mythical journeys of Kúwai and Amaru, and the sacred rituals performed by each generation of human ancestors.

The territory of the Warekena (Walékhena képe) is strongly oriented toward the rivers and other permanent courses of water. The distribution of people (phratries, sibs, and communities) in this territory is determined by their sociopolitical structure. Each phratry (*bakéni* or *bakénai*) has the control and exclusive use of a part of the group territory and over the course of rivers and creeks in the area. The territory of each phratry is also divided among its sibs (*bakéinjepe*), and each of them is located within the area according to its hierarchical position, that is to say, the sib with the higher hierarchical position occupies the lower course of the river, while the one with the lowest position is usually located in the headwaters of rivers and creeks. Each phratry and each sib have a special sacred place for the burial of their dead. The local communities (*dakále*) are distributed, within the territory of each sib, in places (*inákalusi*) appropriate for the economic, sociopolitical, and ritual activities. Ancient local communities (*dakálemi*) were built around a central plaza with one or more big, oval longhouses for the patrilineal extended families and a ritual house fully decorated. Today's communities follow the mission-town pattern (see Figure 2.6).

Place-naming and the geographical description of places emphasize an inventory of the spiritual, ecological, economic, and social resources present in the area. The control over these resources is vested in powerful spiritual entities, the ancestors, and the living members of phratries and sibs. In the San Miguel River region there are places (*inákalusi*) that have spiritual "owners" who are entities responsible for the control of the area. These entities are capable of causing physical and spiritual harm to intruders (non-Warekena Indians) or violators of Kúwai teachings and knowledge. Thus, the Warekena ancestors and living elders are prohibited from speaking any other tongue than the Warekena language to their own people while they are traveling by the Itiniwini River because these spiritual owners can punish or threaten them with heavy rains and thunders, or they even can cause death.

Place-naming is associated with the mythical time of Kúwai and Nápiruli, and also with the historical times of the ancestors and living elders. This association can be observed in different sacred places located in the traditional territory of the group where important processes and events occurred and are recorded by oral history, myth, and petroglyphs. For example, in the San Miguel River basin there are places related to the mythical times, such as the Taphuísia Creek (literally, creek of the shamanic dreamer), the AtúSiwáli Rock (the rock of grandfather Siwáli), and the Machálika-wéni Mountain (see Figure 2.7). But there are also places related to the historical times of the Warekena ancestors and living

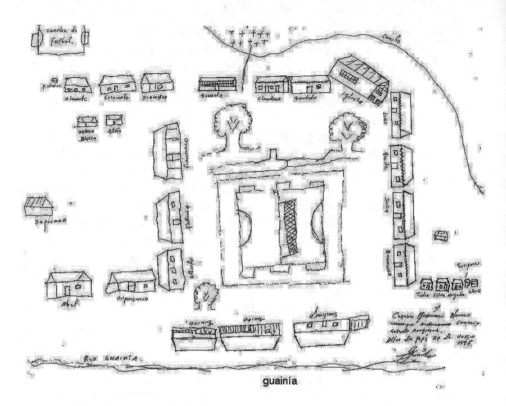

guainía

Fig. 2.6. Wayánapi, the most important township of the Warekena on the
Guiainía River (personal communication, Edilto Bernabé, 1996)

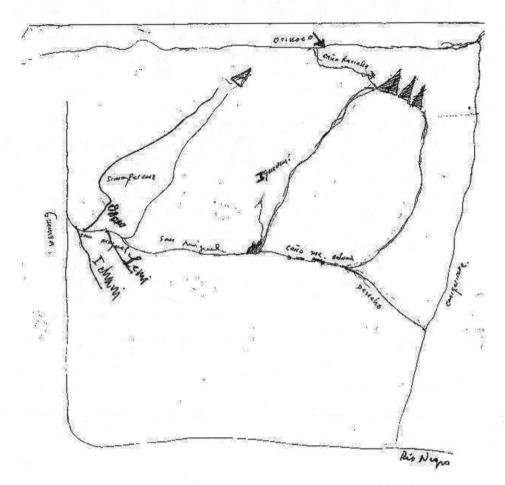

Fig. 2.7. The route to Machálikawéni, a sacred place on the San Miguel River
(personal communication, Edilto Bernabé, 1990)

elders, such as Idhénawi-kuhána kálumi (another way of saying "where Kúwai passes by"), Táli, Makáwa-kápe, Madénawi, and Imo-dámi (the site where Imo the great chief of the Marabitana died), all of them associated with the religion of Kúwai or traditional shaman-warrior-chiefs.

During the period 1969–73, the latest and more important expansion of socioeconomic and political frontiers into indigenous lands in Venezuela began. In the region south of the Orinoco River, this process was called the Conquest of the South by Rafael Caldera, a former president of Venezuela. Caldera's national government began an aggressive development policy geared toward the integration of indigenous peoples and territories into the national economy and culture (Arvelo-Jiménez and Scorza 1974; Arvelo-Jiménez 1980). The idea behind the so-called Conquest of the South was that the Amazon region was underdeveloped because the indigenous groups had backward economies. It was considered that the whole region was practically uninhabited and needed new criollo and foreign migrants with new development projects to people it. This national policy opened up the Rio Negro region to the invasion of a number of intruders and developers who occupied important places of the Guainía, Casiquiare, and Negro basins. But a few years later, these intruders and developers left their colonies and returned to Caracas and other cities of Venezuela, after realizing that the Amazon region lacked the environmental conditions necessary for the success of their cattle-raising and industrialized agriculture activities. These colonizers also realized they lacked a strong economic and political backup from the national government. However, this was an important experience and lesson for the Warekena and other Arawakan populations of the Rio Negro.

The Warekena people soon learned from those experiences that they should take more control over their traditional territory. They also learned to propose their own projects to develop their economy. Thus, they became experienced with new forms of economic and political organizations, such as the cooperatives and the *empresas* or indigenous companies to raise some cattle and to exploit agricultural products. They were also devoted to strictly controlling the access of criollos and foreigners to the San Miguel River.

The Venezuelan national government and its development agents also learned that the region of the Negro River was not suited for their big plans for agro-industrial development. But the national authorities soon realized that the Negro River region also possessed a great natural beauty that could be good for the development of a strong tourism industry. Thus, in 1989 the Guainía-Negro basin was declared a tourist area by presidential decree 625. In this way, the area became open to national and international tourism. According to the Venezuelan legal system, this presidential decree meant that the region had lost its condition of indigenous territory, under special protection by the national and regional governments. In other words, the indigenous peoples had lost their legal rights to their territories, and more invasions of Indian lands were generated in the area. Moreover, during the 1990s the gold rush began in the region, and a number of illegal miners invaded the area with their powerful technical equipment and armies of men (Vidal and Bernabé 1996).

This whole critical situation had a severe impact on the Warekena, but it also generated a number of answers and actions from them that are based on the religion of the Kúwai and the Warekena representations of the sociogeographic space. The first thing the Warekena did was to reunite all the people living in Venezuela and Brazil. The second step they tried was to repopulate the San Miguel River basin and the surrounding areas of the Casiquiare River. This was done by strictly following the traditional phratric and sib territorial divisions and by leaving clear signals of their physical presence and their traditional economic activities in the area. The Warekena also allowed some Wakuénai and Baniva families to occupy certain zones of the lower San Miguel River. Later, the Warekena began a series of continual visits to other Arawakan groups of Venezuela, Brazil, and Colombia, such as the Hohódene of the Isana River, the Wakuénai of Guainía headwaters, the Baré of the Negro River, and the Baniva of the township of Maroa and the Aki River. These visits had the purposes of strengthening the Warekena political alliances with neighboring Arawakan groups and obtaining mytho-historical information to reconstruct the ancient rituals and cultural traditions useful to back up the Arawakan legal rights to their territories. Besides the visits to neighboring groups, the Warekena elders began to hold sacred initiation rituals once a year in the township of Wayánapi (or Guzmán Blanco) or in sacred places of the San Miguel River.

In the political arena of Venezuelan Amazonian society, some Warekena men also participated in the organization of an indigenous political movement for the Guainía-Negro region. This movement led to the open participation of Warekena, Baniva, Baré, Yeral, and Wakuénai men and women in the regional elections to governorship and municipalities. At the same time, Warekena teachers and elders started important research on their history (such as myths and petroglyphs) and spatial representations in order to transmit this knowledge to Warekena children in the schools. They even asked some anthropologists and criollo friends to work on specific research projects to obtain historical and cultural written information, useful for reclaiming their legal rights to their traditional lands.

All these practical actions had the purpose of constructing a database made of chants, prayers, songs, oral and written discourses, and maps of the Warekena territory. Through this database they can repeatedly tell the Indians and criollos the mytho-histories of Aacutetu Siwáli, of Kuámasi, of Mayúkelu and Mawáda, and also of Venancio Cristu Camico, as ways to prove their rights to their lands. The maps emphasized river courses, natural resources of each place (including the name of the spiritual being in charge of the reproduction of animal and plant species), sacred sites (mountains, petroglyphs, rocks, and other historical markers of the landscape), ancient communities, sites of economic relevance, the location of current communities, the Kuwé sacred routes, and so on.

Since the end of the 19th century, most South American countries have been considered postcolonial societies. However, the organization of South American political structures could also be characterized as a profoundly colonial form of power (Nugent 1994:152–153). In other words, in South America "the 'post' of post-colonial is not a sign of overcoming but of reproducing colonialism" (Coronil 1996:68). This is also the case in Venezuela, where, instead of irreversible radical breaks with the past, changes have occurred that do not sever with the past but rather link colonial and contemporaneous events (Nugent 1994:152; Caballero 1995:49–55). For the criollo population of the country, this association between the past and present colonial events has raised ideological sentiments that impel and justify their participation in a colonizing and civilizing process of the indigenous peoples.

In the international arena, Venezuela continues to be viewed as a periphery of the global system whose progress and transformation depend on internal adjustments. In the national political scene, Venezuelan Amazonia was and is still considered to be inhabited by subjugated individuals with subaltern cultures that are viewed as a source of cheap labor and raw materials. It is also thought of as a place for juridical, political, or ideological penetration and expansion of the national society in search of its economic development.

One example of this political and economic expansion was the 1970s Conquest of the South that was implemented to conquer Venezuelan Amazonia and its inhabitants (the Indians). This and other national and regional political mechanisms against the Arawakan peoples and other Amerindian groups of Venezuelan Amazonia were part of the processes that gave rise to many indigenous political movements to reinforce their cultural identities. These movements also promoted and reinforced sociocultural strategies for interpreting and representing the history and sociogeographic space of the Arawakan peoples. In the case of Warekena and other groups of the Guainía-Negro basins, their tradition of inscribing history into the landscape and their ways of representing the cartography of the cosmos, the earth, and the Amazon region helped them to build up practical and successful actions against the national colonial powers that tried to deprive them of their legal and historical rights to Warekena territory (Walékhena képe).

But the most important aspect of the Warekena traditional knowledge (the religion of Kúwai, the sacred routes and places or Kuwé Duwá-kalumi) is that it constitutes their cartography to organize and interpret the past and present of the Americas. This cartographic knowledge was and still is contested by Western cartography and the topography of colonial powers.

3

Three Patamuna Trees

Landscape and History in the Guyana Highlands

NEIL L. WHITEHEAD

This chapter addresses the intersection between ecological and historical anthropology. In order to do this I use the materials from my current fieldwork among the Patamuna of the Guyana highlands, a Cariban-speaking people numbering around five thousand persons. A key concept in this attempt to integrate ecology and history is *landscape*. This term has been widely used, perhaps even abused, of late and therefore has gained a wide currency in anthropology and other disciplines, such as geography, ecology, or history. As a result the idea of *landscape* in cultural anthropology can be understood in divergent ways.

For example, Carole Crumley (1994:6) in the edited volume *Historical Ecology* suggests that landscape history and historical ecology are identical, with *landscape* being understood as the "material manifestation of the relations between humans and the environment," whose changes need to be charted through time. However, William Balée (1998) in his introduction to *Advances in Historical Ecology* likewise emphasizes the theoretical importance of the concept of landscape for the possible integration of diverse disciplinary research findings, but he also notes that *how* this is done is all important.

In contributing to the Balée volume I concentrated on this latter question, arguing that the methodology of historical ecology must make human decision making, and the consciousness that drives it, the independent variable in our analysis of environmental dynamics. The varying "ecologies" (understood as a *practice*) that drive those decisions and associated environmental impacts then become a special subset of study for cultural history, as reflected by works such as Keith Thomas's *Man and the Natural World* (1983), Feld and Basso's *Senses of Place* (1997), or Robert Brightman's study of Cree hunting, *Grateful Prey* (1993). But to equate a historical ecology with a landscape history, however expansive that notion of landscape might be, is to miss the point that an ecology represents human practice *in* the landscape. The fact that no human practice takes place in a "pristine" environment, but always in a landscape shaped by the past ecological practice of others, only serves to emphasize the importance of understanding the historical dynamics of human usages. However, this does not entail that the totality of such human usages is equivalent to the particular sets of data, such as landscape forms, that are used to reconstruct them. In other words, simply to chart changes in landscape through time places phenomena, rather than persons, at the center of explanation, and so that explanation remains evolutionary rather than historical.

However, it is not the purpose of this chapter to debate the theory of the concept of landscape at length, only to stress the value of the concept of landscape for both anthropology and history. Even with theoretical differences over how the idea of landscape should be modeled, all can agree that its fundamental utility and relevance across disciplines is that it directs our attention to the way in which both the past and present are embedded in not only ecological practices and processes but also the cultural classification and interpretation of the environment that is partly created by those culturally informed practices. This, in turn, means that the landscape is more than the natural physical environment and refers also to the immanent presence of the biota and topography, as well as the dynamic activities of humans, fauna, flora, and the spirit world. Historical consciousness is also present in a landscape, reflected in the recounting and memory of the way that those interrelationships have developed through time.

For these reasons research in historical ecology needs to go beyond issues of the quantification of demography and subsistence practice, or investigation of Native classifications of flora and fauna, to take account of the way in which ecological practice is governed by mythic and ritual understanding, which itself is historically changing. This latter point about temporal change needs emphasis since earlier anthropological analyses have certainly made much of the way in which ritual might govern ecological practice, as with Roy Rappaport's (1984) discussion of the Tsembaga in New Guinea. However, these analyses did not address the fact that mythic and ritual practice is not unchanging, anymore than is the environment in which it is enacted.

My emphasis on indigenous historicity – defined as Patamuna consciousness about the past, how it is recounted, and how it is made relevant to the present – is intended to make good this kind of functionalist oversight. In Amazonia the tendency to emphasize synchronic adaptation over historical "involution" (Geertz 1963) was present also in Gerardo Reichel-Dolmatoff's (1985) pioneering discussion of cosmology as ecological analysis and lingers on in Philippe Descola's (1995) discussion of the "homeostatic" nature of Shuar subsistence practice. Somewhat infamously, Betty Meggers (1977) projected a deeply ahistorical view of current ethnographic adaptations back into the past, thereby suggesting a very constrained and limited agricultural and developmental sequence in the archaeological record. However, recent work by a variety of scholars, such as geographer William Denevan's (1992a, 1992b, 1992c) examination of the colonial transformation of Amazonia or ecologist Emilio Moran's (1993) demonstration of the complexity and variety of Amazonia as a habitat when viewed through the eyes of its inhabitants, is reinforced by archaeological studies by Clark Erickson (1994), Mike Heckenberger (1996), and Anna Roosevelt (1991, 1992, 1993, 1994; Roosevelt et al., 1991, 1996), which show the deep antiquity of substantive human impacts in Amazonia. In turn, this archaeological work is complemented by recent ethnographic studies that unravel the intellectual complexity of Native ecological understanding (e.g. Balée 2000, 1998, 1994a; Descola and Pálsson 1996; Viveiros de Castro 1998) and the relevance of the idea of landscape as a site for understanding that complexity (Gow 1995; Santos-Granero 1998). In sum, all these recent studies show how Amazonia should really be considered a cultural artifact, as much as a natural environment; a managed garden, not a pristine wilderness. Consequently, the concept of landscape is key to integrating this new data from both anthropology and other disciplines.

In the historical-ecological landscapes of Amazonia trees loom large, both literally and metaphorically, and this emphasis on trees (Rival 1998) serves to underline that, despite the contingent properties of symbols, their discursive qualities are often closely tied to the natural forms that inspire them. In this sense *trees*, no matter which plant forms make up this cultural classification, are peculiarly appropriate symbols of growth, continuity, and decay – properties preeminent in the cultural construction of historicity. As a result we have come to see that it is not sufficient merely to examine ecological process diachronically, as a succession of changing interactions driven by such factors as environmental constraints, expanding population, or a cultural incapacity for surplus production or accumulative economics. Rather, those changing ecological and economic process are embedded in historical consciousness and sociopolitical choices. Thus human history and decision making with regard to a complex mix of factors, such as political and economic interactions, ritual requirements, and mythic understanding, and which only partly include ecologically significant practice, must be analyzed before the meaning of ecological technique can be properly understood. The concept of landscape is thus critical to this enterprise for the way in which it focuses on the synergy of people and their habitats in culturally producing a physical and intellectual context for the nourishment and subsistence of both bodies and minds.

1. THE SOCIAL ECOLOGY OF THE PATAMUNA

The Patamuna of the Guyana highlands (Pakaraima Mountains) are socially and culturally embedded in their landscape by means of the historical and ecological forces that shape their identity. This intimate connection between ethnic identity, landscape, and an active engagement with the past is forcefully presented by Patamuna in the context of the oral performance of historical and ecological knowledge. Such "performances," loosely conceived as a series of speech acts that occur in formal settings, such as village gatherings, and informally as part of domestic life, also provide an important context for the valorization of cultural idioms of masculinity, especially those of the jaguar hunter (*kaikuci yakamana'yi*), chant owner (*alleluia'san*) and eminent man (*kàyik*).

Work in progress attempts to compare the kinds of narrative devices and symbolic idioms that occur in these different forms of oral performance and to examine how they are linked to the wider social and cultural purposes of gender and ethnic differentiation. Particular attention is being paid to Patamuna ideas and metaphors of landscape, animality and divinity, and sociopolitical incorporation. Research in an earlier phase of this project suggested that, for example, Patamuna orators can elegantly manipulate debate by using the sign *jaguar* as a metonym for all three of these issues. In the case of the landscape, the presence or absence of jaguars delimits zones of human activity, and jaguar hunting becomes partly a forceful assertion of those use-rights.

In the course of fieldwork it became apparent that indigenous historical consciousness cannot be easily separated from other cultural discourses, such as those relating to gender and ethnicity, and is anyway overlain by a historicity that connects the living directly to the dead, the divine, and their faunal and floral spirit forms. The continuing presence and past actions of these ancestors and spirits (*yumu*) are overtly manifest in the landscape in the form of such archaeological features as petroglyphs, burial sites, megaliths and stone alignments, cave sites, and ancestral villages. But they are also present in the living forest and savannas as spirit forces controlling the distribution of game animals, fish, and minerals (*totopù*), as well as constituting specific kinds of threats or obstacles to gardening and gathering (*atai-tai*). The presence of jaguars, boas, anacondas, iguanas, and their transformations as guardians or jealous owners of specific locales, called *esak* by the Patamuna, thus guides the practical subsistence choices that Patamuna men and women make.

In this way the environment itself also offers a series of mnemonics for the recall of historical events, just as subsistence practices and resource management become tokens of Patamuna identity and use-rights in that environment – it is in this sense that the Patamuna practice both a natural and social ecology. The repeated intrusions of loggers, ranchers, miners, balata-bleeders (rubber gatherers), and, most recently, eco-tourism have therefore presented a number of challenges to Patamuna understanding of themselves, others, and their past. Similarly, Patamuna oral history of their aboriginal occupation of this region is structured around their own intrusion and encounters with both the "First Beings" (*totopù, atai-tai*) and a non-agricultural people, the Kawaliyanas. This historiographical motif then provides the context for narrative of the origins and purposes of a distinctly "Patamuna way" in which manioc agriculture is strongly contrasted to Kawaliyana gathering and hunting.

This way of being in the landscape is now directly threatened by forms of economic development that have vastly increased the mobility of Patamuna individuals and their engagement with the global economy. Nonetheless this active engagement with outsiders is also seen by some as fundamental to the future survival of a Patamuna identity, either through the lure of quick cash in the gold and diamond mines or through the uncertain benefits of eco-tourism. It is precisely these kinds of issues that are then mediated in and through the forms of oral performance that have been the focus of the project so far, particularly the unfolding of an indigenous historiography that constantly renegotiates the representation of the "first-time" or originary condition of Patamuna society.

This is evinced in the narration of the growth of external trade contacts and marriage exchanges with the Kawaliyanas, the times of warfare with the Karinya, Makushi, and Ye'kuana, and the presence or absence of the spirits of forest and savanna. The landscape topoi that act as mnemonics for the recall and negotiation of these various themes are numerous and do not fall into any one class of landscape feature. They include the three trees that gave the title to this chapter, the spirits of the *atai-tai* and *to-topù*, and the petroglyphic *timehri*, or "writing of the ancestors," among others. Broader aspects of the environment, such as the contrast between savannas and forest, the archaeological traces of their past in the form of abandoned villages, battlegrounds, and former ritual sites, also structure both ecological practice and discourse.

2. PATAMUNA LANDSCAPES

If we first consider the broadest categories of forest (*tichipileng'yek*) and savanna (*toi*), then it is apparent that the Ireng River, which is located at the southern end of the Yawong valley and forms the political border between Guyana and Brazil, also marks the point at which the high rainforest of the Yawong and Paramakatoi region gives way to the hard, burnt savannas that march endlessly south toward the Amazon (see Figure 3.1). To anyone who walks the paths (*asanda*) of this region, the contrasts between these two ecotones are very evident, and so the complementary identities of Makushi and Patamuna derive partly from the consequences of an adaptation to the one or other of these habitats. Consequently the Patamuna are known to the Makushi as *Ingari-kok*, "people of the cool wet place," and with their neighbors the Akawaio are known as *Ka-pohn*, literally "sky-people," in reference to the mountainous nature of the terrain north of the Ireng River.[1] The term *Patamuna* contains further reference to the importance of historical ecology in the constitution of identity since it may be translated as "owners of the land."

In turn, the political meaning of these ecologically molded identities, or their forgotten antecedents, has sometimes led to open warfare. The Ireng River therefore also traces the distribution of many "bone dumps" that are testimony to the military significance of the savanna-forest frontier, as well as the favorability of the savanna terrain for the conduct of indigenous warfare. Such political contrasts, embedded in both history and ecology, become the occasion and means for the elaboration of ideas about the Makushi and Patamuna, even though there is intermarriage now, even as there was warfare in the past.

Fig. 3.1. (top of page) Forest-savanna transition in the Guyana highlands
(Photograph by author)

Fig. 3.2. (bottom) The cashew tree at Tusenen (Photograph by author)

i. Acajou – *The Cashew*

The theme of warfare allows me to introduce the first of the three Patamuna trees – the cashew (*Anacardium occidentale*), which, when encountered, is always an occasion for the recall of days of warfare and, in particular, the tactic of the *wenaiman* (revenge team).

It was in the Yawong valley that the last *weypantaman* ("killing fight")
with the Makushi occurred, at Kulauyaktoi in the 1920s. The Patamuna
kàyik at this time was actually born a Makushi, but he had married
into the Patamuna. He was known as Laiman, and his "Second," his
brother, was named Salaula. The Makushi *kàyik* was called Waila. Salaula
was killed at Monkey Mountain by Waila and his crew in the series of
Makushi raids that preceded the final battle of Kulauyaktoi. As a result
of the death of Salaula, Laiman decided to hunt down Waila. Meanwhile
Waila sent men to attack Laiman again, although he did not know that
Laiman was already coming for revenge. Laiman reached Kulyuaktoi, an
attack point near the village of Tusenen, which was defended by a dense
hedge of bamboo called *yalá*. Here he encountered Waila and his raiding
party. Laiman killed Waila in combat and, being "heated" by this killing,
asked if there were any others who were still with Waila. One of them
was brave enough to say that he was still a follower, so Laiman pulled his
gun and humiliated the enemy by shooting him in the face.

As the Makushi survivors fled with the wounded, they were contin-
uously ambushed in their retreat, and all were eventually killed "on the
line" (*asanda*) back to their village in the Kanuku Mountains. This technique of secretly pursuing an enemy raiding party was known as *wenaiman*. Conspicuous in this secret harassment of the fleeing Makushi
was one old man in particular who used his blowgun to silently strike
down the raiders. However, he was eventually killed by the Makushi and
then was transformed into this cashew tree, which can be seen on the
outskirts of Tusenen today. These magical transformations may have resulted botanically from the common practice of always walking with a
supply of seeds for planting in new places. But the prevalence of cashew
trees in the savannas also means that this memory is frequently recalled.
The sight of a lonely cashew in the savanna thus both produces and reinforces the image of the lone Patamuna bravely resisting the Makushi
raiders, and in this way the cashew works as a mnemonic for the remembrance of the days of warfare.

Such sites are then linked to the presence of many "bone dumps" of skeletal remains that can be seen on the southern side of the Ireng River, especially at Korona Falls and as far south as the Powis River, which are a silent testimony to the ecological nature of the frontier with the Makushi.

ii. Akyau – *The Palm*

The second tree that allows me to introduce more of the Patamuna topoi in the Yawong valley is the *akyau* palm (*Astrocaryum aculeatum*). The *akyau* recalls another indigenous group that once inhabited the Yawong valley – the Kawaliyanas ("those of Kowa"). They were the first "real people" of this region, and the Patamuna who originally formed Paramakatoi village only numbered some five households. The Patamuna came from the north, having broken away from a group that settled nearer to Kowa Mountain, because the hunting was good in the Yawong valley, and there they encountered the Kawaliyana nomadic hunters. They are recalled as a people without horticulture, living on the fruits, fish, and game of the forest. The palm *akyau* was gathered as a customary item of diet, and the Kawaliyanas are said to have worshiped this tree, circling it in dance to give thanks for its bounty (see also Cormier, in this volume). Also noted by the Patamuna was the use of *icha* fruits (*Eugenia patrisii*, a member of the guava family) and plantains to produce an alcoholic drink. The Kawaliyanas are otherwise unknown in the historical record but appear to have been Cariban speakers like the Patamuna.[2]

The refusal of agriculture is therefore the key to how the Kawaliyanas are represented in Patamuna thought; they stand in counterpoint to the settled farming, centered on manioc, that the Patamuna see as critical to their identity. In a similar fashion emphasis is given to the fact that the Kawaliyanas never had guns, that they used the naturally poisonous *lapo* wood (*Bothriospora corymbosa*) instead of *ourali* (curare) as arrow points, and that they used a massive club, *kawa'yak*, in warfare. This then illustrates the way in which the Kawaliyanas represent a kind of sylvan primitiveness in Patamuna thinking, not unlike the figure of the "Wild Man" in Western cultures (Bartra 1994). The Patamuna people say the Kawaliyanas were very alert to an obligation to share all hunting kills, even to the point of making this a reason for warfare. If only a single hair was left from the carcass of a deer that had not been shared with the Kawaliyanas, they would find out and take revenge for this failure to carry out the obligations of reciprocal exchange.

The Patamuna also recall that the Kawaliyanas showed contempt for those who planted gardens in the forest, used cassava bread and cassiri drink, and settled in villages. The Kawaliyanas did not build houses for themselves, preferring to just make shelters in the forest when they needed them. So conflicts with the Kawaliyanas, as in the case of hunting, are pictured as deriving from the tensions that arose from these contrasting ways of exploiting the resources of the Yawong valley and the surrounding region. The "fierceness" of the Kawaliyanas is explicitly illustrated partly through a hunting homily – to the effect that, among the Kawaliyanas, even those hunters who did not get much while out hunting would still be expected to share as generously as if they had been successful. This was not just something they expected of outsiders but was a belief that disciplined their own hunters.

In this way, the "fierceness" of the Kawaliyanas becomes a warning and a lesson for Patamuna people in their own quest for peace, security, and prosperity. In a kind of Native Hobbesian image of the war of all men against all men, Patamuna say that the Kawaliyanas were actually so fierce that they finally died out, largely because of excessive infighting. This social implosion is thought to be due to the fact that they were not able to organize themselves as effectively as those committed to farming and living in settled villages. In these ways the *akyau* palm, and the other plants not used by the Patamuna, become mnemonics for reflection on the vanished Kawaliyanas, the validity of the Patamuna way, and an understanding of the resources of the Yawong and how they should be used.

iii. Kumaka – *The Ceiba Tree*

The third Patamuna tree, the *kumaka* (*Ceiba pentandra*), has a similar moral meaning and is also connected to hunting, but in this case it is the correct behavior of Patamuna hunters that is in question.

A giant *kumaka* stands at the center of the Yawong valley and, as in other places, serves as a prominent visual marker in the landscape. At the most general level the *kumaka* is a living connection between the earth and sky, between men and divinities, for the Patamuna, as it was for the Mayas. Consequently the kumaka tree figures prominently in creation tales where it becomes the First Tree from which birds, reptiles, and mammals were all created by Makunaima, the First Ancestor. This tree is also the place where bush spirits, such as the *atai-tai* and *totopù*, may conceal themselves while moving around the valley, or real killers, *kanaimà*, lie in ambush. The tree in this picture, which is dead, also has a special

Fig. 3.3. The *kumaka* in the Yawong valley (Photograph by author)

story attached to it that deals with its death as an aspect of Patamuna gender relations.

The tree marks the point in the valley floor on the approach to Paramakatoi where hunters returning with their kill would stop to rest, and it was expected that the women and wives from the village would come down the steep mountain to carry these loads up to the village. One time a hunter, a *kàyik* – that is, an eminent man and famous warrior – stopped here with a hunting party that had been gone many days. All the other men were welcomed by the women with cassiri beer and cassava bread except this man. In a fit of rage at this laziness of his wife he raised his gun and let fly both barrels into the kumaka tree. As a result it began to die, and this event is viewed wistfully by the Patamuna as reflecting their onward rush away from tradition into the uncertainties of modernity and development. However, should this tale be recounted by a woman, it becomes the failure of the *kàyik* to control his anger that is the cause of the death of the *kumaka* tree, and so the tree acts as a multifaceted topoi for the recall of traditional myths about the origins of persons and their habitat. At the same time it allows debate on the consequences of development (the possession of guns) and the consequences of a lack of self-control by men, or laziness on the part of women, which in turn might threaten the destruction of Patamuna identity, which relies on a complementary cooperation of the sexes.

Thus the consideration of these three trees draws attention to the way in which tree symbolism is particularly apt for the representation of change, growth, and decay since landscapes change, as do trees, and this inherent dynamism allows a direct and convincing connection to be made between human history and ecological processes.

iv. Atai-tai, Totopù, Ulupelu, and Timehri

As already mentioned, there are other kinds of topoi in the Patamuna landscape, and these also respond to the processual nature of landscapes and human lives, but in the Patamuna view those ecological processes are far from culturally anonymous or "natural." This idea is constantly reinforced by the way in which bush spirits, such as the *atai-tai* and *totopù*, mark the presence of key resources, such as peccary herds, diamond and gold sources, or old gardens. Such spirits are *esak* – that is, owners of those resources – and so the intervention of shamans is required to gain the permission of these bush masters for the removal of their resources. In turn, the presence of these spirits and their willingness to engage in dialogue with Patamuna shamans is taken as diagnostic of the correctness of Patamuna resource exploitation. Indeed, even historical materials suggest that ecologies governed by shamans are an ancient feature of Amazonian societies. For example, Lawrence Keymis, lieutenant to Walter Ralegh in his 16th-century exploration of Guyana, relates the following about his search for sources of gold: "The aged sort, to keep this from common knowledge, have devised a fable of a dangerous Dragon that haunteth this place and devoureth all that come near it. But our Indian, if when we return, we do bring store of strong wine (which they love beyond measure) with it will undertake so to charm this Dragon, that he shall do us no harm" (Keymis 1596:17). The "Dragon" here can be identified with the *esak* for gold, and the request for drink as the offer to make a shamanic propitiation of that spirit.

The Patamuna today also relate that such a dragon – called Ulupelu – guards a cave in the Yawong valley that is a source of gold and diamonds. So in the current moment, where all kinds of new economic development are being discussed, the claim to have sighted the Ulupelu, *atai-tai*, or *totopù* becomes a strong way in which to mark a disinterest or opposition to expanding the cash economy or experimenting with cash crops such as cabbage or squash. In this context the recent "death" of the *totopù* at the ancient village of Wandapàtoi is a direct expression of this changing scene.

Fig. 3.4. Ulupelu's lair (Photograph by author)

Wandapàtoi was long known as the place where the *totopù* had their origin. The village sits on the edge of a high plateau that is riddled with caves, and the *totopù* is thought to live in these caves. Since the coming of the missionaries in the 1960s the village was largely abandoned even though the presence of the *totopù* made it a deeply significant place, and even though it was the site for a foot race, the *kakú*, that took place between all the villages of the Yawong and was a means for their ritual integration. It was also here that the famous shaman Scipio called out a huge herd of peccaries after mediating with the *totopù*. In the *paiwarri* (manioc-beer) feast that followed, the *totopù* came to dance and drink with the humans, which was always considered a great blessing and evidence of the harmony between the Patamuna and their habitat. But the *totopù* was given too much rum, a creole's drink. He fell, was killed, and was placed under the falls at Wandapàtoi, where no more peccaries have been seen. *Totopù* graves are thought to mark the presence of minerals and are also sometimes marked by petroglyphs, but even with the loss of the *totopù*, ancestral spirits still guide the Patamuna through their presence in abandoned villages, whose gardens are still used, and in their written signs that appear as petroglyphs, or *timehri*.

For example, a series of petroglyphs along the Siparuni River are linked in a by a set of complex symbolic motifs, including human and animal figures as well as abstract designs. The petroglyphs occur consistently from the head of the river downstream to its conjunction with the Essequibo, but they cluster particularly around the falls of the river, with some being only seasonally visible, and also occur on prominent rock outcrops along the course of the whole river. The Patamuna view the Siparuni as an ancestral location, reporting many village sites, replete with pottery remains, along the whole stretch of river. They also still use the Siparuni as an important source of fish, and it is been hypothesized that petroglyphs played a key role in the controlled exploitation of natural resources. Consequently the *makunaima timehri*, "the marks of the ancients," survive as living elements in the Patamuna landscape. In this way an important connection is also sustained with the deep past (see also Vidal, in this volume).

3. PROPHETIC HISTORY

For the Patamuna the construction of history is as much about the present and as it is about things past. In this way prophecy is history

Fig. 3.5. *Timehri* in the Yawong valley (Photograph by author)

since the meaning of what has been can only be understood in relation to the things that are and are to come. In this way the Patamuna
historicity is strongly marked by the practice of prophecy, and so the
form and content of history is concerned with sustaining, into the future, a Patamuna way. Such a historical vision emplaces individuals and
social groups in a landscape charged with historical significance, but
that landscape – through prophecy – may be renegotiated, changed, and
reordered. Prophetic vision can also interpret and thus control external
forces for change, enabling the construction of stable relationships with
others, such as the Makushi or the Kawaliyanas in a way that creates
continuity in Patamuna identities. History is as much concerned with
shamanic practice and prophecy as it is with cataloguing sociopolitical
events (see also Whitehead 2002; Wright 1998).

These kinds of history making include not only material, physical
events but also shamanic warfare for the order of the cosmos – that is,
a struggle between *iwepyatàsak* (prophets), the *alleluia'san*, who can re-
make the human world through continual innovation in shamanic song
and ritual form, and dark shamans, the *kanaimà*, who sustain the cosmic order through a continuous exchange of life force – *ekati*[3] – with the
first beings, particularly *Kaikuci'ima*, Lord Jaguar, master of the forests,
and Makunaima, creator of plants and animals (Whitehead 2001, 2002).

Alongside the history of warfare with political groups is an occult combat in which enemy shamans battle through the use of spirit forces. A shaman has a number of spirit proxies who can appear as animal predators to attack their foe while he is ascending the spirit ladder (*karawali*). If that ladder can be "cut" while the enemy shaman climbs it, he will die. In the case of *kanaimà*, the killers are also men and can be left in great spiritual danger by the death of their *kanaimà* shaman. Such leaderless *kanaimà* are then killed by the *kwayaus* (warriors) of the valley. By the same token, an alleluia prophet and his followers may be ritually mutilated by such killers and, unable to resunder their bodies, are spiritually as well as physically destructed by the *kanaimà*. History therefore becomes literally *embodied* through the material presence of given individuals, and their existence becomes a "proof" of Patamuna historical vision. This is not equivalent to the "heroic" histories of kings and chiefs that represent certain kin groups or lineages as powerful, but a recognition of the way in which individuals become the agents of dark and shadowy forces, through transformation (*weytupok*) into jaguars, anteaters, butterflies, and snakes. In turn, Patamuna life-cycle rituals locate bodies in a cultural framework that envisions bodies and their transformation as sites through which the significance of the past may be understood. Patamuna bodies are produced through the socializing forces of marriage, childbirth, and the couvade, but this intent may be disrupted, and a historical disjuncture may occur when persons not so socialized (i.e., not *ka-pohn*; see note 1) intervene in the unfolding of individual and collective destiny. Individual destiny itself is differentiated from the collective precisely through reference to the alarming appearances of such ghosts, bush spirits, *kanaimà* shamans, or enemy shamans.

Guyanese Coastlanders such as miners and soldiers, as well as foreigners such as missionaries and anthropologists, also appear as disjunctive forces in Patamuna life, and Patamuna historicity understands such discontinuity not simply as change, progress, or development but as a portent of emergent threats – to individual lives, to the integrity of the kin group, and even to the Patamuna as an ethnic community. One of the first white men to traverse the Yawong valley is referred to as a "cannibal" who led a group of Karinya into the highlands to trade for balata, but who also threatened the *ekati* of Patamuna people.[4] The ambush of these outsiders at Kali'nasulatàpù (the place where the Karinya got barbecued) and their military defeat are clearly recalled, and in terms of Patamuna historicity this represents a mimetic equalization of the power relations between themselves and those who would "eat them up." The mutilation of Patamuna bodies in *kanaimà* ritual is also interpreted as an attack on the body politic of Patamuna society as historically constituted through human action. *Kanaimà* killing thereby recalls not just issues of political or economic power but also the destructive force of those dark and occult potencies that menace the humanity of Patamuna life. The power of alleluia chants to overcome these dark potencies and the ability of *kanaimàs* to capture their victims are, however, historically contingent. In this way this shamanic power and prophecy are seen as a contingent, historical practices that will also have an end. As a result, it is said that when the alleluia chants return south to the land of the Makushi, their place of origin, this will also be a sign of the end of all things, the end of historical time itself. However, it remains possible that a new prophetic vision might show a new means to sustain *ekati* in the face of the divine hunger of the originary beings such as Makunaima. The writings, the "texts" of Makunaima left in the form of *timehri* (petroglyphs), are demonstrations of the historicity of shamanic practice, and as the year 2000 approached so a new prophecy circulated in the Yawong valley.

Bagit Paul, once a Native pastor, "received" a rock crystal through which he saw the destruction of the Pakaraima Mountains in a great flood. Everyone would be carried away except those who, through fasting, the rejection of Western medicines, and constant song, would find the path of spiritual redemption. This vision is echoed in other Native prophecies. In the 19th century "false" prophets were reported by British missionaries to be active in the highlands, preaching the end of time and the material redemption of the Amerindians. Among these was "The Impostor, a white man." It is therefore significant for understanding Patamuna historicity that my own presence among the Patamuna was itself testament to the possibility for change and that my own coming was subject to prophetic vision. This points to other complex aspects of Patamuna historicity, for the interpenetration of Western and indigenous historicities continues to produce, as it has since earliest contacts, representations of the agents of colonial and later national society as powerful, even shamanic, figures within Native historicities (Whitehead 2000).

It should be apparent that the notion of a landscape as a cultural production of the natural allows us to integrate archaeological, historical, and ethnographic materials in new ways. We can also see that certain focal points – topoi – become preeminent in ecological and historical discourse, as in the case of the three trees. As a result, human ecological processes – hunting, fishing, mining, farming – constantly recall these topoi as discursive tropes in myth, ritual, and other oral performances. In this way ecological practice becomes thoroughly entangled with historical memory.

More generally, the active conjunction of ecological practice, historical and mythic idioms of representation, ethnic affirmation, and definitions of gender, with changing forms of oral performance, raises a number of theoretical issues that have recently preoccupied anthropologists. These issues include the forms and dynamics of non-Western modes of historical consciousness, the relation between indigenous and external ecologies and the social use of ecological idioms, the grounds for a humanistic as well as scientific ecology, the importance of performance as well as form in indigenous ecological discourse, and the historicity of that performance. The general relevance of such a project for anthropology thus lies in its emphasis on Native forms of historical consciousness and the way in which they are present in forms of oral performance that might otherwise appear to be ahistorical in content. The work of "myth" is far more historically complex than had sometimes been allowed, but the forms of that complexity are still relatively undocumented. Myths of the landscape contribute to the "sense of place" that, as Feld and Basso (1997) have recently illustrated, makes human activity in that landscape replete with cultural significance and personal meaning. So, too, it has been the intention here to suggest ways in which human ecological practice that is reflected in the landscape can also be a historical commentary and form of political positioning. The choices that guide that ecological practice are not simply taken with regard to their technical efficiency or rationalist instrumentality, but they also achieve a proper sense of identity and being as Patamuna, in the face of rapidly changing circumstance. Moreover, as the debate between Sahlins (1995) and Obeyesekere (1992) reminds us, even knowing the forms of historical consciousness does not answer the question as to how such cultural structures are present in action and agency. The emphasis given here to performance upon and discourse about landscape is intended to move us beyond that distinction.

NOTES

1. The term *kapohn* also distinguishes the human from the nonhuman and possibly human.

2. There is said to be one surviving speaker of the Kawaliyana language, intelligible to Patamuna, but I have as yet been unable to interview this man.

3. *Ekati* refers to notions of spirit essence among many Cariban-speaking peoples and for the Patamuna is a property of all life forms. *Ekati* may become detached in dreams or if someone faints, but it also can be purposefully separated, by both *piya* (curing) and *kanaimà* shamans, in order to travel great distances and kill enemies. The physical and magical force of kanaimà attack is particularly effective because it totally drives the *ekati* out of the victim, through acts of ritually proscribed mutilation to the still living victim, and so makes the *ekati* available for "consumption" by *kaikusi-yumu.*

4. This usage of the notion of *ekati* to refer to a collective essence of being Patamuna is an important extension of the meaning of the term. It neatly illustrates the way in which "traditional" categories are deployed to encompass the challenges of "modernity," thereby creating alternative modernities to those promulgated by the priests and prophets of "development and progress."

Contact and Power

4

Power Encounters

BERTA E. PÉREZ

It is already well established in anthropology that cultures and societies can no longer be ethnographically studied as ahistorical and self-contained – isolated local islands – nor can their interactions and relations with national and global power (or vice versa) be analyzed only from a unidirectional and unidimensional perspective. As Whitehead indicates in the introduction to this volume, we now need to pay particular attention to the kinds of historical consciousness, or "historicities," rather than continue to extend our analysis to the histories that are precisely created and made meaningful by these historicities. The importance of examining historicities – or the modes in which certain kinds of historical consciousness are expressed – is that these are precisely anchored on the experiences lived by distinct groups who have shared a particular region, such as Amazonia, and on the sociocultural significance by which these groups radically select their own respective past "from the immensely rich swirl of past human activity" (Price 1973:5). In addition to providing a better framework of analysis in anthropology, as rightly suggested by Whitehead, this special focus on historicities can serve as a stepping-stone toward the development of a theoretical basis from which to link local and global realities, such as the historical relation of power based on domination and resistance or on conflicts, negotiations, and resolutions.

Within this framework on historicities, the expression of power has formed part of the Aripaeño's historical consciousness. The Aripaeño are descendants of runaway black slaves, or maroons, and currently live in Aripao, located on the east bank of the Lower Caura River in the northwestern region of Bolívar state, Venezuela (see Figure 4.1). Similar to their ancestors in resorting to *grand marronnage* as a mechanism of resistance against slavery and, subsequently, in creating a physical space in an alien environment that would enclose a cultural heritage born of a process of ethnogenesis, present-day Aripaeño continue to have the capacity to

81

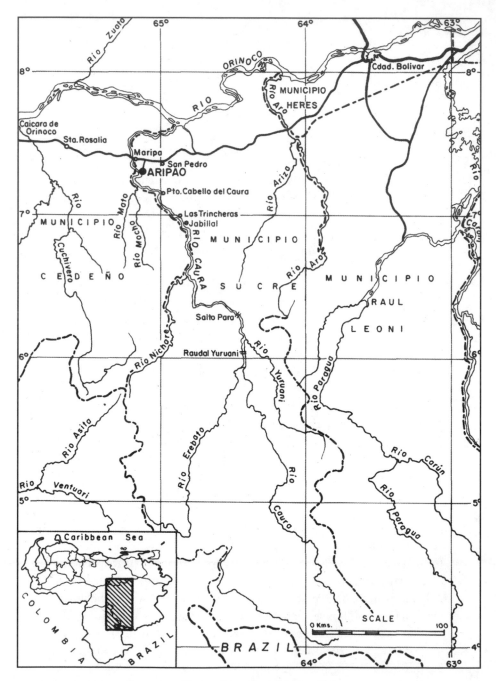

Fig. 4.1. Location of Aripao

defend their own cultural reproduction, representation, and production. That is, they make their own decisions over those cultural elements that they consider theirs and over those elements that they have appropriated as their own for having a maroon spirit or ethos (Pérez and Perozo 2000a). This spirit is characterized by the control that they manifest over their own physical and cultural survival as well as toward the preservation of who they are and what is theirs, while still being receptive to foreign cultural elements by means of negotiation, rather than through imposition by the external world.

Hence, the historical reconstruction of the Aripaeño and their involvement as active agents in the "making of history" in the Guianas has been a focus of my research (Pérez 1995, 1997, 1998, 2000a, 2000b; Pérez and Perozo 2000a, 2000b). Both aspects indicate that the Aripaeño are very much a product of an earlier process of globalization (or of international conflicts) that gave rise to the Atlantic slave trade in the colonial period and show that the encounters of power between the Aripaeño and the members of the status quo, specifically, are a continuation of that same process. This process is defined as the expansion of an economic model that privileges the market conditions or the exploitation of human and natural resources for the benefit of capital accumulation. Under such a scenario, the Aripaeño forebears, for instance, in their status as maroons, saw themselves obliged to embrace two foreign political systems. They formed part of the indigenous political system of the region and yet were also compelled to participate in the colonial political system. Although both political systems have been modified and transformed through time and space, the descendants of the Aripaeño continue, as a matter of their cultural survival, to engage in a political practice that reflects the dynamic relationship between domination and resistance or scenarios of conflict, negotiation, and resolution.

Whereas indigenous political systems in Amazonia are often characterized by the formation of horizontal or nonhierarchical alliances among distinct ethnic groups, the Western political system is exclusionary and oppressive to those groups that are not a part of the established order or initial status quo. The main purpose of this essay, through the examination of a particular event that occurred in Aripao in the year 1996, is to demonstrate that the Aripaeño have maintained cultural continuity partly through the negotiations that they make using both indigenous and Western political models. The case study of this event also illustrates the forms of political performance of the Aripaeño in conflict situations and demonstrates that the essence of their present decision making and actions has not varied much from that of the past. This event came about when a woman from Caracas settled in an area that the Aripaeño consider as their communal land.

The work of Arjun Appadurai (1997:178–199) on the "production of locality as a property of social life" and "production of neighborhood as a property of social forms," for example, is relevant to understanding many facets of the Aripaeño's life, including the relations of power implicit in the encounter with the woman from Caracas. In this sense, I posit that the Aripaeño's "locality-producing activities are not only context-driven but are also context-generative," just as Appadurai asserts when he refers to other cultural groups, such as the Yanomami (1997:186). As a result of their traditional way of life, the Aripaeño produce a wider set of contexts beyond the space that they have established as their current locality and neighborhood within the Caura region. But the cultural consolidation of that space in which these newer contexts are generated does not exempt the Aripaeño from experiencing encounters of power with representatives of the Venezuelan nation-state and even with other cultural groups within the region. The latter point suggests that cultural heterogeneity still prevails (Appadurai 1997; Comaroff 1996; Comaroff and Comaroff 1992, 1993; Sahlins 1999), even though cultural homogeneity is what globalization often connotes. And this pluralization, or the rise of localism (Comaroff 1996), becomes evident through the historicities that the distinct cultural segments reveal in accordance with the experiences that each of these has had with members of the established order and even with each other.

The Aripaeño, as a local example of the global village, have not necessarily rejected the influx of outsiders nor the incorporation of elements of modernity into their community or region. Yet, their major concern is that the integration of these external factors would cause disruption in the ebb and flow of their traditional horizontal and decentralized way of life. This does not imply the existence of an absolute political equilibrium among the Aripaeño, nor between them and other cultural segments or individuals that inhabit the region. But it does show that "being maroons" or having a "maroon" ethos (Pérez and Perozo 2000a) has helped the Aripaeño to persevere, even in situations that have national or global implications.

In order to understand the aforementioned specific event that becomes the core of my analysis, a brief historical, geographical, and cultural sketch of the Aripaeño is necessary. Aripaeño forebears escaped from the Dutch colonial plantations of Surinam or Demerara sometime after the middle of the 18th century. As either explicitly or implicitly inferred by some scholars (Bilby 1997; Price 1973; Whitten and Corr 1997), it is not unusual to find that part of the physical and cultural survival of maroon societies often depended on pacts, treaties, or alliances made with other indigenous groups and colonizers. In the case of the Aripaeño forebears, the social and political context in the Orinoco basin during the 18th century was highly complex in that the resolutions arrived at from the political actions taken were not fixed, but rather were fluid and fluctuating. That is, the political outcomes or agreements made among distinct cultural segments depended on their shared interests and common enemies at a given time (Pérez 1995, 1997, 1998, 2000b).

So during their *grand marronnage*, the Aripaeño forebears were likely to have remained away from the areas controlled by the Kari'ña, a Carib indigenous group.[1] The reason is that the Kari'ña had made alliances with the Dutch in order to combat the threat of the Spanish Crown from conquering and controlling the Orinoco River basin, which the Kari'ña fiercely defended (Morales 1979; Whitehead 1988). At the same time, the arrival of Aripaeño forebears into the Upper Caura River was facilitated through alliances previously made with distinct indigenous groups such as the Ye'kuana, a Carib indigenous group. The Ye'kuana, for example, were victimized by the Kari'ña for the socioeconomic alliances made with the Spaniards (Pérez 2000b). Although more research is needed for the period between the end of the 18th and the middle of the 19th century, relationships among Spaniards, Amerindians, and Aripaeño varied considerably. While the Ye'kuana broke off their trade networks with the Spaniards following a rebellion against the Spaniards in 1776, the Aripaeño also formed alliances with the Kari'ña, especially following the Kari'ña loss of military power over the Caura region by the middle of the 18th century.[2] Nonetheless, following their dual strategy, the Aripaeño also united forces with the Royalist Spaniards to fight against the Republicans in the Venezuelan War of Independence. Despite the Spaniards' defeat, the Aripaeño stayed and even consolidated their position along the Caura River, within the newly formed republic.

Part of Aripaeño forebears' survival as maroons depended on two particular factors. One is their insertion in a horizontal or nonhierarchical indigenous political system known as the "System of Orinoco Regional Interdependence – SORI (Arvelo-Jiménez 1981, 2001; Arvelo-Jiménez and Biord Castillo 1994; Arvelo-Jiménez et al. 1989; Morales Méndez and Arvelo-Jiménez 1981). This system transcended the purely ethnic level of sociocultural integration through the establishment and maintenance of articulatory mechanisms such as trade, ritual services, marriages alliances, political treaties, raids, and warfare among distinct ethnic indigenous groups. These inter-ethnic relations were nonhierarchical, and they, in turn, permitted permanent political and cultural autonomy for each of the distinct ethnic groups involved. Such characteristics gave Aripaeño ancestors a promising context in which to seek refuge and form economic and political alliances. In fact, some Aripaeño men claim that although their ancestors feared or considered as enemies some indigenous groups (e.g., the Kari'ña), there were others (e.g., the Ye'kuana) with whom they established trade and marriage alliances.[3]

The other factor in the maroons' survival was the likelihood that they would gain the status of "freed slaves" or of "political exiles" upon their entry into the Caura region – which was then Spanish territory. Thus, the Spaniards, who were at war against the Dutch over the control of the Guianas for political and economic gains, protected and allocated available land (e.g., San Luis de Guaraguaraico) to the original Aripaeño (López-Borreguero 1886; Wickham and Crevaux 1988). Hence, the Aripaeño's participation in the horizontal and decentralized indigenous political system and in the vertical and centralized political system of the Spanish Crown involved negotiations and alliances with indigenous groups and with Spanish missionaries, respectively (for more details, see Pérez 2000b).

It was precisely in this community where Pantera Negra (Black Panther) – the Aripaeño's ancestral and messianic female mulatta figure – was raised and where, through her persona and deeds, she marked the beginning of a historical landscape from which present-day Aripaeño derive their claims to a distinct cultural heritage and identity (see Figure 4.2). In Appadurai's terms (1997), her creation of a locality and of a neighborhood became the "ethnoscape" from which her descendants

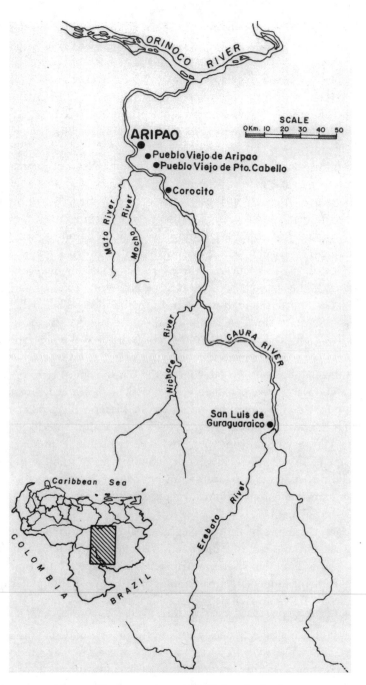

Fig. 4.2. Former settlements of Aripaeño forebears

were to produce, represent, and reproduce similar contexts of social life and social forms.[4] According to present-day Aripaeño, their forebears had formed, at the very least, five settlements in the Caura region.[5] These are San Luis de Guaraguaraico, Corocito, Pueblo Viejo de Puerto Cabello, Pueblo Viejo de Aripao, and Aripao. Thus Aripao's formation dates to the last six generations of Aripaeño, and the ancestors have left a legacy that the modern Aripaeño embrace and guard symbolically, historically, and in daily practice.[6]

A central feature of this legacy entails Pantera Negra, the offspring of an upper-class Dutch white woman and a black slave foreman who worked at the Dutch colonial plantation owned by the father of Pantera Negra's mother. Upon the couple's discovery of the pregnancy, they fled in the company of other blacks from the plantation and settled in the Caura region, probably by the end of the 18th century. Pantera Negra was born during this journey to freedom or *grand marronnage*. Upon the death of her parents, Pantera Negra became the ruler of San Luis de Guaraguaraico, the maroon community founded by her father. Although she maintained social, political, and economic alliances with both the Spanish missionaries and Carib Indians of the area, the stability of these relationships with one or the other faction was sometimes upset through her ambition to control the Caura region. Her apparent beauty and warriorlike personality were particularly feared by men; as a beautiful woman, she used her feminine qualities to entice and enchant men for her own purposes, and moreover, as a dreadful, malelike figure, she mercilessly killed anyone who crossed her. However, Pantera Negra's life came to an abrupt end as a result of a love triangle and the jealousy that she created in her two lovers – one her cousin and the other a Carib Indian named Panchito, whom she had seduced as part of a strategy to defeat the Spaniards.

In fact, the figure of Pantera Negra reveals a transformation of her life cycle – from birth, life, death, and rebirth – into a temporal, historical continuum that relates to Aripaeño's landscape, a landscape that ranges from the immediate surroundings of Aripao to far-flung sites such as San Luis de Guaraguaraico (Pérez 1997, 1998; see Figure 4.3). Pantera Negra thus demarcates and permeates Aripaeño's ancestral territory with mythic (or almost magical) features that are grounded in historical events and that serve as important markers of their heritage and identity (Pérez 1997). In this sense, I define their landscape as historical in that it is filled with the physical existence of certain significant elements

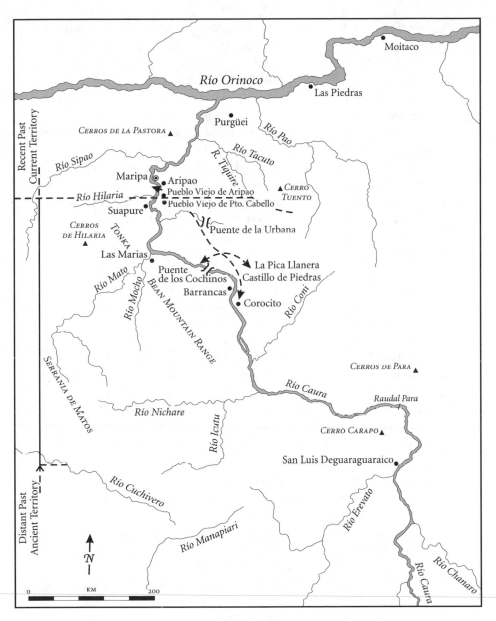

Fig. 4.3. The historical landscape

of nature – such as trees, water resources, and animals – and elements *in* nature, such as material culture. And as such, it thus enfolds events and places that relate to the past (e.g., Paso de Maripa, La Pica Llanera, Puente de los Cochinos, Castillo de Piedras, Barrancas, Corocito, Pueblo Viejo de Puerto Cabello, San Luis de Guaraguaraico), as well as giving the Aripaeño a sense of rootedness that allows for the formation of new landmarks (e.g., Aripao, Pueblo Viejo de Aripao, Suapure, Potreros) that relate current affairs to their more recent past. When the Aripaeño recount their history, their landscape is not only a reference point but also a part of their cultural history (see Pérez 1995:132; 1997). For the Aripaeño, then, this historical landscape is a product of some 250 years of a historical relation of power based on domination and resistance or on conflicts, negotiations, and resolutions with different cultural forces or individual actors during distinct historical periods and changing political settings.

The Caura River basin continued to feel the impact of erratic or sporadic events of later cases of globalization. From near the end of the 19th century to the middle of the 20th century, the Aripaeño experienced one of the most "devastating" economic impacts. Although unique for its sociocultural and ecological components, this impact is representative of a historical period in the Amazonia characterized by the exploitation and extraction of natural resources and the subjugation of the inhabitants into quasi-slavery conditions through the imposition of a socioeconomic system known as debt/peonage (*aviamiento* or *endeude*; see Arvelo-Jiménez and Biord Castillo 1994). This economic event thus centered on the exploitation and extraction of rubber, timber, and tonka beans – (or the seeds of *Coumarouna odorata*, which lured many immigrants (*llaneros*, or plainsmen) from other regions such as Guárico and Anzoátegui states to the Caura region.[7] The Aripaeño and other indigenous groups living in the area also participated in this trade. The harvesting of these forest products, however, enhanced the formation of new social, economic, and political networks between the original population and the newcomers without losing their own cultural autonomy. Although the Venezuelan government prohibited the exploitation of timber in the area and temporarily halted the export of tonka beans in the early 1940s, these changes in the economy of the Caura region neither disrupted the socioeconomic and political alliances already made between the Aripaeño and the newcomers nor surpassed the importance of Aripaeño local production (e.g., fishing, hunting, agriculture, smallscale cattle ranching, and gathering of forest products). The exploitation and extraction of rubber, however, was transposed to countries in Southeast Asia.

Another impact that the Aripaeño witnessed was marked by the beginning of democracy in Venezuela during the 1960s. This new political era was recognized for its focus on leading Venezuela into the stage of modernity and toward its direct participation in the global market. Although some governmental projects, such as the Urban and Industrial Development (or *Desarrollo Urbano e Industrial*) in the 1960s as well as the Conquest of the South (or *La Conquista del Sur*) in the 1970s, were aimed at adjacent areas (e.g., Imataca, La Gran Sabana, and Los Pijiguaos) outside the Caura region, their influence was nevertheless felt in this area. For instance, in the 1960s the Aripaeño saw the construction of an asphalt road right into their town. Prior to this time, and still largely true today, fluvial routes as well as land trails were the only means of communication between the Aripaeño and people from other communities, both indigenous and *llanero*. The road was intended as a direct gateway for easier and quicker contact between the Aripaeño and the external world, for it intersects the main highway that connects Caícara de Orinoco (in the extreme west of Bolívar State) with Ciudad Bolívar (in the extreme east of that state). This also meant the introduction of other forms of development, such as rural housing programs, a rural health service, and government-subsidized food markets, commercial agricultural projects (rice, corn, and beans), and animal husbandry (small-scale swine and fish farming) programs. Yet, all of these economic programs have failed for various reasons, and such failures have made the Aripaeño skeptical of outside interventions that do not involve their direct participation.

Moreover, the Aripaeño have also seen, since the early 1970s, an exodus of many of their people to other towns and cities, particularly to Maripa, Caícara, Ciudad Bolívar, and El Tigre, in search of other opportunities and services. Such emigration includes young adults who leave to obtain a university education or employment, elderly people who move in order to get better medical attention, and middle-aged individuals who hope to gain a better and more stable job. These migrants keep close socioeconomic and political ties with each other through their spatial consolidation in the same shantytowns (or *barrios* – e.g., Sabanita and Los Coquitos in Ciudad Bolívar) of different Venezuelan cities. They also maintain these ties with their people in Aripao through their visits during the holidays and through the practice of "circular migration."[8] This exodus and circular migration practiced by these migrants offer some explanation for the fact that Aripao has a population of about three hundred people and yet still is populated by descendants of the same ancestral families, such as the Tomedes, Pérez, Caña, and España families, that were part of the original foundation. The majority of the present population consists of children under 18 years of age and some elderly individuals. The adult population is mostly employed by the government as teachers, nurses, public officers, policemen, and janitors – very few are small-scale entrepreneurs. Yet, many Aripaeño still engage in their subsistence tradition of fishing, hunting, small-scale slash-and-burn farming, small-scale cattle ranching as well as chicken and swine farming, and annual gathering of tonka beans and *moriche* (*Mauritia flexuosa*) fruit. It is through the practice of these traditional activities that their customarily egalitarian and decentralized way of life becomes more apparent. The Caura River and the interfluvial zones are still the predominant means through which the Aripaeño maintain direct communication and reinforce their alliances with indigenous and *llanero* groups, and these social priorities are more significant than interests of trade and subsistence.

Hence, the Aripaeño have always been compelled to participate in the vertical and centralized political system, though under distinct historical periods – the colonial period and the Republic. But just as in the former period, the political system of the nation-state also brings about unfamiliar challenges and new struggles for the Aripaeño. Nevertheless, they continue, just as their forebears did, to partake and maintain close socioeconomic and political ties with indigenous groups and *llaneros* in the system of Orinoco regional interdependence (SORI), even though it has been modified, transformed, and reduced by the increasing presence of national and international forces.

POWER ENCOUNTERS

Despite the penetration and influence of the outside world, the Aripaeño have managed to sustain their identity as maroons (Pérez and Perozo 2000a). The Aripaeño identify themselves as being reserved, mysterious, cautious, jealous, malicious, skeptical, and suspicious – qualities that an outsider or a stranger would find difficult to overcome in order to gain the Aripaeño's trust or to become part of the group. These qualities reflect a sense of autonomy, authority, and control that the Aripaeño still exert over their formal and informal decision making in terms of rights, duties, and privileges related to immigration, socioeconomic and political alliances, and resources in their territory. Nevertheless, the Aripaeño also perceive themselves as being amicable, cordial, hospitable, and respectful, especially when their cultural codes are respected by others with whom they have established alliances and negotiations. Through the production, representation, and reproduction of their social life and social forms in a historical landscape, the Aripaeño have finely intertwined these paradoxical qualities within the myth-history of Pantera Negra and the life of their ancestors, together reflecting a complex collective memory.

Overall the Caura region is far from being totally "modernized" and "globalized" as yet, although this may become a reality as there are active government plans to develop the area of the Orinoco-Apure confluence. It will be instructive to know whether the Aripaeño's maroon ethos can prevail over the coming waves of modernity and globalization. However, it is my belief that the teachings of Pantera Negra will come alive under such conditions. Pantera Negra could be transformed again by the Aripaeño from a passive force into an active force, especially in situations where they feel their integrity is threatened by external circumstances (Pérez 1997:236–237). The affair of the woman from Caracas, or the Caraquena, as she is known, may be the start of precisely this process.

This particular event involved the people of Aripao as well as outside actors, and the outcome of this power encounter subsequently spurred the Aripaeño to develop new tactics and strategies in defense of their landscape. The incident began with a woman from Caracas who came and settled in Potreros, which is about four kilometers south of Aripao (see Figure 4.4).[9] Potreros is an extension of land, about six kilometers long and two kilometers wide, surrounded by natural springs to the north and east, a stream to the south, and the Caura River and lagoons to the west. The Aripaeño have considered it as communal land and have used it for small-scale cattle grazing ever since the late 19th century. At present, there are about five families living there in order to watch over the free-roaming cattle that belong to them and other Aripaeño.

This Caraqueña is very much like Pantera Negra. They are both symbolic powerful female figures, in terms of their beauty and warriorlike personality. As a beautiful woman (with blond hair, white complexion, and hazel eyes), the Caraqueña uses her feminine qualities to entice and enchant men for her own purposes; moreover, as a warriorlike personality, she mercilessly fights with anyone who crosses her. In certain aspects the Caraqueña is a mirror image of Pantera Negra in terms of her desire

93

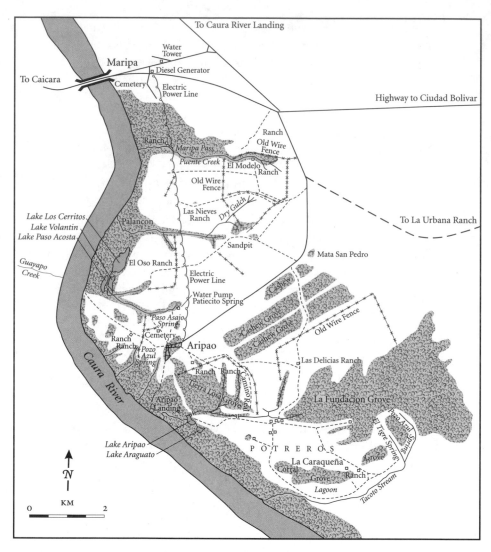

Fig. 4.4. Potreros and the surrounding area

to conquer a "foreign" territory and to impose her wishes within it. Yet, she represents and operates under the vertical and centralized political system (or status quo) in her desire to conquer a "foreign" territory, as opposed to Pantera Negra, who represented the traditional horizontal and decentralized lifestyle and who, in turn, was compelled to participate in the colonial political system. In other words, it seems like the Caraqueña leaves no room for negotiations; and while Pantera Negra is the founding ancestral figure of the Aripaeño (or of an ethnic group), the Caraqueña may presage other personages and events that will be the tokens of a modernity and globalization yet to come into Aripao.

Whether the Caraqueña obtained permission to settle in Potreros, apparently either from the parochial council or the local agrarian union of Aripao, it was irrelevant to the Aripaeño. Although some Aripaeño men claim that she enticed some of the male members of the agrarian union in order to avoid having to deal with the council altogether, usually the council approves granting up to ten hectares to any individual or family. In the case of an outsider, the council members must either know the person or believe in his or her good intentions. The problem really began, however, when the people of Potreros and Aripao noticed that the Caraqueña began to expand and fence more than the allotted ten hectares. As one Aripaeño man explains: "For example, Epifanio was not known, but he seemed like a good person. And up to now, he has demonstrated outstanding behavior. Another person is Salazar, who has been in Potreros for many years, and he, too, has had an outstanding behavior. The only problem that we have now is with the 'Caraqueña,' who is a lawyer and believes that she is the owner and master of the area. . . . all of the sudden we noticed that she began to expand and fence" (JL, interview, March 3, 1997).

While Epifanio and Salazar are *llaneros* and thus share with the Aripaeño that traditional horizontal and decentralized way of life, the Caraqueña is a product and a part of the national status quo. As a result, some Aripaeño became very angry and decided to confront her and persuade her to leave. Those involved in the effort to remove the Caraqueña utilized two political strategies simultaneously. They filed a complaint at the Instituto Agrario Nacional (IAN, the Agrarian National Institute) alleging her abusive use of land, and they took the law into their own hands, as this strategy had worked well against other intruders in the past. To this end the council members and some people of Aripao and Potreros decided, in the company of the National Guard, to visit the Caraqueña's ranch and demand her immediate departure; they threatened to burn down her place if she did not comply. While the Aripaeño believed that the Caraqueña left Potreros for good as a result of their threat, a few days later she came back with some representatives of the IAN and with the title of her land in hand. Some Aripaeño claim that she used her influence at the IAN because she happened to be a former employee of the government institution. This was later supported from my own observations when the Caraqueña mentioned to me that she formerly worked for the IAN and now is a legal consultant for it. In any event, both strategies to remove her proved to be unsuccessful, for she had violated none of the Agrarian Reform laws, and anyway such laws did not recognize the perceptions that Aripaeño have of their land. Through her own initiative, the Caraqueña told me about the encounter she had with the Aripaeño and claimed: "I bought 372 hectares from the IAN where I am planning to bring in my 200 head of cattle; in turn, the institute granted me the final title. The Aripaeño believe that all this land is theirs, and it is not. This land belongs to the IAN. . . . This is all wasteland [*baldía*]. The Aripaeño think that this is communal land [*ejido*]" (ED, interview, March 3, 1997). In order to find additional information about land tenure in Potreros and Aripao, I contacted one person from the IAN, who clarified the situation: "in the region of Aripao, no one has title to private property; on the contrary, the titles granted, including that of the 'Caraqueña,' are those of 'limited land rights' [*titulos definitivos de uso, goze y disfrute*]" (LH, interview, March 24, 1997).

Although the Aripaeño had no choice but to accept the verdict, an ecological fact gave them hope: Potreros is not suited for intense cattle ranching because the majority of the savannah is flooded during the rainy season, and because there is not enough good pasture during the dry season to maintain a large number of cattle. In this way many Aripaeño opined that the Caraqueña's 200 head of cattle would not survive after the first year and as a result, she would be forced to leave Potreros.

It would seem by the outcome of this event that the Aripaeño resigned themselves to the Caraqueña's settling in Potreros. That is, they immersed themselves into their daily activities and routines and seldom mentioned her again. Even the male members of the agrarian union who had previously supported her apparently recanted their claims to knowledge of the Caraqueña's real intentions or her breaking of Aripaeño's cultural codes. Yet, the Caraqueña did not overlook this lack of support, and she denounced them to the National Guard for deforesting Potreros. They were actually cutting tree stumps, just as she did for her own fencing, in order to fence in their father's ranch, known as Las Delicias. Whenever I asked about the Caraqueña, some Aripaeño would simply reply, "Oh, she does not come as often as she used to," while others would claim in a disinterested tone, "Oh, she abandoned everything and left." Their sentiments are an expression of cultural alienation and separateness, another strategy that they applied in their silent resistance toward the Caraqueña.

I noticed, however, that the Caraqueña had stopped making improvements on the land and that she had not brought her cattle to the ranch. The answer to the Caraqueña's inaction may have been related to the fact that some Aripaeño slowly began to occupy or fence sections of the savannah in 1997 and again from 1998 to the present. Although these Aripaeño claim to have obtained the title of "limited land rights" from the IAN, the key aspect of the fencing is that it has blocked all access by car to the three ranches located to the north of Potreros. The only route is right through the heart of town, where there is a road to the new bridge to Potreros, although it is gated and locked. However, these obstacles present no problems for the Aripaeño. The water resources (e.g., natural springs, streams, and lagoons) used for their fishing, hunting, and gathering activities, which are closed in by the wire fences of the ranches, can still be reached by the Aripaeño, either on foot or in dugout canoes (*curiaras*) and without acquiring permission from their kin – or anyone else. The Caraqueña, on the other hand, exclusively drives a vehicle to travel to and from her property, which obliges her to ask permission to pass through any of the gates. However, she has cultivated a certain male ally, who is an outsider to the community but who has married a female Aripaeño. Through his marriage and social alliances with the Ariapeño, and as a small-scale cattle owner, he has direct access into Potreros. This has eased the Caraqueña's access into Potreros, but nonetheless the location of the wire fences to the north of Potreros is a new strategy of passive resistance against the coming and going of the Caraqueña.

Since the 1960s – with the asphalt road built into Aripao – the Aripaeño have experienced the introduction of many modernities into their community, such as rural housing, electricity, radio, television, running water, and, most recently, telephones. They have also encountered the beginning of penetration or settlement by outsiders in their region as a result of international markets and government programs directed toward the economic development of southern Venezuela.[10] Yet, the Aripaeño are not necessarily resistant to outsiders. Men such as Epifanio and Salazar, for example, were accepted by the Aripaeño and allowed to live in the area. However, the Aripaeño defend their territory against people who do not follow the cultural norms. The Caraqueña is in antipathy to their traditional way of life and their systems of mutual dependence. In their eyes, she represents individual, rather than communal, benefit or gain.

Moreover, small-scale cattle ranches are not a new phenomenon in the life of the Aripaeño, as these have existed prior to the 1960s. As a matter of fact, some Aripaeño have maintained, at different times, ranches located to the north, northeast, and northwest of Aripao (e.g., El Modelo, Las Nieves, El Oso, Críspuli – see Figure 4.4). But the fences were simple constructions (e.g., gates without locks and small logs with loose wire), because the purpose was to keep the cattle and pigs inside, rather than to prevent outsiders from entering or settling on the land. Yet, the recent acquisition of land from the IAN by the Aripaeño, as in the case of the ranches found to the north of Potreros and another ranch recently built to the west of Aripao as well as the modernization of ranch security (e.g., professionally installed fencing, locks, and private property signs), are all too familiar signs of a pressing need to reaffirm that they are here to stay and to safeguard their ancestral land.

The incident with the Caraqueña is not an isolated event. On the contrary, there have been many such situations that the Aripaeño have encountered throughout their history where they have responded to external political and economic power. Their political responses to these events are a product of an ancestral legacy symbolized by the epic of Pantera Negra, who, in essence, (1) provides a historical and cultural continuity from Dutch Guiana, where she was conceived, to Aripao, where the Aripaeño currently live; (2) demarcates the Aripaeño's ancestral landscape from San Luis de Guaraguaraico to their current location; (3) guides them toward the formation of social, economic, and political alliances as well as networks with other cultural groups in the Caura region, while still maintaining their own autonomy; (4) points to the existence of an asymmetrical relationship of power that involves Amerindians, Afro-Americans, Europeans, and criollos; and (5) signals to the Aripaeño that their cultural and political *mestizaje*, or racial and cultural mixing with others, is a strategy for survival.[11]

It is important to add that the Aripaeño's forebears were a product of a world capitalist system that began in the colonial period and in which they were forced to become slaves or, simply, commodities. They rebelled and were victorious against such inhumane treatment, just as their descendants continue to resist any outside influence, intervention, or penetration that is contrary to their own cultural premises. Even though they participate in the modern world capitalist system, their political and economic involvement is still imposed from the outside and severely limited in scope.

Although Aripao has the status of Foreign/Rural County (Municipio Foráneo) – and the Aripaeño thus have political and administrative power through a parochial council, a local agrarian union, a subprefecture, and a police station – they are still at a disadvantage. On the one hand, they occupy a territory that is considered to be "wasteland" by the Venezuelan nation-state; on the other hand, they may not have any claims or original rights (*derechos originario*) to land tenure because they are descendants of people from another territory or continent. Yet, it is perhaps no coincidence that their administrative territory (see Figure 4.5) coincides with the territory that the Aripaeño consider to be an extension of their close socioeconomic and political ties with others in the region, particularly *llaneros* and Amerindians living in Puerto Cabello, Las Trincheras, and Jabillal, as well as those communities that lie outside their prescribed territory, such as San Pedro del Tauca and Suapure (see Figure 4.6).

Nonetheless, this conforms with what the Aripaeño conceive of as their ancestral territory or historical landscape – simplistically stated, their former settlements, such as San Luis de Guaraguaraico, Corocito, Pueblo Viejo de Puerto Cabello, and Pueblo Viejo de Aripao (see Figure 4.3). These landscapes, superimposed on the administrative territory, reflect an acknowledgment by the Venezuelan nation-state of the deep historical roots that the Aripaeño have in the Caura region. This historicity is founded on 250 years of a history making and a distinct cultural heritage born of a process of ethnogenesis – none of which the Aripaeño are likely to give up easily and which are partly shared with other indigenous groups and the *llaneros*. The Aripaeño's close relationship to the land and their commitment to a traditional way of life, which evinces the rootedness that their present situation has to their past, may aid them in the quest to make manifest an ancestral territorial demarcation and, therefore, a truly legitimate claim for a recognition of the historicity of their landscape by the Venezuelan nation-state.

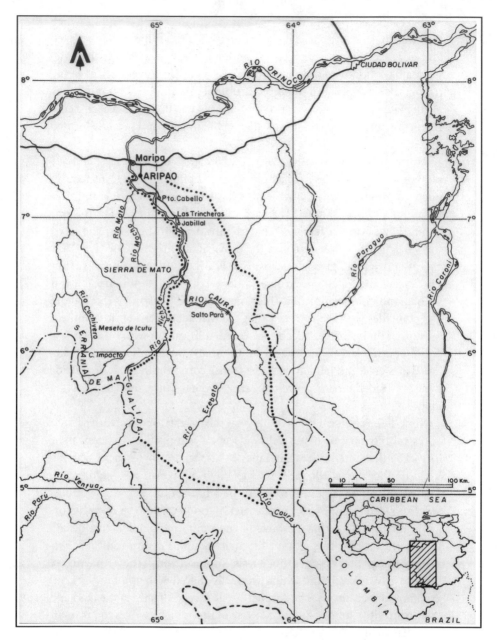

Fig. 4.5. Aripao's political and administrative territory

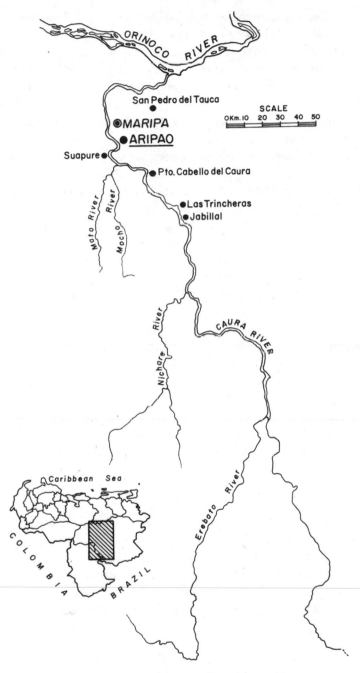

Fig. 4.6. Aripao and surrounding communities

The Caura region does not yet suggest an image of modernization and globalization. However, the region is increasingly being affected by government programs (e.g., eucalyptus planting, mining, urbanization, and a space shuttle) and the play of international markets in lumber and gold. It is for this reason that other recent Venezuelan examples of development, such as in the Gran Sabana (tourism, mining, electrical power transmission, and a highway to Brazil) and Imataca (mining and forest exploitation on a small, medium, and large scale) are important. Even though the Caura region is still somewhat pristine, the experience of these other regions is important – before the inhabitants of the Caura are literally bulldozed into modernity. It is therefore important to highlight tradition, such as in the case of the Aripaeño, in the hope that it may improve the quality and outcomes of any negotiations or alliances between the key players in development of the region – CVG (Corporación Venezolana de Guayana), its business associates (mostly Canadian companies), and the peoples of the Orinoco.[12]

People such as the Aripaeño, in the words of Comaroff and Comaroff (1992), "fashion their own vision of modernity and globalization" (5). This suggests that there is also an "endogenous historicity [for] all social worlds" (24), and for this reason, Comaroff and Comaroff continue, "If a neo-modern anthropology is to work creatively at the frontiers of ethnography and the historical imagination, it must be founded on a conception of culture and society that takes us beyond our traditional stamping grounds" (30). Even as we agree with these notions, we must remember that the Aripaeño participate in the modern world capitalist system not by their own choosing.

ACKNOWLEDGMENTS

A version of this paper was presented at the Annual Meetings of the American Society for Ethnohistory (October 18–22, 2000), in London, Ontario, Canada, in the plenary session titled "Histories and Historicities in the Amazonia." Special thanks are due to Marshall Sahlins for initiating and organizing these annual meetings and to the Wenner-Gren Foundation and IVIC (Instituto Venezolano de Investigaciones Científicas) for funding my participation in this event. I would also like to thank Neil Whitehead and Manuela Carneiro da Cunha, organizers and chairs of the plenary session in which I participated, for their invitation and for the wonderful feedback I obtained from them as discussants of that session.

In addition, my thanks extend to Alberta Zucchi for her excellent comments and editing of the version of this manuscript that was presented at the meetings. Also, my gratitude goes to Abel Perozo for his wonderful ideas and discussions on the theme, and last, but not least, to Carlos Quintero for making the maps.

NOTES

1. Some form or degree of alliance made between the Aripaeño and the Kari'ña prior to the latter's political defeat over the Orinoco River basin is not discarded. For instance, Whitehead (1998:22 n. 17) suggests that the Caribs were at times warned by the Dutch in Essequibo against the sheltering of runaway slaves who belonged to the plantations of the colony.

2. This is shown in the history of both Pantera Negra and her lover Panchito, a Carib Indian. Also, these intercultural relationships are evident today in the socioeconomic and political alliances made between the Aripaeño and the Kari'ña. For example, there have been intermarriages among them.

3. Although the Carib indigenous groups (e.g., Kari'ña, Ye'kuana, and Pemón) in Venezuela share a similar kinship system that establishes endogamous marriages among bilateral cross-cousins, their interactions among themselves and with other groups within the SORI are likely to have made marriage alliances become more flexible. That is, such a system likely facilitated exogamous marriages – or the union of men and women of different ethnicity (also see Medina, in this volume). At the very least, our recent data gathered on contemporary Aripaeño's kinship, which have not yet been analyzed, reveal intermarriages with Kari'ña, Ye'kuana, and *llaneros* (or plainspeople of other Venezuelan states). Rather that being seen as either an accident or a recent incident, these contemporary intermarriages are likely to be an outcome of their continuous interactions within the SORI; although the SORI has been transformed and modified since colonial times, it still operates, for example, in the Caura River basin.

4. By "ethnoscape," Appadurai means, "the landscape of persons who constitute the shifting world in which we live: tourists, immigrants, refugees, exiles, guest workers, and other moving groups and individuals constitute an essential feature of the world and appear to affect the politics of (and between) nations to a hitherto unprecedented degree. This is not to say that there are no relatively stable communities and networks of kinship, friendship, work, and leisure, as well as birth, residence, and other filial forms. But it is to say that the warp of these stabilities is everywhere shot through the woof of human motion, as more persons and groups deal with the realities of having to move or the fantasies of wanting to move" (1997:33–34). This definition applies more specifically to the Aripaeño's situation in the colonial period (when African individuals were

brought as slaves into a new continent conquered by distinct colonial forces). Today, the Aripaeño perceive themselves and are considered by the nation-state as Venezuelan citizens, and small cells of them can be found throughout different Venezuelan cities and towns. Yet, their rights to land as an ethnic group remain unknown as the new constitution only (and finally) recognizes ancestral territory of the indigenous peoples.

5. There are not yet hard data available to answer what the layout was like in former Aripaeño settlements, nor whether the layout was similar to or different from that of indigenous settlements. However, the Aripaeño settlement pattern was likely to be dispersed household compounds, composed of extended families of no more than three continuous generations, and in which each oscillated as satellites around a founding center. This statement is supported by Aripaeño oral accounts and by historical sources written by chronicles or explorers of the New World. It was not until Aripao, for instance, began to be exposed to modern structures and elements (e.g., rural housing, a health service, a primary school, and a Catholic church) that the Aripaeño decided to concentrate in a closed compound that simulated a city or town, a Westernized tradition. In order to confirm or disprove this hypothesis, archaeological research has just begun this year.

6. In addition to Pantera Negra, this legacy entails a traditional way of life based on intercultural relations with indigenous groups (Kari'ña and Ye'kuana) and other cultural segments (Spaniards in the colonial period and criollos or, more specifically, *llaneros*, or plains people – from the states of Guárico and Anzoátegui – during the Republican era; and a subsistence tradition of small-scale slash-and-burn farming (or *conucos*), small-scale cattle ranching, fishing, hunting, and annual gathering of tonka beans (the seeds of *Coumarouna odorata*) and *moriche* (*Mauritia flexuosa*) fruit.

7. The exploitation of tonka bean trees involves two sides of the same coin: traditional use and global market use. The Aripaeño use the tonka bean tree in almost all of its aspects. That is, they use the timber for cutting boards and stools when the tree is rotten or too old to produce; the flowers to decorate and to perfume the inside of their households; the seed for stomach ailments; the fruit to eat; and the ashes of the fruit's skin to mix with other ingredients in order to make soap. The international market specifically uses the tonka beans for making perfume, aromatizing tobacco, and medicine.

8. By *circular migration* I mean that there are some Aripaeño emigrants who come back to live in Aripao, or simply that many of them send their children or grandchildren to be raised by their family (e.g., mother, mother-in-law, sister, sister-in-law, or female cousin) left behind.

9. Depending on the context in which an Aripaeño speaks, Aripao may be the town itself or any extension of land that points to either their current locality-producing activities or their ancestral territory (Pérez 1997).

10. More recently the Aripaeño have rejected the current government plan to relocate survivors of the 1999 flood in La Guaira. The government, at this point, has complied.

11. As a whole, the Aripaeño have important ethnic markers such as mythic-history(ies), ancestral territory or territoriality, a black maroon identity and ethos, and customs. There have not been any linguistic studies conducted yet. Although the Aripaeño speak the Spanish language, I am told by the Aripaeño themselves and by other people who have lived in the area that they did have a distinctive dialect (i.e., they spoke strangely or *hablaban raro*). Even though I am not a linguist, I do hear particular sounds in certain consonants that are not common in the Spanish language.

12. However, it has been a rather difficult task to construct the tradition of the Aripaeño, for even the colonial missionaries did not leave behind any documents about them.

5

Rebellious Memories

The Wapishana in the Rupununi Uprising, Guyana, 1969

NÁDIA FARAGE

What when I name forgetfulness, and recognize withal what I name;
whence do I recognize a thing, did I not remember it?

Saint Augustine, *Confessions*

In the first days of the year 1969, Lethem, a tiny town in the Rupununi region, on the Guyana border with Brazil, was taken by an insurgent army, composed mainly by Wapishana Indians and led by local right-wing white ranchers.[1] The precarious communication links with the rest of the country and all government buildings were taken over by the insurrectionists; public servants were imprisoned, and some were shot dead. The rebels broadcasted a declaration of independence for Rupununi.

The insurrection, however, did not last more than three days. Soon, the Guyana Defence Force was sent from the coast; Lethem was battered by artillery fire, and the leaders went into exile in Venezuela. In flight, the Wapishana swam across the Tacutu River, seeking refuge in the villages along the Brazilian side of the border. Some were imprisoned, and some reportedly were killed.

As a consequence of the failed rebellion, from this point on, an important population flow started, heading for the Brazilian villages. So, although brief, this episode affected Wapishana sociology. In fact, the population influx shaped the present demographic and social profile of the Tacutu valley: at least three villages are composed exclusively of Guyana refugees and a large number of inhabitants of the other villages were born and grew up on the Guyanese side of the border (see Figure 5.1).

The distinction between Guyanese and Brazilian is politically operative for the Wapishana, especially in the outbreak of conflict among

Fig. 5.1. Wapishana settlements (E. Migliazza 1970, J. Forte 1990)

kindred: in these situations, in spite of the passing of time, the Wapishana still consider themselves refugees, and their common origin aligns political loyalties; conversely, those born in Brazil refer to those from Guyana, not without derision, as "runaways." On a larger scale, nevertheless, all of them regard the savannas that lie between the Branco and Rupununi Rivers as their territory: the fall of the regime in Guyana, in 1992, did not trigger any return movement.

In this essay, I inquire into the construction of Wapishana social memory about the Rupununi uprising, focusing mainly on its rhetorical codification, by which I mean a systematic whole of discursive conventions relying on conceptions of time and the human condition.[2] Thus beyond the clash of meanings and values about the past I address the rhetorical devices that constrain what is speakable about the past. If "in speech is History made," as stated by Marshall Sahlins (1981:5), I suggest that the rhetorical codification, by means of which the discourse about the past is constructed, can be a strategic locus to depict historicity.

THE WAPISHANA IN THE BRITISH COLONIZATION OF RUPUNUNI

In 1884, when traveling across the Branco/Rupununi savannas, the French naturalist Henri Coudreau noticed how Brazilians feared a British invasion of the borderland, at that time under dispute by the two countries. How wrong they were, he observed; in all the Rupununi area, there were no more than two British subjects, and they were more interested in Amerindian labor than in territorial annexation: "The two British houses in Rupununi gave me the impression that they were much more worried to pay the least possible to their Indians than to teach them to murder the language of Shakespeare and to devote a fetishistic reverence to the religion of Her Most Gracious Majesty" (Coudreau 1887, 9:269; my translation).[3] From the Mountains of the Moon to Pakaraima Mountains, he concluded, maliciously, there were not "more than ten Indians able to understand, in English, more than the two words 'match' and 'Goddam' (283; my translation).[4]

Written sources do not give further information about these two 19th-century British residents in Rupununi. It is certain that since the first decades of the century the exploratory travels by Waterton (1984), Hilhouse (1978), or the Schomburgk brothers (1903; 1922–23) had brought back knowledge about the Rupununi savannas and its inhabitants to the administrative center of the British colony of Guiana.[5] However, a systematic effort to colonize the area, based on land occupation, would not occur in that century.

In the beginning of the 20th century, the Scotsmen H. C. P. Melville and John Ogilvie, together with three Brazilian ranchers who had settled there after the arbitration of the border in 1904, were the only white owners in Rupununi (Clementi 1919:80–81). This was due, above all, to the fact that the economic and political focus of the colony was on the coast, a situation that would not be radically altered during the 20th century. Colonial economy along the coast had been based on sugar production (see Mandle 1973), which, until 1838, depended on African slave labor and, from then on, *coolie* labor – mainly that of East Indians brought in massive waves into the colony during the 19th century. The Amerindian population, inhabiting a remote and economically marginal area, was not recruited to work in the sugar plantations.[6] For a long time the Amerindians living in Rupununi, particularly the southern Wapishana, were considered by the colonial administration to be wild Indians untouched by civilization.

The reference for the colonization of Rupununi is the Scotsman H. C. P. Melville, whose trajectory gives a romantic tone to subsequent travel books, such as the one by the popular British writer Evelyn Waugh (1987). After arriving in the Rupununi around the late 1880s, Melville probably bartered manufactured goods for Wapishana products, which he traded in Georgetown. Later he would devote himself to cattle raising. Soon he was appointed by the colonial government as magistrate and protector of Indians in the Rupununi District, positions that he held for a long time. So, it seems, for some decades, he alone was an outpost of colonization on, to quote Rivière (1972), that "forgotten frontier."

Melville's cattle raising took place on Wapishana lands and benefited from their work: the subsequent literature attributed Melville's political influence over the Wapishana, as well as his access to their labor force, to his marriage to an Atoradi woman (a Wapishana subgroup). Later, Melville took a second Wapishana wife and, with his two wives, brought up the large family on which we focus here, since the social relationships thus created were on the basis of the 1969 uprising. Labor relations, plus alliance through marriage with Melvilles – this is what Lucy, an elderly Wapishana woman who nowadays resides at Canauanim village in Brazilian territory, tells us: "the Wapishana called Melville the boss" – she says – "he was the father, but there were two mothers; first he took the oldest sister, then the younger; they gave him all his children."

Due to difficulties of communication with the coast, Rupununi cattle production was conducted on a small-scale basis, a situation that would change only after World War I. In 1914, with the onset of war and the consequent shortage of food along the coast, Melville obtained from the colonial government and British businessmen the necessary capital to create the Rupununi Development Company, which would start entrepreneurial cattle raising in the southern savannas of Rupununi, the very heart of Wapishana land. In addition, at that time Melville got funds to open a "cattle trail" to take Rupununi livestock to the Georgetown market. Nevertheless, this piece of infrastructure remained precarious between the wars; only the establishment of air communication in the 1940s consolidated the integration of the region into the colonial market (McCann 1972). At that time, Melville sold his interests in the Rupununi Development Company and returned to Scotland; his children stayed behind, still holding lands in the Wapishana territory and trading with Wapishana people until 1969. When Evelyn Waugh (1987:25) traveled across the Rupununi in 1932, the Melville sons and sons-in-law held all key positions in the district, as well as the monopoly of commerce. Nobody was certain whether Dadanawa and Wichabai were Wapishana villages or Melville homesteads.

Not only territorial space intermingled, but above all the social space between the Melvilles and the Wapishana: the remembrances of many Wapishana, now at mature or advanced ages, outline a situation of pa tronage, in which labor was based on the multiplication of kinship ties through adoption of children and marriages. The Wapishana had become children, brothers, uncles, brothers in-law. Perhaps the most vivid example is given by Edward, in Pium village, who in the 1990s kept on the wall of his house the unlikely picture of two children, dressed in old British fashion, which he proudly showed to visitors: his brother and sister John and Amy Melville.

This universe sustainained itself in an insulated region, socially and geographically remote from the main political stage along the coast. The uprising in 1969 linked the region to that stage.

ETHNIC GROUPS AND POLITICAL PARTIES IN GUYANA: A SKETCH

The Guyanese environment of party politics in the 1960s must be understood from the perspective of the struggle against British colonialism.

Since the second half of the 1940s, intellectuals and nationalist militants – Cheddi and Janet Jagan, Forbes Burnham, and Sidney King, among others – had been devoting themselves to the creation of a nationalist and left-wing party, the People's Progressive Party (PPP), whose immediate goal was the independence of Guyana (Bradley 1961:2–4).

Conceived as a working-class party with a socialist horizon, the PPP fought against fission lines based on ethnic criteria, which would deviate it from its main target, British colonialism. The militant and organized PPP won the majority of the Assembly in the 1953 elections, which also gave it the majority of colonial ministries. In that same year, the PPP prime minister, Cheddi Jagan, was forced out of power by British armed intervention under the pretext of his leading Guyana into communism; many party members were imprisoned and their publications forbidden. However, primarily because the party represented the fight against the British, the PPP again won in the 1957 and 1961 elections.

In the mid-1950s Forbes Burnham and Cheddi Jagan began to diverge politically. This started an internal fight in the party, which resulted in a rupture. Burnham and others created then another party, the People's National Congress (PNC). Initially, as Bradley (1961) states, divergence was more ideological than ethnical, and thus many East Indians followed Burnham, and African descendants followed Cheddi Jagan; this trend was reversed as Forbes Burnham, Sidney King, and other PNC activists little by little embraced the discourse on Afro-American unity that flourished in the Caribbean. Ethnic conflicts then exploded in violence in the streets during those years (Sanders 1972:31).

Ethnic issues gained ascendancy over the discourse of ideology and class. In this context of conflict, another party appeared, the United Force, which brought together the small right-wing white entrepreneurial elite under the leadership of Peter D'Aguiar, a rich sugar entrepreneur. This party would constitute the principal political force among white ranchers and, importantly, the indigenous population in the Rupununi (Sanders 1972:45). A United Force–People's National Congress coalition won the 1964 elections; under its administration, the colony of Guiana became an independent member of the Commonwealth in 1966 (Wearing 1972:32–33).

For the 1968 elections, everything pointed to the PPP's victory. In those last years, however, the party had openly declared its Marxist-Leninist ideology and had become affiliated with the Communist International (Bradley 1961). As anticommunism had been growing within and outside the country, the prospect of Cheddi Jagan's victory certainly cast a shadow over Guyana from the point of view of the United Kingdom and the United States, as they feared another defeat analogous to the recent Cuban revolution. So, both countries decidedly supported Forbes Burnham's candidacy.

The elections were marked by ostensible fraud, which, according to Jagan (1969:37–39), was planned and implemented by the CIA. The fraud was mainly based on the extension of the vote to Guyanese living overseas. Granada Television Ltd. (1969) documented that many overseas voters simply did not exist; their identities and addresses were false, and even the dead were taken out of their graves to vote. Locally, the opposition ballots were simply discarded. All this assured Forbes Burnham's victory in December 1968.

Teddy Melville and his cousin Jimmy Hart did not accept the results of the election and took a radical stance as the United Force publicized the fraud and broke with the recently elected government. This could explain the insurrection of the right-wing white ranchers affiliated with the United Force, as they feared a government of the Afro-descendant majority that, although supported by the United Kingdom and the United States, still belonged to a left-wing spectrum. But it does not explain sufficiently the Wapishana presence.

In a militant analysis, Cheddi Jagan (1969) observed that the active participation of the Wapishana in all this was due, above all, to the anticommunist proselytism of Catholic missionaries, who were greatly accepted by the indigenous population in the Rupununi; this proselytism would had led them to massively support the United Force. From a Marxist-Leninist point of view – echoing Marx's views on peasants in *The Eighteenth Brumaire of Louis Bonaparte* (1964) and Engels's views on the Bakuninists in Spain (1972), Jagan could not see autonomous reasons for Wapishana actions. The Amerindians were bound to be co-opted by others as long as they did not constitute a class, and for this reason, they did not have revolutionary potential either.[7] The weakness of this argument has already been exhaustively demonstrated by Sahlins (see Sahlins 2000). It would be useless to insist that historical experience is necessarily linked to agency, or as Bruce Albert (2002:15) summarizes: "no society, as long as it survives, can fail to capture and transfigure everything proposed or imposed on it within its own cultural terms, independently of any political confrontation (war, rebellion or protest)."

In his turn, Guyanese anthropologist Sanders (1972) argued that the

Amerindians had supported the white ranchers in their rebellion against the government mainly because historically they had always considered the whites as allies and superior to them. From my point of view, this explanation is plausible but not good enough. As we have seen, there was indeed alliance between the Melvilles and the Wapishana, but the alleged superiority is contradicted by the fact that the Melvilles – in their first and second generations – took Wapishana wives and, in Wapishana reasoning, would stand as debtors to themselves, as their affines.

Even so, this alliance politics still would have to be considered against the backdrop of party politics, as well as against the decolonization process, which did not assure Amerindian land rights, nor even a political place for the Amerindian population in the recently created nation. Such a line of interpretation is suggested by the Wapishana benevolent evaluation of British colonialism even to this day: "the Queen went away," says Ana, "but kept sending for the Wapishana tractors and other tools which never got to come to us."

Land was the alleged core motive for the uprising, as the renewal of land leasing for Rupununi ranchers by the PNC government was uncertain. This was a motive that aligned Amerindians and ranchers, the latter also mentioning their Amerindian ascendancy to assert their land rights. Nevertheless, I do not further examine the political project that would had led the Wapishana to rise up in arms against the recently established Burnham regime. My main concern is the present construction of memory of the uprising, as is made clear below. For the moment, let us go back to the days of the insurrection.

Binot, a man of mature age who is now a resident in the Wappun village in Brazil and who lived in Aishalton village at the time of the uprising, reveals that the insurrection had been prepared some time in advance. Binot says that on Christmas Eve of 1968, Teddy Melville had been at a party in the village, where he distributed guns to the adult men and summoned them to a war. On this occasion he also cut the phone wires. Indeed, in the occupation of Lethem, all communications between the Rupununi and Georgetown were cut.

This explains why on January 3 the news that came into the capital was rather vague: "a party of Guyana Defence Force soldiers and policemen was air-dashed to the Lethem area in the Rupununi yesterday afternoon following reports of disorder in the district. An unconfirmed report stated that there was shooting some time in the afternoon. Wireless Communication between the area and Georgetown is out of order and as a result no accurate account of the incident was available up to late last night" (*Guyana Graphic,* January 3, 1969).

The report indicated disorder only, without subjects or causes. Once the focus of the rebellion was detected and the agents identified, official discourse grew into nationalist hysteria: "rats in the Rupununi," shouted the press, claiming "to unmask the traitors" and to send more men to guard the frontier (*Guyana Graphic,* January 6–7, 1969). The neighboring countries were also alarmed; Brazil sent troops to confront the turbulence on the frontier. But in the epidemics of nationalism that took over the press, the prevailing hypothesis was that Venezuela supported the rebels, a hypothesis that seemed to be confirmed when, some days later, that country officially gave asylum to 50 insurrectionists (*Guyana Graphic,* January 8, 1969). From Caracas, Valerie Hart – a defeated United Force candidate in the 1968 elections – declared that the Rupununi uprising was "a bid for freedom." The party, however, immediately expelled her.

We have to note that the United Force, right from the start, made an effort to dismiss the rebellion and to depict it as a local initiative. Nevertheless, Peter D'Aguiar, on January 3, had departed for Trinidad (*Guyana Graphic,* January 3, 1969). From London, he declared to the Canadian TV program *World in Action* that he was in shock over the killings in the Rupununi, and he added, "while the Amerindians have genuine grievances particularly concerning the titles to their land and have suffered provocation, I can only deplore any attempt by foreign powers to exploit their grievances" (*Guyana Graphic,* January 8, 1969). By taking this line, D'Aguiar was the only voice that tried to characterize the movement as an indigenous rebellion. Such an argument did not convince the press, which suspected a separatist plot involving the ranchers, the party, and Venezuela. Nor did the argument convince the government of Forbes Burnham, which was about to proceed openly against the members of the United Force. In the absence of Peter D'Aguiar, his teenager daughter was prevented from traveling back to school in the United Kingdom (*Guyana Graphic,* January 13, 1969). After two days of fire from bazookas, machine guns, and flamethrowers, the uprising was defeated (Ridgewell 1972:222). The rebels were in flight: the press reported that three hundred Wapishana crossed the border toward Brazil, but their number could have been much higher (*Guyana Graphic,* January 9, 1969). Imprisonments and prosecutions began; the Burnham regime consolidated, opening a hard time of counterinsurgency for Rupununi people. The Wapishana were by then targeted by plans of integration by the Guyanese government at the same time that, paradoxically, their access to industrialized goods was abruptly cut.

In those disturbing days of January, the pro-government newspaper *Guyana Graphic*, in an article significantly titled "Decolonizing the Cattle Kingdom," proposed the systematic introduction of colonists of African descent in the Rupununi (January 9, 1969). Indeed, in the following years, the Guyanese government would encourage mining by African descendants. The Burnham dictatorship would never recognize Amerindian lands. "We came for the salt," say the Wapishana today in Brazil, an oblique way of saying they fled from the extreme shortage of goods suffered while in Rupununi. In Brazil, they also experienced adverse conditions: most of the time they sold their labor for degrading wages on the cattle farms of the region and had their names converted into Brazilian ones in order to avoid the accusation of secrecy.

"The time when the Teddies uprose," or "the time of Teddy's war," an expression that encapsulates the Melville family, is an important temporal reference in many biographies among the Wapishana in Brazil today. It marks, as we saw, the beginning of a time of shortage, political persecutions, and consequent population movements. However the episode of the 1969 uprising is never given more than a brief mention in their biographies. The reference, when it happens, is marked by detachment, as in the following account by John, now a resident in Jacamim village, who in the time of the uprising worked for Teddy Melville in Dadanawa: "The blacks won the elections; the Melvilles did not accept the results. That is why they crossed the river. At that time, we Amerindians also crossed the river. The Melvilles had given guns to the Wapishana in order to kill the blacks. They killed five soldiers."

Binot, a man I mentioned previously, at the time of the rebellion worked on the farm belonging to Jimmy Hart, a first-hour insurrectionist. He spoke of the visit of Teddy Melville to Aishalton village on Christmas Eve and added: "after I do not know what happened; I was not there; I only heard about it." Most of the adult men said the same.

Of course, they have pressing political reasons to keep silent about the uprising in everyday discourse. Still, the Wapishana also keep silent about it, for less obvious reasons, in their formalized discourse about the past, which they conceive as properly historical. But this unexpected silence gains a different value if we take a closer look at the formalized discursive modality.

In what follows, I present a narrative told by Lucy, the elderly Wapishana woman mentioned previously, who now resides in the Canauanim village in the Branco River valley. Despite the conspicuousness of the repression in Rupununi, Lucy's narrative, among the repertoire I collected, is the closest reference to the episode I could get:

> I lived there, with John Melville and his wife, Dona Diva. Yes, Dona Diva was his wife. I lived with her. I worked for him; it was a very good time when John Melville took care of us. He was Wapishana, Atoradi. But his wife was a Brazilian.
>
> He was good to his wife, but when he drank rum, when he got drunken, he was not good; he got angry, he took his gun and shot everywhere. Everybody runned away from him. He was bad-tempered that Melville, but his brother Teddy Melville was good. He and Charlie Melville, Lally Melville, George Melville, these were John's brothers. I knew them; I worked for them. I lived in Wichabai, in Dadanawa. Then his wife took me there, I went there, to the mouth of the river, to Georgetown; I went with them, they took me. Then, I lived with them until he died, poor John Melville. He died, and his wife came back to her father's. I do not know the name of the place where Teddy Melville is; he has not died yet; all his relatives died, his parents, all of them died, there is nobody left; only him, but I do not know where he lives now. Now I do not know; he lives in a town; he got married. *Uru'u utokon* [this is the end].

I must observe that narratives belong to a larger rhetorical codification, which encompasses three formalized discursive genres (for a detailed analysis, see Farage 1997). The Wapishana classify this narrative within the genre called *kotuanao dau'ao*. Before we look at the conventions of the genre, let me briefly outline the social access to narratives. Age is the basic criterion to narrate. Only the oldest ones – be they men or women – have large repertoires of narratives. The oldest ones, "the ones who know the histories," are called *kwad pazo* (the ones who tell), an expression that the Wapishana translate for historians. Only a full adult – a grandfather or grandmother – can be a *kwad pazo* because, for the Wapishana, knowledge derives from life experience.

The *kwad pazo* are called and call themselves *kotuanao* remnants (remnants of the old) because they are narrators as well as co-participants of a past the younger people do not share by their own experience. This expression is crucial to understanding Lucy's position as a narrator.

The expression *kotuanao dau'ao* (what is told about the ancient ones) indicates that, for the Wapishana, narratives are not a legacy from the past; on the contrary, they are conceived as what is produced today about the past. Nevertheless, there is one strong convention for the narrative genre, which relies on the notion of "old." First of all, *kotuanao* (the old, the antique, the one who does not exist anymore) is opposite in meaning to the word *kainao* (the living, the one who exists). The duration of time is divided by this clear-cut opposition between *kotuanao* and *kainao*. In this conception, the word *kotuanao* refers to the dead ones. This means that recent or biographical reports that involve living people are not considered *kotuanao dau'ao*.

In genealogical terms, the Wapishana consider *kotuanao* as the dead people in the second ascendant generation to the narrator. The dead people in the first ascendant generation can occasionally be said to be *kotuanao*, if the narrator is very old and considers that the dead people being discussed belong to a distant past. It is important to note, however, that not all dead people are *kotuanao* – only the ones about whom there is no biographical memory. Accordingly, *kotuanao* is a generic category of emptied dead people about whom no personalized memory remains. That is why old narrators are said to be the remnants of the old; they are able to remember individual bodies that social memory refuses.

Now we can understand why the recent uprising of 1969 could not be a theme within the genre *kotuanao dau'ao*, whose thematic reference is the remote past. Let us turn to Lucy's narrative about the Melvilles. In spite of its biographical tone, it was performed as a *kotuanao dau'ao* narrative and so was acknowledged by its audience. The inadequacy of a biographical tone according to the central convention of the genre was compensated for, from the point of view of a younger audience, by the fact that Lucy is an aged woman; age made her a "remnant of *kotuanao*," whose experience could only be shared through language.

In analyzing Piro narrative, Peter Gow (1990) argues that the notion of a radical rupture between the dead and the living – which Manuela Carneiro da Cunha (1978) demonstrated to be generalized in the lowlands of South America – in Piro representations of the past is expressed by the construction of a language link with the dead in opposition to the substance relations that connect the living ones. In addition, Gow suggests that this opposition between the dead and the living is operative not only in the narrative transmission but also in its composition.

Indeed, narrative performance among the Piro actively shapes memory as it creates distance in relation to the past.

In an analogous way, the Wapishana narrative genre is guided by an opposition between the experience of the senses and the experience of language. "You cannot see *kotuanao* with your eyes," the saying goes. The central premise for such an opposition, as I argue in other works (see Farage 1997, 2002), derives from the Wapishana notion of death and the dead. For the Wapishana, the main attribute of a corpse and its specter or ghost (*ma'chai*) is deterioration or putrefaction, which it can spread among the living. The grief about dead ones, their memory, can make the living vulnerable to lethal *ma'chai* attacks. In order to avoid them, it is imperative to forget the dead ones: from the Wapishana point of view, forgetting is indeed the ideal attitude in the face of death and thus toward the past. Free from their once individual face, the dead can collectively reach the condition of old people, the *kotuanao*. Through the remoteness created by oblivion, they do not threaten anymore the time of the living. This same process of detachment works in the narrative genre. Thus vivid memories, experiences shared by so many living bodies and individualities, like that of the 1969 uprising in all its consequences for the present existence, can not be told.

I must stress that the passage of the dead to the condition of old people can be detected in narrative, but reciprocally it is enacted little by little by the act of narrative itself. As for the Piro, it seems that for the Wapishana the transformation of the past into narrative – that is, an experience of language – grants the necessary remoteness of the past; to speak of it is to circumscribe it in a place where it cannot affect the present.

Does Lucy's narrative proceed differently? Her narrative emphasizes that what she once saw, the world she experienced by her senses, is now dead. The Melvilles, the social universe of the Rupununi cattle ranch; Georgetown, the mouth of the river Essequibo at the time of the British: all are gone. They are all dead, she says. In so doing, she places herself in a position of a "remnant of old" linked to her listeners by language. At the same time, she points out for her listeners the present time as the proper time for the living ones. In effectuating the remoteness of the past, Lucy's narrative also rhetorically effectuates its oblivion. The conclusion is Saint Augustine's: "Which way soever it be, notwithstanding that way be past conceiving and expressing; yet most certain I am that I do well remember this same forgetfulness, by which whatsoever we remember is defaced" (10:16).

1. The Wapishana are Arawakan/Maipurean speakers living in the savannas that lie between the Uraricoera River valley in Brazil and the Rupununi River valley in Guyana. Their numbers are estimated at between 10,000 and 11,000 (Forte 1990; Farage 1997).

2. This essay is a partial result of a work in progress, funded by Conselho Nacional de Desenvolvimento Científico e Tecnológico in Brazil. The main arguments on Wapishana rhetorical codification were originally presented in Farage 1997; particularly, the discussion in the last section of this essay about narrative conventions in the construction of the past also applied to the contact between the Wapishana and the whites (Farage 2002). I thank Audrey Colson, Bruce Albert, Mauro Almeida, José Luiz dos Santos, and Rae Swem for their comments and their corrections regarding the English writing.

3. Original in French: "Les deux maisons anglaises de Rupununi me font l'effet de se préoccuper beaucoup plus de payer le moins possible leurs Indiens que de leur apprendre à écorcher la langue de Shakespeare et à fétichiser la religion de Sa Très Gracieuse Majesté" (Coudreau 1887, 9:269).

4. Original in French: "plus de dix Indiens capables de comprendre, en anglais, autre chose que les deux vocables 'match' and 'Goddam'" (Coudreau, 1887, 9:283).

5. The region did come to prominence in the first half of the 19th century due to the beginning of the dispute on the borderline between Great Britain and Brazil, whose point of departure was the temporary establishment of a Protestant mission in an area that Brazil claimed to be its territory. This led to the neutralization of the area in order to wait for diplomatic arbitration, which happened only in 1904. For a detailed study of the episode and its connections with the British policy against African slavery, see Rivière 1995.

6. Until 1793, Amerindian slavery was allowed in what was then the Dutch colonies of Essequibo, Demerara, and Berbice, although the bulk of labor for the plantations was supplied by African slaves (Whitehead 1988; Farage 1991).

7. The analysis of insurgence without a party program had classically the same theoretical fate (see Hobsbawm 1970, 1976).

The Cultural Transformation of History

6

Decolonizing History

Ritual Transformation of the Past among the Guajá of Eastern Amazonia

LORETTA CORMIER

It is axiomatic that historical representation is a selective process. Cultural meanings are embedded not only in the events and personalities chosen to be of sufficient significance to be remembered but also in the process itself of remembering the past. Whitehead (1995:56) has argued that historical anthropology has a distinctive role in general anthropology in that it deals uniquely with "others" who are distant in time or place. If the postmodern critique that Western ethnographic and historical narratives often reveal as much about the observer as the observed is valid, then indigenous historicities may also serve to reveal native tropes. It is not only the content of the encounter with the historical other that should be understood, but also the form of that encounter.

The Guajá Indians of eastern Amazonia encounter the past through the somatic experiences of dreaming and ritual visitation of the past. The past is viewed as an alternate spiritual realm existing simultaneously with the present. Here, historical consciousness is emplaced and embodied in sacred landscapes, sacred beings, and sacred ways of being. The past is enacted in the sense that is both performed and created. Guajá agency in ritually transforming the past serves, in part, to reverse acculturation and to preserve cultural identity.

THE VIEW FROM THE SHIP: A BRIEF HISTORY OF CONTACT

The Guajá Indians are a Tupi-Guarani foraging people living in eastern Amazonia in the state of Maranhão, Brazil. The Guajá began coming into prolonged contact with non-Indians only over the last twenty-five years. Sporadic written records of contact with the Guajá exist over the last several hundred years, but they remained largely isolated from non-Indians until the 1970s. Early evidence for probable antecedents of the modern-day Guajá is found in a mid-18th-century missionary report of the "Uaya" in the region of the Tocantins River, to the west of their present location (see Balée 1994b:25). Between the 1850s and the 1960s the Guajá were intermittently seen near their present location in the vicinity of the Pindaré, Tocantins, and Gurupi Rivers in the western portion of Maranhão, Brazil (Dodt 1939; Gomes 1985, 1988). Contact with non-Indians increased with the construction of the BR-222 roadway through their territory in 1969; that same year, approximately 40 Brazilian families settled the area along the Pindaré, although it was designated as a protected area by the now defunct Indian Protection Service, SPI (Serviço de Proteção aos Índios) (Gomes 1988; F. Parise 1987).

The current Brazilian Indian Agency, FUNAI (Fundação Nacional do Índio), began attempts to make official contact with the Guajá in 1973. In general, these early FUNAI reports, as well as other first-contact reports, describe the Guajá as nomadic hunter-gatherers, living in groups of 10 to 20 people and relying heavily on babassu palms, howler monkeys, and tortoises as subsistence items (e.g., Beghin 1951, 1957; Dodt 1939; Carvalho 1992; Meirelles 1973; Nobre de Madeiro 1988; Gomes 1988; Nimuendajú1948; V. Parise 1988). Nimuendajú's (1948) evidence of the Guajá goes back as far as 1912 and was obtained from descriptions of other local Indians of the Guajá.

The consequences of contact were devastating to the Guajá in terms of loss of life and loss of land. Although some deaths occurred due to organized bands of local Brazilians who set out to kill the Guajá (Gomes 1988), infectious disease has had the most serious effects. FUNAI records of events of the 1970s are harrowing, describing numerous corpses scattered along the Pindaré River, presumably due to introduced diseases (F. Parise 1988; V. Parise 1973a, 1973b). It is not known how many Guajá died during this period. However, after the creation of the first indigenous post for the Guajá by the FUNAI in 1976, the effects of introduced disease were documented. The population in contact with the post was reduced by more than two-thirds, from 91 to 28 individuals, with most of the deaths attributed to a single influenza epidemic (F. Parise 1988).

Perhaps the single most important event for the Guajá in recent history occurred in 1985 when the state-owned Companhia Vale do Rio Doce (CVRD) began construction of a railway for the Ferro Carajás mining project. The Carajás railroad runs from the coast at São Luis to the interior where iron is mined. Although no mining is currently taking

place in the Guajá area, the railway was built through the Guajá foraging grounds, and it has been accompanied by illegal land confiscation,
deforestation, development, and disease. Since operations commenced,
approximately 2,350 square miles of forest *per year* have been cut down
and burned for use in pig-iron smelting factories (see Balée 1994a:2). The
train has facilitated settlement of the area, and the Guajá habitat has been
and continues to be threatened by illegal invasions from the impoverished locals.

Today, there are approximately 200 Guajá with at least periodic contact with one of the four indigenous posts established by the FUNAI. It
is not currently known how many Guajá remain uncontacted, but it has
been estimated that there are approximately 50 to 75 uncontacted Guajá
who remain full-time foragers (Matos dos Santos 1997; Damasceno da
Silva [chefe de P.I. Awá], 1997, personal communication; Gomes 1996).
The FUNAI has introduced agriculture to those Guajá in contact, and
they are now involved to varying degrees in horticulture (particularly
of manioc) and are incorporating Western material goods into their way
of life.

Undoubtedly, the construction of the roadway and railroad was not
the first contact that the Guajá have had with non-Indians. Strong evidence exists that although the hunting and gathering mode of subsistence
of the Guajá has been in place for at least several hundred years, prior to
this time, they were probably agriculturalists.[1] Presumably, the adoption
of a foraging way of life was a voluntary or involuntary reaction to colonization, warfare, and disease. Balée (1994b, 1999) has provided convincing ethnobotanical and linguistic evidence that historical factors have led
to Guajá culture loss and regression from a previous horticultural mode
of production.[2] However, perhaps the strongest evidence that the Guajá
have undergone culture loss is that they no longer possess the critical cultural skill of indigenous fire-making technology and instead must carry
firebrands. In addition, a possible survival from an agricultural mode of
subsistence can be found in the Guajá belief in the existence of a group
of supernatural beings they call the *manio'i*, who live underground. Although the Guajá now use the term *tɛrama* to refer to manioc, it seems
very likely that the term *manio'i* is an older Tupi-Guarani cognate for
the domesticated plant, suggesting metonymy with respect to the underground habitat for *manio'i* beings. Apart from the belief in their existence
in the ground, the nature of the manioc beings is otherwise unelaborated
in the Guajá cosmology.[3]

Gow (1991:3) has argued that ethnographers have tended to employ a faulty dichotomy of acculturated historical peoples and traditional ahistorical peoples. His argument is particularly appropriate here. The use of the terms traditional and acculturated are problematic in describing Guajá historical chronology. If they were, in fact, agriculturalists prior to early events in European colonization, they reacted through dramatic culture change; this change was not through acculturation, but through its antithesis in retreating from Western influence. There is a basis for describing the Guajá as deculturated agriculturalists, but it is more accurate to describe them as reculturated. Although the assumption seems warranted that they have experienced culture loss, they have adapted to a foraging way of life. The adaptation to foraging did not involve merely a change in their mode of subsistence, but their social organization, environmental relations, cosmology, and value system are consistent with a foraging way of life.

Thus, the Guajá encountered in the 1970s were not a people without history; they were shaped by the events of earlier colonial influence. This also makes the term *acculturation* problematic in describing the sequelae of the culture contact of the 1970s, particularly with regard to their adoption of agriculture. Should the authentic culture of the Guajá be considered that of the early precontact agriculturalists, or that of the foraging mode of subsistence that has been in place for at least the last several hundred years? The argument could be made that the introduction of agriculture is restoration of their earlier precontact mode of subsistence as much as it is acculturation.

Although it is clear that an acculturated-historical / traditional-ahistorical scheme is an invalid dichotomy for understanding the Guajá historical chronology, ironically, the Guajá themselves make a distinction that is, to a limited extent, analogous. In the Guajá ontological beliefs, they view themselves as existing simultaneously in the earthly realm and the spiritual realm. Their earthly forms have undergone the effects of acculturation while those of the spiritual realm remain "traditional" in their interpretation of what it means to be authentically Guajá. Time also takes on different dimensions in these two realms, but rather than a historical/ahistorical dichotomy, it is perhaps best described as a time-quotidian/time-protean distinction. In the sacred realm, the past is multiform and malleable, and Guajá agency in the multidimensional past is important to creating their cultural identity.

In the Guajá conception of space-time, the cosmos is divided into two main layers: the *wī* (earth) and the *iwa* (sky). *Wī* and *iwa* are not merely spatial categories, but also temporal and spiritual distinctions. *Wī* is the present-time earth, whereas *iwa* is both the sacred past and a sacred dimension of the present. The celestial sphere is the home of the divinities, dead ancestors, and even dead plants and animals. It is also the home of past and present alters of the living Guajá. The Guajá view themselves as existing simultaneously on the earth and in the sky. The Guajá notion of the self is complex, as individuals are believed to be manifested in multiple states with alters who have semi-overlapping consciousness with each other. Three basic modes of being exist: the earthly bodies of the living, the earthly bodies of the dead, and the multiple sacred bodies in the sky.

The Guajá believe that at the moment of death, individuals bifurcate into two contrary forms: the *hatikwayta* and the *aiyā*. The *hatikwayta* can be roughly glossed as the soul or the spirit, whereas the *aiyā* are malevolent earth-bound manifestations of the dead. These *aiyā* are cannibal ghosts who eat the souls of the living and are believed to be the primary cause of illness and death among the Guajá. However, they are a necessary evil, because *aiyā* cannibalization brings about the separation of the earthly body from the spirit and gives one's *hatikwayta* its final eternal divine form.

At first glance, this scheme brings to mind a Freudian tripartite division of the "mind" into the id, superego, and ego. Although there is a rough parallel in the negative *aiyā*, the idealized *hatikwayta*, and the intermediate earthly body, these are not viewed as intra-psychic competitors within one's unconsciousness vying for control. Rather, the earthly body is hypostatic in that it is the primary state from which the other forms of being are derived. The *aiyā* cannot be manifested by living beings and can come into existence only with the death of physical bodies. The *hatikwayta* forms also depend on the existence of the earthly living body for their genesis. In addition, although the earthly living body can be considered an intermediate way of being, it is not an intermediary between modes of being. These alters are believed to have largely independent existences that are neither controlled nor directly negotiated by the earthly living body.

Hatikwayta is a plural concept. The *hatikwayta* are integrated into the physical bodies of individuals and also have multiple temporal manifestations in the celestial sphere. The *hatikwayta* are considered to permeate physical earthly living bodies as well as to have multiple temporal manifestations in the *iwa*. Co-consciousness with one's *iwa hatikwayta* is achieved in two ways: through dreaming and through ritual visitation of the past. Among Guajá men, dreaming is interpreted as the flight of one's earthly *hatikwayta* into the *iwa*. In dreams, dead relatives, divinities, and even one's own alter may be encountered. Dreaming is enacted through a ritual performed repeatedly in the dry season they call *karawa*. The Guajá explain the *karawa* ritual as being the same experience as dreaming, where one's *hatikwayta* takes flight to interact with others in the past.

The plural forms of the self in the *iwa* may pose somewhat of a logical paradox from the Western perspective. The Guajá say, "yaha ha'i iwabe" 'there are many of me in the celestial sphere.' Thus there is only one *iwa*, but multiple representations of the self at any "time." The *iwa* experience can be considered a form of ritualized remembering (see Cormier 1999). From the Western perspective, memories of different times, different places, and different life stages are interpreted as mental imagery taking place in the single locus of the "mind." For the Guajá, there is a single locus for this multiform, multitemporal experience: the *iwa*. However, since this is not viewed as merely mental imagery for the Guajá, but as a physical reality, the *iwa* forms have independent existences from the Guajá.

The *hatikwayta* can be considered a manifestation of both the spiritual self and the remembered images of others. The *hatikwayta* are multiform in part because they are relational memories. Although one may see oneself in the *iwa*, this is not the goal of going to the *iwa*. It is not one's individual identity that is important, but rather, encountering the *iwa* beings. Thus, the remembered *hatikwayta* do not have an a priori existence but come into existence through the experience of remembering. If the *karawa* experience is a ritualized form of remembering, then the *hatikwayta* would of necessity be plural in order to account for the varied memories of individuals. What one individual "sees" in the *iwa* will not be the same as what another "sees." In addition, although there is individual choice in who and what is remembered in the *karawa* ritual, the dream experience should be under less conscious control and therefore should generate an even greater degree of individual variation in recounting these experiences.[4]

At this point, it should be stressed that in arguing that the Guajá experience the past through ritual, this is not to suggest that they are unable to remember past events outside of dreams and ritual activities. However, the sacred past takes precedence in their historicity. The word *past* is an inadequate gloss for the sky world because it is not perceived in terms of the Western time's arrow version of history. The Guajá language itself lacks a past verb tense, which is consistent with their interpretation of the past not as other time, but as other place.

The independent nature of the existence of past selves in the *iwa* also relates to their idealization of *iwa* way of being. For the past forms of oneself and others, unpleasant events that are remembered as occurring on earth did not happen in the celestial sphere. For example, the Guajá recalled the event of a child born with a cleft palate. However, the Guajá say that when that child's alter was born in the *iwa*, she had no cleft palate. All *iwa* forms are enhanced. Everyone in the *iwa* is said to be beautiful, healthy, and extremely fertile. Men have additional spouses and children in the *iwa*, and women are said to be continually pregnant. Thus, there are some individuals believed to exist in the *iwa* who have never had earthly counterparts. The forest is also different in the *iwa*. There, the palms have no spines, the canopy is low, and it is easy to hunt game and gather fruit.

Iwa time is protean in that it exists in multiple states. All beings in the celestial sphere are eternal, but these beings cannot be characterized as living in a state of mythic timelessness. Although the divinities have their genesis in time immemorial, they are able to both visit and intervene in life on earth and time on earth. Likewise, the Guajá are agents in the past when they travel to the *iwa*. They are not merely witnesses to past events, but they interact in the past. The past does not have a static existence but is interpreted through the ongoing experiences of dreams and ritual engagement in the past.

GUAJÁ HISTORICITY: REMEMBERING OR FORGETTING?

"History, for them, is forgetting," concludes Anne Christine Taylor (1993) in her analysis of Jivaro identity, mourning, and memory. She addresses the paradox that although one often finds active mechanisms in place among Amazonian peoples for erasing the memories of the dead, the dead often play a substantial role in religious life. Two common, and often related, processes are found in Amazonia that facilitate forgetting the personal identities of the dead: genealogical amnesia and varied onomastic practices. Genealogical amnesia is extremely widespread in lowland South America, and naming practices include teknonymy, inheritance of names, name recycling, multiple name sets, and outright taboos on the names of the dead.[5]

Taylor (1993:654) describes the dead among the Jivaro as "altered egos" who play a structural role as an alternative social organization with values that are either absent or at odds with the social organization of the living. This is similar to the argument made by Hill (1988:10) in describing South American mythic histories as an attempt to reconcile a view of "what really happened" with "what ought to have happened." Although this is also true among the Guajá, it is more than a dialectic between the real and the ideal. Among the Guajá, it is not only the dead who play a role as altered egos in the world of the *iwa*, but the Guajá themselves are agents in both the world of the living and the world of the remembered.

This idealization and erasure can be considered a ritualization of memories and likely relates to their profound genealogical amnesia (Cormier 1999). Although encounters with dead ancestors are central to their religious life, the Guajá have difficulty recalling the names of their dead after several years have passed. The Guajá even have difficulty recalling the names of their own parents. The Guajá have no taboos on the names of the dead, no teknonymy, and no other onomastic practice that would discourage providing the names of the dead. Nor do they exhibit any anxiety upon either stating or hearing the names of dead ancestors. A few were able to recall the names of some of the dead. On several occasions, informants who were asked the names of their dead parents later returned and provided the names they were initially unable to recall. In addition, FUNAI records contained some genealogical history. There was no anxiety displayed upon hearing these names, and some were able to confirm them as their relatives, although others did not remember. Thus, while there is no active rule prohibiting recalling the names of the dead, it is, nonetheless, normative to forget.

A pattern does exist in the process of "forgetting." The dead are initially recalled as individual personalities, then recalled in terms of their affinal relations to living, and, finally, take on a more generic status as the *awa harɛ piharɛ*, the Guajá kin. This process was observed in several deaths that occurred during the research period. Immediately upon the death of an individual, he or she would be the subject of much discussion and grieving in the days following the death. Shortly thereafter, sightings would be reported of the individual's *aiyā*, still using the individual's personal name. For those who had been dead for several years, the *aiyā* were referred to with kinship terms of reference, such as "Kaimaru's *emeriko*" (Kaimaru's wife), rather than using the dead individual's personal name. Similarly in the *iwa*, when specific individuals are visited, they tend to be described through a kinship term of reference rather than a personal name.

Although the dead play an important role in Guajá religion, individual personalities fade. Their presence is analogous to a sculptor's clay. The existence of the dead is a substrate necessary for Guajá historicity, but their presence requires sufficient pliancy in order for the Guajá to act as agents in creating history. The *iwa* experience is an intense form of both remembering and forgetting, but moreover, it is a process of historical transformation.

DECOLONIZING HISTORY

Comaroff and Comaroff (1992:50) have argued that ethnicity always has its genesis in specific historical forces, which are simultaneously structural and historical. Although it would go too far to argue that the way the Guajá experience the past is determined by the watershed crisis of the settlement of their indigenous area, their experience of the past is most certainly an important manifestation of the Guajá reaction to these pivotal events. The *iwa* experience is an ethnic affirmation and a display of extreme ethnocentrism. While the Guajá have had little control over the invasion of the territory and other changes in their way of life, through the *iwa* experience, the Guajá have the power to separate foreign elements from their existence.

The ethnocentrism of the *iwa* experience is much more profound than merely interpreting the past from the Guajá perspective; they deny even the existence of a sacred past for others. Prerequisite for entering the sacred realm of the past in either life or death is the existence of the *hatikwayta*, which non-Indians lack. The Guajá believe that whereas endemic plants and animals have *hatikwayta* forms that are transported to the *iwa* at death, non-Indians lack them and have only a temporary, ephemeral existence in the earth-time present.[6] Thus, local Brazilians, FUNAI officials, anthropologists, and other Westerners simply do not exist in the past.

The *iwa* reverses the effects of contact not only by excluding non-

Indian people from their history but also in removing all material evidence of them. Acculturation has brought many diverse changes to the Guajá. As previously mentioned, one of the most important has been the FUNAI's introduction of domesticated plants and animals. This was done, in part, due to the concern that the circumscription of their territory will make their traditional hunting and gathering lifestyle difficult to maintain.[7] The Guajá in contact with non-Indians are now involved to varying degrees in manioc cultivation and processing, as well as cultivation of a number of additional domesticated plants such as corn, papaya, and rice. Domesticated animals have also been introduced, including dogs, cats, and chickens. Although the Guajá are growing more dependent on domesticates, there are no domesticates in the celestial sphere. Dogs, cats, chickens, and other domesticated animals are considered to be the pets of the *karaí* (non-Indians), and thus, like the *karaí*, they lack *hatikwayta* and an existence in the past. Domesticated plants are also absent from the *iwa*.

For the present-time *iwa* alters of the Guajá, they live a life that parallels that of the living, but without Western influence. For example, two items of Western material culture that have been introduced are shotguns and cloth hammocks. When an individual goes hunting on earth with a shotgun, his present-time *iwa* alter is said to hunt simultaneously, but with a bow and arrow. Likewise, if a Guajá sleeps in a cloth hammock, his or her *iwa* alter is said to be sleeping in a *tikwita* (*Astrocaryum vulgare*) fiber hammock in the *iwa*.

Although the Guajá are idealized versions of themselves in the *iwa*, their activities there are rather mundane. Life in the *iwa* is neither an escapist fantasy from their daily lives nor a means for heroic exploits that would undo or alter history in a dramatic fashion. The lack of dramatic action does not make their activities in the *iwa* any less significant, for it is not so much what is done, but how it is done. Even in the most commonplace of activities, the *iwa* acts as a cultural filter removing any non-Guajá elements from their past. As such, they systematically decolonize their history.

AMBIVALENCE: THE JAGUAR BECOMES THE TRAIN

Although cultural contact has clearly been destructive in numerous ways to the Guajá, they also express the value they place on some aspects of contact, most notably Western material goods. This is so despite the exclusion of Western material culture from the *iwa* experience. One way this ambivalent attitude has been manifested is in a change in the creation myth recounted by some informants. In the original creation myth, the creator/culture hero, Mai'ira, creates a wife from a tree. The woman-tree is impregnated by Mai'ira and conceives male twins.[8] When Mai'ira is away hunting, the tree-wife walks alone in the forest and is confronted by an anthropomorphic jaguar (*yawárɛ-awa*) who eats her and takes the twins, whom he raises. In his grief over the loss of his wife and sons, Mai'ira leaves the earth for the *iwa*, never to return. In the new version of the creation myth, the source of Mai'ira's grief is the coming of the train.

The train can be considered a "historical metaphor" becoming a "mythical reality" (Sahlins 1981). The substitution of the train for the jaguar is metonymic in the shared opposing attributes of predation and protection. The jaguar is an ambivalent figure in both Guajá mythology and their daily lives; it is the object of both fear and identification. Jaguars are enemies because they prey on the Guajá, both in mythic representations and in literal encounters with jaguars in the forest. However, the Guajá also seek to emulate the predatory skills of the jaguar. Despite its dangerousness, the mythological jaguar is also a nurturer in its parental role, its ability to destroy predators of the Guajá, and its magical sustenance of the physical body.

The mythological jaguar is a dubious parent. He kills the mother and displaces the father, yet his role as adoptive father becomes important to Guajá cultural identity. The people of the train have also been dubious characters. Paternalism is perhaps an apt description for the relationship of the Guajá people to the larger Brazilian society where they have the legal status of minor children. However, the paternal or parental role is best understood from the Guajá perspective. In their relatively egalitarian society, parents do not exert real authority over children. Parents guide, teach, protect, and advise children, but they do not directly discipline them. That is not to say there are no consequences for failure to abide by the parents' wishes or the general cultural norms. Gossip, ridicule, and other expressions of displeasure are powerful motivators for compliance, but parents are not authority figures.

The people of the train, like the mythological jaguar, are clearly viewed as the cause of Guajá misfortune, but they are also viewed as having a role in its remedy. This dual nature of the people of the train may also account for why they substitute the train for the jaguar, rather than for the *aiyā*. The *aiyā* would seem a clearer choice for a purely destructive force. It could be argued that one reason the people of the train were not substituted for the *aiyā* is that imparting *aiyā* to non-Indians would go too far in humanizing them. Although indigenous plants and animals have *hatikwayta*, only the Guajá manifest *aiyā*. Thus, it would endow Westerners with a spiritual aspect that only the Guajá possess. However, the attribution of *aiyā* has occurred with the mosquito. In the wet season, FUNAI personnel have begun to spray the Guajá village area with insecticides to control the mosquito population. The Guajá have merged the Western scientific knowledge that mosquitoes bring malaria with their own cultural meanings. Although traditionally no forms of life are capable of generating *aiyā* except human beings, some Guajá now say that mosquitoes are manifestations of *aiyā*.

The Guajá recognize that the people of the train are the source of introduced infectious respiratory diseases.[9] The coming of the train brought non-Indians who killed both directly and indirectly through disease transmission. However, the non-Indians are also the source of the medicines to combat these diseases. Although the Guajá continue to heavily utilize indigenous plant remedies for illness, those in contact do actively seek out Western medicines and recognize their efficacy in alleviating or ameliorating illness. The jaguar also has a role in Guajá traditional medicine. Its most important role is that it is the only being in the cosmos capable of permanently killing an *aiyā*. In addition, the Guajá describe a kind of magical contagion that occurs when the jaguar is eaten. It has the ability to provide those who consume it with strength and is the only food believed to have the ability to confer its properties by being eaten. However, there is ambiguity in eating jaguar as well. Young boys and the grandparent generation are encouraged to eat jaguar, but it is taboo for others because it is believed to interfere with fertility.[10]

Finally, there is a parallel between the people of the train and the mythological jaguar in the critical role in the teaching of subsistence technology. The jaguar, as adoptive father, was responsible for teaching the twins how to hunt. The twins are believed to be the genitors of all the Guajá people; thus without the jaguar, the Guajá could not be hunter-gatherers. Similarly, the people of the train are teaching the Guajá about agriculture. Although the Guajá do not view the mythological jaguar or the people of the train as having legitimate authority over them, a parallel exists in this parental role of teaching the Guajá subsistence strategies. Although the *iwa* purges domesticates, it is possible that with Guajá increasing reliance on them, they may one day incorporate them into their *iwa* forms of life. One young adolescent who had grown up in the village with agriculture stated that there was manioc in his *iwa*.

REVITALIZATION, CULTURE CRITIQUE, AND CULTURAL IDENTITY

In a sense, the anti-Western nature of the Guajá *iwa* experience bears similarity to a revitalization movement through its conscious effort to suppress the effects of acculturation through ritual. More specifically, it has nativistic features in its restoration of the precontact way of life. Although it shares some features of revitalization, the *karawa* ritual is not a new ritual, not a syncretic ritual, and not a ritual designed to bring about change in the contact situation. It could have this function. The divinities could be asked to intervene and eliminate foreign influence, but they are not. Rather, the divinities are asked to bring game to the Guajá, to decide marriage alliances, and to heal the sick, but not to rid them of Westerners.

Further, although the *iwa* experience effectively eliminates Westerners and Western material culture from the sacred realm, the Guajá do not behave strictly this way in their day-to-day lives. Although the Guajá have killed intruders, they have basically good relations with the FUNAI and visiting researchers. In addition, as previously described, they also express a great desire for all manner of Western material goods. But they do not ask the divinities for machetes – they ask the FUNAI. Although some Guajá have chosen to remain isolated, some of those in contact express lament over even temporary absences of items of Western material culture that are being incorporated into their lives. For example, one hears complaints from those on long treks of the difficulties of going without manioc or packaged salt, although these are items that have only recently been introduced to them. One informant who described how her alter sleeps on a *tikwita* hammock in the *iwa* used the opportunity to complain that she was in urgent need of a cloth hammock because the *tikwita* fiber was much too rough for her baby.

Although the *iwa* does seem to serve as cultural critique, contrasting the way things are with the way they should be, it can be at variance with the expressed desires of the Guajá for Western material items. Similarly, although it is certainly an ethnocentric reaction to culture contact, this cannot be a complete explanation if the Guajá do not hesitate to incorporate Western material items into their daily lives. In addition to its nativistic features and provision of structural contrasts, the *iwa* experience is important in creating difference. The *karawa* ritual is more than wishful thinking, an escape hatch from an unpleasant reality, or a reflexive encounter with the idealized self. It is a means to create cultural contrast. Here, differences between the Guajá and non-Guajá are exaggerated. The *iwa* mimesis is an "over the top" performance, if you will, where alters amplify Guajá distinctive features.

The *iwa* experience is not just a reaction to contact with non-Indians, for it is also important in constructing cultural differences with other Amazonian Indians. The lack of domesticated plants in the *iwa* is particularly telling. Although the Guajá did not know how to grow domesticated plants when they were contacted in the 1970s, that did not mean that they had no knowledge of the existence of domesticates. Prior to the 1970s, local Brazilians and neighboring enemy Indians described the Guajá as crop stealers, even though this was quite a dangerous practice (Beghin 1957; Nimuendajú 1948). Thus, the ethnocentrism of the *iwa* experience is directed generally at all non-Guajá cultural items, not merely Western cultural items. And further, these foreign cultural items are eliminated from the *iwa* experience despite their desires and great efforts to attain them in earthly life.

In Graham's (1995:114–118) work, *Performing Dreams*, she describes the dream experience as being interpreted differently depending on one's status in Xavante society and being an expression of age grade solidarity. Similarly, the *iwa* experience creates differences not only between the Guajá and outsiders, but also in relations of power within the group. As previously discussed, the Guajá, as a foraging people, are relatively egalitarian. Gender hierarchy does exist, but these differences are difficult to see in Guajá daily life. This is particularly so in their sexual lives, where women freely have multiple sexual partners of their own choosing outside of marriage.[11] However, gender differences do exist in access to the sacred realm. Women are said to be, by their nature, unable to reach the *iwa* or its inhabitants through ritual. They must ask their husbands or male relatives to do their bidding with the divinities. Thus, their access to the power of the divinities is always indirect. Women's dreams are also interpreted differently. All men's dreams are believed to be the flight of their *hatikwayta* to the *iwa,* but women's dreams are passive experiences. When they dream, they are said either to be seeing through the eyes of one of their *iwa hatikwayta* alters or to be spirit-possessed by a divinity, and in that way, they see the *iwa* through the eyes of the divinity. Although women have a high degree of freedom and independence in their daily lives, it is in the sacred realm where the differences are made. The *iwa* experience does not so much reflect or mystically justify gender stratification as create the stratification itself. Thus, the *iwa* experience creates difference both within and between group relations.

In conclusion, Guajá historicity decolonizes the past. However, the tremendous changes brought about by contact with non-Indians have not created the way the Guajá experience the past; rather, the experiences of contact have been incorporated into their existing structures for interpreting the past and for asserting their cultural identity. Although Western history records and interprets the critical events that shape the trajectory of time's arrow, the meaning and purpose of the past differ for the Guajá. Through ritual and dreaming, the Guajá become active agents who re-create and transform past events and thus present cultural meanings. Although encountering the past does serve to counter acculturation, it also serves to reinforce norms, values, and social relations within the Guajá culture. In sum, Guajá historicity is religious expression and political agency, it is culture critique and ethnocentrism, and it is remembering and forgetting.

NOTES

1. A number of studies have argued against the existence of independent hunter-gatherers in the tropical forest (e.g., Bailey and Peacock 1988; Bailey et al. 1989; Hart and Hart 1986; Headland 1987). Balée (1988) has argued that the Guajá are adapted to anthropogenic forests, in their heavy reliance on the babassu palm, which grows in old fallow fields. Further, anthropogenic forests are also a concentrated source of plants the Guajá identify as being eaten by monkeys, an important prey food (Cormier 2000a, 2000b). Thus, while not in direct trade relations with agriculturalists, they are indirectly dependent upon the forest habitats created by agriculture.

2. Balée (1994b, 1999) provides four lines of evidence to support this culture loss in comparing the Guajá to the linguistically related Ka'apor, who share one of the Guajá reserves: the existence of Tupi-Guarani cognates of domesticated plants in the Guajá language; Guajá terms for nondomesticates modeled on terms for domesticates; fewer plant names known by the Guajá than the Ka'apor; and underdifferentiation of generic plant names by the Guajá in comparison with the Ka'apor.

3. One informant suggested that the above-ground world is the spiritual realm for the *manio'i* in the same way that the celestial sphere is the spiritual world of the Guajá. However, the Guajá do not suggest that the *manio'i* influence earth events or affect earth time. Rather, I suspect this is an example of perspectivism common in Amazonian thought. Thus, what appears to be *iwa* to the *manio'i* is what appears as earth to the Guajá.

4. The degree of conscious control involved in dreaming is an important question, but it is beyond the scope of this work. The Guajá describe all experiences (dreaming and ritual) in the *iwa* as "good" *katu*. When questioned about bad dreams or nightmares, they stated that children sometimes awaken in the night in fear, but that this is not an *iwa* experience.

5. A few examples of groups with naming practices that impede recalling names of ancestors are the Araweté: teknonymy (Viveiros de Castro 1992); Jivaro: name recycling and inherited names (Taylor 1993); Ka'apor: teknonymy (Balée 1994b); Mehinacu: teknonymy and inherited names (Gregor 1974); Mundurucu: taboos on names of the dead (Murphy 1956); Sirionó: teknonymy (Holmberg 1985); Suyá: inherited names and multiple name sets (Seeger 1981) Yanomamö: teknonymy and taboos on the names of the dead (Chagnon 1997).

6. The status of non-Guajá Indians, the *kamara*, is less clear. Some Guajá believe it is possible that members of neighboring tribes do have souls and an *iwa* of their own.

7. I am hesitant to voice criticism of the FUNAI for introducing agriculture to the Guajá, although it is drastically altering their way of life. I must credit the local FUNAI for their attempts to preserve the Guajá indigenous area. In doing so, they have risked their own personal safety, since they have been the targets of numerous death threats from many angry and impoverished local Brazilians who seek to settle and extract resources from the Guajá lands.

8. I use the term *impregnated* here because in the Guajá view, conception is achieved by males. Females are not believed to have a direct role in conception but rather are viewed as a receptacle for the semen, which is believed to create the child.

9. Although the Guajá recognize that infectious respiratory disease comes from non-Indians, the Guajá still believe that it is the *aiyā* that ultimately kills a Guajá. Similarly, they believe that snakebite causes swelling, but that death does not come from the snakebite, but from the *aiyā*.

10. The classification as a "grandparent" begins around the early 30s and does not necessarily coincide with actually being a grandparent. For both women and men, attaining a certain age confers what the Guajá consider an ability to eat foods that would be harmful to them when they were younger. Thus, women as young as their early 30s are "grandparents" who can eat jaguar even though they are still in their reproductive years. It should also be noted that the jaguar

is not the only food that is considered to interfere with fertility. However, the jaguar is the only food that has this dual quality of being able to both help and harm.

11. Among the Guajá, it is actually viewed as necessary for women to have multiple sexual partners during their pregnancies in order to obtain sufficient semen to make a fetus.

7

Guyanese History, Makushi Historicities, and Amerindian Rights

MARY RILEY

This essay examines and analyzes how the Makushi in the northern Rupununi savannas of southwestern Guyana selectively use events and scenes from their collective past to galvanize the Amerindian rights movement in the present. Makushi Amerindian men and women speak both of events that occurred in the mythological past (that is, before the world came to be as it is presently known and experienced) as well as those events that occurred in the verifiably historical past, but the contexts in which the mythological past is evoked are often different from those in which it occurred in a recognizably historical time frame. Although some of the events they recollect are verifiably historical (e.g., intertribal warfare and village raiding, Brazilian enslavement of Amerindians, the arrival of missionaries in the Rupununi in the early 19th century), this essay examines how the Makushi order and speak of all past events, whether or not they are historically verifiable, and examines the reworking and refashioning of what is being said by Makushi men and women about Amerindian life, philosophy, world view, and political life in the present age, in the early years of the new millennium.

Additionally, although the discussion and recollection of the Amerindian past occurs both in mundane conversations (e.g., just-so stories) and during "formal" events (e.g., culture shows performed for a public audience or at nationally visible Amerindian conferences), all of these narrations of Amerindian life in the past serve a number of purposes of the individual Amerindian speaker or the Amerindian community. I argue that not only do the Makushi construct and reinterpret their past in ways that seek to explain the present world in which they live, but that these explanations also figure into the collective discussions among increasing numbers of Guyanese Amerindians concerning land rights, the value of indigenous knowledge, autonomy, self-determination, and cultural heritage preservation. Another function of the whole of these narrative expressions – performing culture shows, the telling of just-so stories, and anecdotal stories about the Makushi in historic time (during the colonial era) – is to accentuate the notion that Amerindians are ontologically different from the rest of the Guyanese population. Because of this basic difference between Amerindians on one hand and all other Guyanese citizens on the other, Guyanese Amerindians are therefore more than justified in actively cultivating and encouraging a separate identity from that of the national motto: "One nation, one people, one destiny" – which some Guyanese Amerindians view as being solipsistic or glibly assimilationist (LaRose and McKay 1999:33).

In order to better understand how the Makushi are using the past to bolster their rights to land claims, territorial claims, resource rights, political autonomy, and self-government, we need to step back further to examine the relationship between knowledge and power. If it is surmised that the collective past of the Makushi people contains a reservoir of indigenous knowledge – of Makushi subsistence; of knowledge of plants, animals, and the environment; of past historic and mythological events; of how to live well and honorably among kinsfolk and villagers – then we must examine how this reservoir of knowledge is embedded within the physical, cultural, and historic landscape of the northern Rupununi savannas (which the Makushi have permanently occupied only since the late 17th century). The position of the Rupununi as a cultural landscape – in the eyes of both Amerindian and non-Amerindian Guyanese – also must be considered when examining the formation of Amerindian identity and the physical, cultural, and historic separation of (Rupununi) savanna-dwelling Amerindian groups (such as the Makushi in Guyana) from (Coastlander) non-Amerindian Guyanese.

"WILD" LANDSCAPES AND THE PLACE OF THE RUPUNUNI IN GUYANESE SOCIETY

The Rupununi savannas hold a special place within the Guyanese imagination, as well as in the imaginations of many Westerners who chanced to visit or travel through this remote area over the past three centuries. The striking beauty, remoteness, and vastness of the Rupununi have been noted in several travelogues, governmental reports, and other historical documents (Brett 1868; Bridges 1985; Henfrey 1965; Hilhouse 1978; Im Thurn 1883; Ralegh 1997; Schomburgk 1922, 1923). Perhaps because of this past regard for the Rupununi savannas, the Rupununi has incontrovertibly come to represent within Guyanese national consciousness *the* Guyanese interior (as opposed to all other interior regions of Guyana).

Because the Rupununi is the interior *par excellence*, all that is regarded as being the dead opposite of what is considered to be normative, civilized, and conforming is projected onto the physical and cultural landscape, onto a region and a people – the Rupununi and the Amerindian groups who live there. The notions of "primitive" or "uncivilized" may be expressed sympathetically, such as "Amerindians are children of the forest and so close to nature" or, alternatively, in a derogatory sense, such as "Amerindians are backward and do not know how to progress into the modern era." In both cases, the relatively forbidding and inaccessible location of the Rupununi within the country of Guyana has aided in cementing the Rupununi as being the "wildest" place, because of its remoteness from the life of Coastlander society in Guyana and because of the presence of Amerindian groups continuing to live in the traditional ways, as well as the presence of the *vaqueiro* (cowboy) culture and ranching industry, which evoke images of the lone, free cowboy life and vast, lawless places for the Guyanese citizen as much as it does for the North American citizen.

This characterization of the Rupununi is somewhat ironic, because many Rupununi Amerindians, out of either necessity or fun, do periodically migrate to the towns of Bonfim and Boa Vista in Roraima, Brazil, to earn some cash for a few months or years and have become quite familiar with modern conveniences such as electricity, running water, telephones, and, increasingly, the Internet. The modern conveniences of electricity, running water, and telephones have gradually become available, in limited amounts, within the frontier town of Lethem on the Guyanese side of the border, throughout the 1990s. A few Amerindians living in the village of St. Ignatius even have access to the Internet since one line of electricity and one computer were introduced to the village in 1998. Although the Rupununi may represent wildness and freedom within the mind of Coastlander Guyanese, one Amerindian woman recently e-mailed me and stated that for her, the Rupununi was not "wild," but it was free, as opposed to the congestion found in the Coastlander city of Georgetown. But even more important to our discussion of the region's physical and cultural landscape, the Rupununi savannas were simply home to her.

In the next section, I present a brief overview of the relationship between the production of knowledge and the creation of power and how this may apply to the ways in which the Makushi assert their claims to their ancestral lands, resources, and unique cultural heritage.

SITUATED KNOWLEDGE AND POWER

The subject of much discussion and scrutiny over the past two decades in anthropology has been the construction of knowledge and the historical and sociocultural influences in epistemology. This has taken the form of several guises: the postmodernist works of Marcus and Fischer (1986) and of Clifford and Marcus (1986); the work of Marshall Sahlins discussing decidedly Western constructions of history (1985) and the artificial divisions between past, present, and future on the linear timeline that is so normalized to Western perceptions of self, reality, and our "place" (temporally and spatially) in existence. Although I do not intend to reiterate here what has become oft-tread-upon ground in anthropology for about the past 20 years, I do want to remark upon the comments of one social scientist (Csikszentmihalyi 1995) with regard to the process of knowledge building:

> Knowledge, or the symbolic representation of what we believe to be true about reality, is biologically and socially constituted. It is biologically constituted in that our senses precondition what we can experience and set limits to what aspects of reality we can actually observe. Knowledge is socially constituted in that the symbolic representations of facts and their relations are formulated in terms of historical traditions that are largely accidental and *always at the service of some local interest or another*. It is not that the laws of physics, for instance, are arbitrary fabrications; what they claim about the material world does, indeed, correspond to our experience of it. But the laws of physics deal only with those dimensions of the world that we are able to grasp in terms of our current sensory and intellectual equipment, and are concerned with expressing knowledge in terms that will allow humans, or a specific subsection of humanity, to control the reality thus grasped.
>
> If knowledge is socially constituted, it follows that it will change, like other biological and social structures, in response to relevant changes in the environment. The process by which organisms acquire knowledge is selected, stored, and transmitted through ceaseless actions with the environment. (P. 123; emphasis added)

There are several points that Csikszentmihalyi makes that are relevant for the purposes of our discussion of Makushi historicity, which is basically the ways in which indigenous peoples create, relate, and interpret their history to themselves and to others (Whitehead, introduction, in this volume). Knowledge is both biologically and socially constituted, and although the ways in which history is created, interpreted, and transmitted in society may be subject to societal conventions or "traditions," the creation, interpretation, and transmission of the collective past for any sociocultural group is never value neutral. The existence of *any* collective history of a people serves several purposes at once – philosophical, ontological, and perhaps eschatological, but both history and knowledge possess decidedly political dimensions as well.

In addition, with regard to historicity, Fortier (1999) succinctly reviews the recent theoretical underpinnings of historicity and community. For Fortier, the community in itself does not exist until it begins to become conscious of itself and, in the case of Italian immigrants in Britain, when they begin to write about themselves, in an effort to communicate to themselves, about themselves, and for themselves. What is also significant to note is that Fortier conducted her study among a group of Italian immigrants in Great Britain, so that written accounts created by and for the then newly immigrated Italian community also contribute to her analysis of community, as well as information recovered from interviews with members of the Italian community. Anthropologists are increasingly able to rely on at least written media (e.g., newspaper articles, Web sites, archival material), but generally our major sources of information on Amerindian history, or at least history as Amerindians create, interpret, and transmit it to the next generation, are from oral narratives supplied to us by Amerindians themselves. The oral tradition within Amerindian societies has (or has traditionally) enjoyed the same authoritative power as the printed word has done for societies in the West (Urban 1996:25).

The just-so stories, local histories, and culture shows that I recorded during my time in the field operated on more than just a political level. However, for the purpose of this discussion, it is the political aspects that I examine further, since I want to illustrate the connections between overt and covert use of selected narrative expressions of the Amerindian past to fuel the present battles for political and cultural survival.

THE CULTURAL LANDSCAPE OF THE MAKUSHI

The Makushi of the north Rupununi savannas continue to live with a fair amount of their "traditional" life intact. In the early morning hours, the roosters begin to crow, and Makushi women rise early to start on the morning's tasks. Most Makushi villages still rely upon the traditional subsistence pattern of horticulture with complementary hunting and fishing, so farming dictates the daily and seasonal rounds of work in village life. A fair number of villages in the north Rupununi savannas are small settlements, many of which are relatively recent in age and number as few as 40 persons. There are about 15 villages that number from a few hundred to over a thousand people (most notably, St. Ignatius), and there are many more settlements with smaller populations. The Rupununi savanna lands are geographically contiguous with the Gran Sabana in Venezuela and the Rio Branco savanna in Roraima, Brazil (where Makushi villages also are located), which borders the Rupununi to the southwest. All Makushi households require at least some cash to cover expenses; work performed for cash temporarily takes men and women outside of the village, such as working as a ranch hand or *vaqueiro*, as a miner, or in domestic or construction jobs in Brazil. The general tendency for Rupununi Amerindians to move around in order to find work, escape drought or famine, or pursue other economic opportunities (either as individuals or, in some cases, as families) is also a traditional pattern, attributing to a high degree of movement and autonomy within the Rupununi district and along the border between Brazil and Guyana.

Houses are still constructed using traditional, locally obtainable materials, such as bush vine, palm fronds for roof thatch, wood collected in the montane forest for posts and rafters, and clayey mud for making sun-baked bricks. (In the past, wattle and daub wall construction was the norm). Despite the rectangular shape of Amerindian houses, these houses are still considered "traditional" in opposition to the "modern" (and non-Amerindian) houses, which are built using materials such as corrugated zinc sheets for roofing, mortar, and kiln-fired bricks made in Brazil and finishing with cement-poured floors instead of clean-swept dirt floors typical of Amerindian houses.

The fact that Amerindians live in a way that is vastly different from that of any other ethnic group that has lived in Guyana has been used to both positively and negatively stereotype Amerindians as a group. Folklore accounts of Amerindian culture always include cultural traits that are the most salient features of Amerindian culture: the beliefs in *kenaimas* (evil spirit-beings), *taling* ("blowing" for good or evil intentions), and *piaiman* (the village shaman); arts and crafts such as basketry, manioc graters, squeezers, and sifters for processing cassava (manioc);

bows and arrows to satisfy subsistence needs; traditional food and drink such as pepper pot (*tuma*), cassava bread, and *casiri* (a fermented manioc drink); living in the traditional Amerindian way, as farmers who live in thatch roof houses; and dancing "the traditional dances," which are thought to be quintessentially Amerindian by many non-Amerindian Guyanese.

The definition of what it is to be an Amerindian was first put forward by the British colonial powers that held the plantation colonies of Essequibo and Demerara throughout much of the 18th century and then ruled the colony of British Guiana without interruption from 1803 until the colony's independence in 1966. The British colonial attitude toward the Amerindians was a mix of paternalism and benign neglect. In order to prevent Amerindians from losing their culture and picking up less desirable aspects of modern (Western) people and their culture, Amerindian groups were to remain on their traditional lands, the assimilation of Amerindians into the larger Guyanese society was discouraged, and non-Amerindian (especially white) contact with the Amerindians was restricted. The exception to this isolationist policy was to allow Christian missionaries to go in and convert Amerindians, since Amerindian religion was viewed to be patently false, and Christianity could only help Amerindians develop within themselves the nobler aspects of modern (Western) people and their society: a work ethic, industriousness, and morality, such as monogamous marriage, non-incestuous kin and conjugal relationships, and unremitting obedience as loyal subjects to the British Crown. It was during the British colonial period that romanticized notions of the "noble savage" Amerindian became more commonplace within the writings of missionaries, explorers, and government officials.

Of course, the very cultural attributes that glorify and romanticize Amerindians by non-Amerindian Guyanese in one breath are the same qualities that are also used to denigrate and condemn Amerindians in the next. Amerindians are peaceful farmers, living off the rainforest and their farm plots; Amerindians are poor, are without ambition and backward, and "don't want to develop themselves"; Amerindians are highly skilled hunters and trackers and are very knowledgeable of (and live in harmony with) their natural surroundings; Amerindians are lazy, shiftless, and dishonest; Amerindians are humble folk, uncontaminated by city or Coastlander life; Amerindians are all *kenaimas* and practice witchcraft; Amerindians are Guyana's first inhabitants and deserve special honor because of this fact; Amerindians are not equal citizens under the law and do not deserve any special protections under the nation's constitution because, in accordance with the national motto, "we are all Guyanese." Although the Amerindian Act was created in the early years of the 20th century, was incorporated into the Guyanese constitution, and then was occasionally revised, Amerindian activist groups charge that the Amerindian Act (most recently revised in 1976) is woefully inadequate in protecting and ensuring the rights and needs of Amerindians under the constitution (Amerindian Peoples Association 1998).

Folklore accounts of Amerindian cultures can easily be reworked to enhance negative stereotypes of Amerindians and to justify local, regional, and national prejudices toward Amerindian Guyanese. Unlike the situation in Brazil, as brilliantly analyzed by Ramos (1998:23, 76), where the Brazilian plan to "emancipate" the Indians is to liberate them from their Indianness, there is a shared idea among both Guyanese and Brazilians that "Even if they [Indians] wanted to become civilized they could not, for it is in their nature to be Indian, and Indians belong in the bush" (76). To remain within the boundaries of folklorified Amerindian culture is then to be denied full access to or any participation in the opportunities, developments, and pursuits of mainstream Guyanese society. Some elements present in this Eurocentric discourse of Amerindian culture – that it is being "lost" or disintegrating because of change over time – have been internalized by some Makushi Amerindians, who equate objects with culture because that is what is taught in the nation's schools about Amerindians. This is also a message that is directly in conflict with what is seen in Makushi villages – a culture that is thriving and, most importantly, that is not defined by the presence or absence of traditional objects, but by the actions of Makushi villagers who are living their culture and valuing it for what it is.

Although the discourse produced by the British colonists has been consistently in the tone of "Amerindians are losing their culture" since approximately the 1840s, that discourse planted the seeds for the present Amerindian movement – predicated on the importance of *difference*. Although the producers of discourse about the nature and character of Amerindians were largely Europeans and British colonists and missionaries nearly up into the present time, Amerindians are now increasingly gaining a voice of their own to speak of their lives, both at local forums in Guyana and worldwide. Forces of globalization, such as the Internet, knowledge of indigenous rights movements elsewhere, and increasing attention placed on biodiversity and conservation issues have also contributed to giving the Makushi a voice that is heard beyond the borders of the Rupununi and the Rio Branco savanna. But although the knowledge of a "world out there" that is sympathetic to their struggle for land rights, for self-determination, and against land encroachment, another set of discourses – village-level, everyday discourses – that accentuates the difference between the Amerindian world, life, and history and that of whites (from abroad) and other non-Amerindian Guyanese is circulated and spread in the context of the everyday life in the villages and, very occasionally, is encoded in the "culture shows" performed for non-Amerindian audiences in Georgetown. Increasingly, indigenous historicities are being consciously produced for Amerindian communities themselves and for the consumption of non-Amerindian audiences (both in Guyana and abroad) who are interested in supporting the cause for Amerindian rights. In the next section I discuss what these historicities contain and how is it contextualized, transmitted, and accorded significance.

AMERINDIAN DISCOURSE ABOUT THE PAST
AND PRESENT TIME

Urban (1996) argues that discourse is the vehicle for cultural stories and meanings but that it also possesses a thinglike quality unto itself, once it is spoken and circulated to others in the community. Therefore, the action of speaking, ceremonial performances, and the like to transmit certain values that are key to Amerindian culture reinforces the values themselves because they do not merely "tell" about or convey meanings through the action of vocalization on the part of the speaker. Certain narratives and narrative performances become objects that are identified, interpreted, and transmitted from one to another in the community.

In this section I illustrate how Urban's points about discourse being both a sensible and intelligible entity (i.e., "out there" in reality, experienced and also known as an abstraction in the mind) can also be applied to the discourse that flows through Makushi performances in culture shows, in instances of telling just-so stories, and in talking about verifiably historical events. All of these narrations, either overtly or covertly, strengthen the idea that the Makushi (more accurately, Amerindians) are distinct from other groups in Guyana, and that by virtue of their distinct history, way of seeing of the world, and living close to the earth in a geographical landscape that can only belong to the Makushi and their past forebears, Guyanese Amerindians should have rights to what has always been theirs, what is asserted to be theirs in the present, and what should remain as theirs in the future.

JUST-SO STORIES

The just-so stories, stories that explain how things came to be the way they are now in the present time, in some ways are the most intriguing because they are relatively innocuous. During my time in the Rupununi, just-so stories were told to me by Makushi villagers of all ages in a relatively spontaneous fashion. There was nothing terribly special about them; they were simply stories of how one animal being, plant being, or landscape-object being either gained the attributes that are characteristic of it in the present day, or stories about the circumstances under which the being in question was transformed into the animal, plant, or object in the landscape seen today. But the stories themselves, or the structure that held the story, nearly always followed the same formula and contained elements that are worth examining a bit more closely.[1]

For instance, the just-so stories often started with little or no reference to time whatsoever. Many stories started by the speaker saying "One morning . . ." or "One day . . ." and then relating the action of the story starting from that point. Only later did I discover that these stories did not occur on just any "one day," but a day in the life of mythological time. The big tip-off for me was that the stories were usually about plants, animals, or inanimate objects, which could all talk to one another. Further, the "animals" mentioned were not yet in the form in which they are commonly spotted (and captured) today. That is, Tiger (Jaguar) was a being *like* a person, but not in the form of the quadruped now seen today. Deer was also a person. Spider, Yawarri (Opossum), Woodpecker, and Hummingbird were also animal beings instead of their present animal forms.

Because the just-so stories started off with little to no reference to time frame, they had a way of truncating the past – that is, a story could have happened much sooner in the past than what we tend to think of when we (Westerners) say "mythological past." In these stories, the Amerindian view of the world is stated and restated, and the past (and the relationships between several different kinds of beings) is reinterpreted in the present. This theme is found in other ritual contexts among Amazonian groups, where language is used to close the distance between members of the same social world and cultural universe (Chernela 2001).

Additionally, the just-so stories were amazing in that they accounted for the tiniest details found upon the indigenous landscape – why does the crab have dry eyes, why does spiky grass grow on the savannas after the rain, why are deer herbivorous and jaguars carnivorous? The fact that so many just-so stories exist for explaining every physical phenomenon imaginable tells the Makushi Amerindian living in Rupununi as well as the non-Amerindian that the knowledge the Makushi possess about their environment is intimate, exact, missing no detail, and leaving it without meaning in the process. It tells the listener(s) as well as the speaker about the authority the Makushi have over their landscape, even if their place in the Rupununi is not "at the top of the hierarchy" or the supreme master of their domain (as expressed in Judeo-Christian thought and theology). Another interesting fact about these just-so stories is that all of the stories tell of action occurring between two or more beings – none of the action happens to one individual alone, as a lone actor effecting the plot and actions in the story single-handedly. I discovered later that (not surprisingly) the form and manner in which the Makushi narrated just-so stories, and the relational aspects among various sorts of beings within the stories, closely resembled the tales within the Orinoco creation cycle, *Watunna* (Civrieux 1980).

CULTURAL PERFORMANCES

In contrast to the just-so stories, which I usually heard told in the context of *kari* parties, or parents telling their children stories, or Amerindians telling me stories because I would be interested in hearing them – cultural performances were not exclusively performed in the setting of the village. Culture shows could have either Amerindian or non-Amerindian audiences, depending on where the show was being held. A culture show held in Lethem or Georgetown, for instance, was aimed toward a non-Amerindian audience, whereas shows performed in Makushi villages only rarely had a non-Amerindian audience. The culture shows functioned in two ways: they depicted Amerindian traditions performed in both the past and present times, and they affirmed Amerindian values by linking the audience members with the reenactment of particularly culturally salient events, such as rites of passage that are rarely or no longer openly practiced (in the case of *village-sponsored* culture shows). In the case of culture shows aimed at non-Amerindian audiences, the skits performed usually met more stereotypical expectations that the audience had of what Amerindian culture was about – but I want to emphasize the acknowledgment of difference and of Amerindians as the gatekeepers of a unique culture and stewards of the natural environment.

The reason culture shows varied depending upon the audience viewing them was due in part to the Amerindian knowledge of what the non-Amerindians knew about them (stereotypical ideas). More importantly, some Amerindian traditions are not well understood by non-Amerindians, and Amerindians would save those skits for an audience that could properly identify and interpret their meaning. For instance, although one of the culture shows put on in St. Ignatius contained a skit showing how a young girl was traditionally "tied high" in her hammock and secluded in a specially built *binab* when she first reached menarche, I never saw this particular skit at a show in Georgetown for a wider audience. (The fact that the skit is in essence about menstruation could also be a factor in its not being performed in Georgetown.) In the Amerindian case, a girl's reaching menarche is highly important because it marks her reaching physical and sexual maturity and her ability to conceive and bear children. In mainstream Guyanese society, the importance of a young woman as a potential mother is eclipsed by her availability as a sex object for young men, or at least those are the messages that stream steadily from the media and on the street.

One skit that is often performed in culture shows, for Amerindian and non-Amerindian audiences alike, is one that shows the *piaiman* "beating the leaves" to cure a sick patient and the subsequent encounter with the *kenaima*, an evil spirit being to whom is attributed all illness and deaths in the village. In Amerindian villages, the skit with the good *piaiman* and the evil *kenaima* (whether the *kenaima* is represented by a person or not during the skit) serves to represent informal institutions at the heart of Amerindian life – the shaman-healer and the patient, good and evil, disorder and restoration to order (via healing), and, to a degree, *taling* (blowing), which is also thought to summon the spirits responsible for illness from the spirit world to the *piaiman*'s presence. Within the skit, as in real life, the family of the ill person calls upon the local *piaiman* to hold a séance at night to determine the spirit responsible for causing the illness and to lure the patient's soul into coming back and reentering the patient's body, if no other methods of treatment have worked to help the patient.

The power of the *piaiman* is shown plainly in the "skit" ceremony. He chants and beats the leaves – two definite signs that show he really is a *piaiman* – and the *piaiman's* soul travels and goes up vertically into the air into the spirit world, shown by a leaf rising up into the air. The spirit that appears at his calling is virtually always the *kenaima*.[2] The *piaiman* then threatens the *kenaima* with physical harm if he does not stop bothering the patient's soul. The *kenaima* then departs, showing that the *piaiman* won that round of the battle for the patient's soul. Then the *piaiman* advises the patient (also addressing the mother or care giver for the patient) what plant remedies to give to the patient to restore health. (In real life, if things do not improve by the next night, the *piaiman* will return the next evening to continue singing over the patient).

At Georgetown, one *kenaima* skit I witnessed added non-Amerindian elements, such as the inclusion of a physician also called in to examine the patient.[3] The physician comes in a car, to the uproar of the audience, Amerindian and non-Amerindian alike, probably laughing for different reasons. Interestingly, the skit about the *piaiman* and the *kenaima* was titled *kenaima*, since belief in *kenaima* is seen to be a quintessentially Amerindian trait that is not shared by other Guyanese citizens. But the plot of the Georgetown *kenaima* skit was also a bit darker in tone, and the mystery behind the term *kenaima* is also projected back onto Guyanese Amerindians as a group, with their mysterious beliefs and incantations in the wild interior.

Other elements of Amerindian culture emphasized in the Georgetown culture show could be said to more accurately represent scenes from Rupununi life in general – two-step dancing, Brazilian *vaqueiro* guitar music, ranching and cattle culture. But since in the eyes of non-Amerindians, "the bush" of the interior is the "natural" abode of Guyanese Amerindians, then all other aspects of life in the interior tend to become kaleidoscopic in a stereotypical picture of Amerindian life, or the Coastlander's view of what Amerindian life must contain.

VALUES EMBODIED IN DISCOURSE

Overall, these Amerindian discourses form a Makushi past that shows Amerindians as independent, their traditional customs in full flourish, with little to no acknowledgment of the presence of non-Amerindian "others" in their lives. While the Makushi would tell amusing stories of how Amerindians and whites are different in their logic and thoughts in the present time, I did not record any stories that accounted for the "origin" of white people in the past. Such stories certainly must have existed at one time, or perhaps they were stories that I was unable to record but that were in the context of culture shows, just-so stories, and, to a degree, historical anecdotes. (These were my findings among the Makushi, but the situation may be different for other Amerindian groups in Guyana; see Moreno 2001.) Although I was able to record oral accounts of specific historical events involving white people (such as the missionary Reverend Youd who came to the Rupununi in 1838), I encountered no mythological explanations for the origin and presence of whites in the Amerindian world, nor any stories explaining the differences between whites and Amerindians.

The just-so stories, as well as the culture shows, show no history of tribal warfare (although this is sometimes acknowledged in informal conversations by the oldest Makushi villagers), nor fleeing from Brazil to Guyana, or other acknowledged historical events. However, the historical facts are that indigenous groups of the Guiana Highlands had developed ongoing, interdependent relationships with one another, which were expressed by extensive trading and knowledge networks, local specializations in the production of goods for trade, and intermarriages between Makushis, other Cariban-speaking groups, and Arawak-speaking groups such as the Wapishanas (Butt-Colson 1973:139–141; Foster 1990:68–74; D. Thomas 1972:10–15), notwithstanding the fact that these networks may have been altered or otherwise influenced by the activities of European powers within the Orinoco basin (Arvelo-Jiménez and Biord 1994:60–65). Even the names that have evolved as "tribal names" (although they are not ethnonyms) – Patamuna, Makushi, Wapishana, Akawaio, Warao, Arecuna, and Waiwai – are thought to be part of a larger system of nicknames by which each group referred to the other (Butt-Colson 1983–84:119, cited in Foster 1990:72–73).

In the past, Amerindian groups themselves were fluidly defined, with shifting, permeable boundaries. Expression of tribal affiliation and membership could have been expressed through the adoption of a distinctive hairstyle, or by the wearing of specific ornaments, attributes that can be changed by the person wearing them, if necessary or convenient. Such fluidity was in fact necessary to the production and reproduction of the "community-of-practice," the locus of transactions between individuals and entire groups of Amerindians, which served to reproduce Amerindian cultures and values in the next generation (Foster 1990:50). In the face of non-Amerindian ideo-political hegemony, with Amerindians of all tribes classified as "one people" different and distinct from other

Guyanese, Amerindians find solidarity with one another in demanding that they have more say in deciding how their lands will be used in the future. As the "first inhabitants" of the lands that now comprise Guyana, and everyone else who is Guyanese being either a descendant of a former slave (brought to the New World by force), colonial master (brought to the New World seeking profit), or an indentured laborer (brought to the New World at a price), Guyanese Amerindians demonstrate the difference between their claims to their own heritage vis-à-vis all of the non-Amerindian "others" who are, as evidenced by their own historicities, far less qualified to assert similar united claims to land, resources, and cultural heritage. When non-Amerindian Guyanese draw upon their collective psychological, mythological, and cultural landscapes, the landscape *of the present moment* is the Coastland. However, the cultural and psychological landscapes of the past include India, West Africa, the Madeira Islands (Portugal), Cathay (China), or any combination thereof, depending upon the ethnic descent of the individual doing the recollecting. These homelands were explicitly referred to by non-Amerindian Guyanese in the course of ordinary conversations about family and community histories. These latter landscapes are even further away, both in space and time, than the Rupununi, and the presence of these "alternate" landscapes (to that of the Coastland) further complicates the identity – or identities – of many non-Amerindian Guyanese citizens.

THE DISCOURSE ON LEGAL RIGHTS – NEWSPAPERS, PRESS RELEASES

What is especially interesting, when considering how and what pieces of history the Makushi selectively use to construct their past in present times, is how the image of the "Ecological Indian" is used time and again to highlight two basic points, which are then tied to larger discourse on the issues of self-determination, land rights, political autonomy, and decision making. First, Amerindians possess special knowledge, which is commonly termed as indigenous knowledge – that is, they have knowledge that no one else does, and this knowledge becomes evidence of their close relationship to their surroundings, a relationship that should be respected by the government into the present day. Second, this culture, history, and life of Amerindians in Guyana is special, different, and unique – and, in parallel with the arguments for how indigenous peoples worldwide should have a *sui generis* legal system in place to handle their concerns, Guyanese Amerindians use the uniqueness of their history, vis-à-vis other non-Amerindian groups in Guyana, to assert rights that other groups in Guyana do not have, nor could they argue for such rights.[4]

With the formation of the Amerindian Peoples Association (APA) and the Guyanese Organization for Indigenous Peoples (GOIP) in 1991 (LaRose and MacKay 1999:32), Amerindians were given a voice – although these organizations were formed in large part because of the need for nongovernmental organizations (NGOs) to exist to channel and distribute international grant money to Amerindians in the interior. Many Makushi with whom I spoke about these organizations expressed the view that they were not certain for whom the APA and GOIP spoke; that is, each group has its mouthpiece, claiming to speak on behalf of all Amerindians, but whether or not they really did was unknown. Another circumstance exacerbating such suspicions was that, with so few communications from the coastland to the interior regions of Guyana, it was difficult to obtain any information on what was happening with these groups. Some Amerindian villages had strong connections to either the APA or GOIP because of personal connections, blood or residence ties with one of the members, or a close alliance of the *touchau* (village headman) with the APA or GOIP. But what these connections were actually doing for all Amerindians in Guyana was harder to discern, for the Amerindian farmers who cared more about simply making a living as a farmer and had less energy to concentrate on larger goings-on, over which they felt they had little control, such as mining or timber concessions on Amerindian lands.

In addition, Amerindians felt that the government was doing little to help them, but to be fair, the Guyanese government has had and continues to have extremely limited resources at its disposal for working on basic problems facing the country, such as rebuilding the nation's crumbling infrastructure and continuing the attempt to buoy the national economy. Notably, many organizations that exist to help Amerindians in Guyana, in economic terms as well as in issues of human rights, biodiversity and conservation, and indigenous rights, are financed by developed countries abroad. This has led some Amerindians to believe that *non-Guyanese* tend to care more about their plight than many Guyanese living in Georgetown. Since the headquarters for both the APA and GOIP are located in Georgetown, their location on the coast may only arouse suspicions that APA and GOIP do not really have the interest in interior-dwelling Amerindians at heart because of their relative physical remoteness.

Also, the increase in international attention to Guyana as a "cash-poor but biodiversity-rich" country has, so to speak, placed Amerindians more on the global stage than ever and has given them a listening audience, thus providing further incentive toward developing historicities that reinforce indigenous rights claims in the present. Concomitant with this attention, in the 1990s there was a marked increase in research on Guyana's biological and genetic resources. Groups such as Conservation International, Survival International, and the World Wildlife Fund, along with a host of other scientific institutions, herbaria, and ongoing projects such as the Iwokrama Rainforest Project, have all been present in Guyana and making the news with their findings that Guyana is one of the most biodiversity-rich countries remaining in South America, with many species of plants that are endemic to Guyana alone.

The legitimating discourses produced by these scientific organizations have influenced Amerindian discourses on indigenous knowledge in two ways. On one hand, this outside research reinforces the view that indigenous knowledge is unique, worth "saving" or preserving, and that those who possess such knowledge of these rare, highly biodiverse areas (i.e., Amerindians) should be the ones who can best manage these areas; on the other hand, because these outside groups are validating indigenous knowledge via studies on the rainforest, the land, and the plants, in a sense they are bypassing the government, which has ignored Amerindians, their concerns, and their knowledge. Ironically, the representatives for these scientific organizations, so often established in North America and Western Europe, are nearly all white – and thus more related to the former colonizers of Guyana than to the Amerindians – yet these people are now seen as being more helpful and sympathetic (and as holding power and influence within international forums) to Amerindians than the present (nonwhite, non-European/First World) Guyanese government. So when a group of white, educated, moneyed scientists and consultants comes to Guyana and provides support to Amerindian groups, this appears to have a direct effect on how Amerindians talk about themselves in the present and what kinds of indigenous knowledge, objects, and ideas are expressed, represented, and reinterpreted within Amerindian narratives and, ultimately, historicities.

As is discussed at length by Medina elsewhere in this volume, many Amerindian communities in Guyana are also starting to map their village boundaries, mainly for the purpose of resolving boundary and reservation issues with the government (Fergus and Mackay 1999:32). The Makushi as well are discovering that another avenue for fighting for their rights as Amerindians means appropriating the tools of the non-Amerindian system – such as the use of the Internet for selling hammocks (Rupununi Weavers Society) or the use of mapping to assert indigenous claims to land and land titles. In a similar vein, the first lawsuit ever filed by an Amerindian community occurred in 1998 against the government for allowing a mining concession to come into the Upper Mazaruni River to do large-scale dredge mining, which caused damage and contamination to nearby settlements (Global Law Association et al. 2000). Amerindians were not informed of or even allowed to comment on the mining company's presence on their land, even though by law (under the Amerindian Act) they are supposed to be consulted whenever any non-Amerindian group wants access to their land. Although it will take some time to resolve this court case, the Amerindian Law Center was established in June 2000 with funds from outside of Guyana and is headed by a lawyer specializing in Amerindian law. It seems that, increasingly, others from the outside are lending help to the Amerindian rights movement in Guyana. In turn, this causes some aspects of Amerindian life and cultural heritage to be upheld as "culture" and not others, as Ramos (1998) discusses, as well as many other sources on Amerindian identity (e.g., Foster 1990; Jackson 1994). All of this may be light years away from the ways in which Amerindians construct, produce, and retell their history at the village level, but through this discursive process, all of the elements that are being funneled into the present process of production, portrayal, reproduction, and consumption of the collective Amerindian past can be seen and are seen to act upon one another.[5]

In conclusion, what can be easily discerned in the above discussion is how the discourse in which the Makushi directly engage is tied to Amerindian interests situated in the present time – the growing power of the indigenous movement, which works at international, national, and, increasingly, regional and local levels of political debate. It appears that the deliberate use of Amerindian motifs, technologies, locations, and landscapes in practices, in expressive performances, or in speech will continue as long as Guyanese Amerindians are engaged in furthering their own rights as a distinct cultural and ethnic group in Guyana, but also as long as the *audiences* to which Guyanese Amerindians present their culture are also "others" and as distant in thought, location, and life as from the Amerindian way of living, being, and doing.

1. As compared to historical accounts told to me, such as the coming of Reverend Youd to Parishara in 1838, this particular "story" was related to me simply and anecdotally, not following any narrative structure characteristic of the just-so stories or culture shows. In this case, too, the speaker did not add a meaningful time reference – at first I thought the speaker meant the 1950s instead of the 1830s.

2. In some skits, a person represents the *kenaima*; in others, no one represents the *kenaima*. That is, the *piaiman* speaks to the air in the skit, but everyone knows that it is the stage in the skit where the *piaiman* is addressing the *kenaima*. In addition to the fact that many may be reluctant to be the one in the skit to represent the *kenaima*, a skit that shows the patient and *piaiman* alone, possibly with family off to one side during the curing ceremony, is more realistic.

3. The physician in itself is not too anomalous – there are regional hospitals in the Rupununi – but the community health worker (CHW) is more likely to make house calls. Only rarely would a non-Amerindian physician come from Lethem to a village – due to lack of available transportation, patients come to Lethem. Also, in the skit, the non-Amerindian physician comes in a Land Rover, which reflects how Medecins Sans Frontières got around when they were last in the Rupununi, but which also is decidedly not the Amerindian way

4. I realize that this argument can be taken too simplistically. Although Amerindian groups in Guyana definitely live differently than other ethnic groups, this is in large part due to their physical and geographic isolation from Coastlander society. So whereas Amerindians live in their traditional homelands (at least traditional for approximately the past three hundred years), they are marginalized from the nation's political process, from resources needed to succeed in society (e.g., a good education, economic opportunities), and from other resources crucial to individual and community self-determination.

5. Especially with the case of North Americans and Europeans, *consumption* seems to be the apt word to describe the process. The "whites from the outside" tend to entertain certain notions of who Amerindians are, how they live, and what constitutes Amerindian living. To some degree, Amerindians play to this audience, and in a sense, the whole play back and forth ends up reifying some concepts of Amerindian life that really are not central to the *Amerindian* definition of what it is to be an Amerindian: Amerindians are only farmers; Amerindians are not interested in development; Amerindians are more naturally attuned to nature (as if nothing is "learned" – it simply occurs by osmosis).

The Archaeology of History

8

Caña

The Role of **Aguardiente** in the Colonization
of the Orinoco

FRANZ SCARAMELLI AND KAY TARBLE

Discussions of the significance of contact and colonialism have played
a major role in the development of anthropological and archaeological theory. Over the years anthropology has attempted to overcome its
parochial concerns with small-scale, isolated cultural phenomena in order to confront issues derived from the global process of Western expansion. Acculturation theory dominated the earlier attempts to analyze
situations of contact. A more critical approach, which drew on world-
system theories, placed stress on the expansion of global mercantilism
and capitalism and on the civilizing projects that accompanied colonial
involvement worldwide. These concerns made important contributions
to the practice of anthropology in general but at the same time revealed
a number of serious theoretical problems. World-system models tended
to be overly economic and to overemphasize the role of the core as de-
termining the processes occurring in the peripheries. At the same time,
due to its incapacity to accommodate indigenous historical agency, the
model precluded the understanding of variations in colonial encounter
situations (Dietler 1995, 1998) and tended to obscure the role of local cultural forces in the formation of the world system itself (Sahlins 1988).

In reaction to these tendencies, recent literature on the historical anthropology of colonialism has underlined the need to move toward less
unidimensional and mechanistic ways of conceiving local histories. To
do so, emphasis has been placed on the role of culture as a historical
product and agent; furthermore, concerns about agency and structure
as mutually constituting historical forces have been incorporated into
the analysis (Dietler 1998:299). This has contributed to the refinement of
the theoretical apparatus used to explore the articulation between local
and global structures of power and the specific historical mechanisms

that contribute to the formation of structures of colonial dependency and domination. In pursuing these objectives, there has been an increasing interest in understanding the role of material culture in historical processes of colonialism (Wolf 1982; Bourdieu 1984; Comaroff 1985; Mintz 1985; Appadurai 1986; Sahlins 1988, 1993; Comaroff and Comaroff 1991, 1992, 1997; N. Thomas 1991; Carneiro da Cunha 1992; Dietler, 1995, 1998). Processes of cross-cultural consumption in the colonial context have gained prominence as indicators of the interactive experience (Dietler 1995). The analysis of consumption constitutes a fertile ground for the investigation of colonial encounters, since patterns of exchange and consumption are often accessible in both the archaeological and written records. Where ethnographic evidence is available, even richer insights can be gained into the place of goods in local value systems and their role in structuring interaction with colonizers (Sahlins 1988, 1992).

At the same time, anthropologists have recognized the ethnocentricity of what has generally been called "history" and are coming to grips with local modes of conceiving and constructing history. In the recent literature on the tropical lowlands of South America, ethnographic and ethnohistorical analyses are contributing to an understanding of pan-regional historicities – models of time, space, and memory, which differ structurally in different areas of the Amazon. Based on these models, such as those offered by Viveiros de Castro (1992) for the Araweté, Turner ("Sacred" n.d.; "Social" n.d.) for the Gé-speaking peoples, Catherine Howard (2001) for the Waiwai of Guyana, and Hugh-Jones (1979) for the northwest Amazon, it can be argued that time-space and memory are constructed out of the reciprocal relations inherent in affinal relations, exchange partnerships, and intercommunal commensality, and ritual, vengeance, cannibalism, and shamanistic practice. The marking of the body and the landscape, the memory of songs and stories, and the cycles of obligations and rights between generations and among affines contribute to a chain of production that is the very reproduction of society itself (Turner 1977, 1984).

One of the challenges facing those interested in analyzing situations of colonial contact lies precisely in the interface between historicities. In order to comprehend the reactions of the societies in contact, more research must be done into the different worldviews and value systems that were mediating the actual transactions taking place and, at the same time, contributing to forge new structures. In this case, our research focuses on one aspect of intercultural exchange in the Middle Orinoco region of Venezuela, where, as on other parts of the colonial frontier, indigenous and colonial agents sought to gain value and exercise control over each other through the exchange of material goods. European strategies for domination were designed both to suppress and seduce the local population. Military and religious strategies for these ends are well documented for the colonial frontier in Latin America (Rey Fajardo 1971, 1974a, 1974b, 1988; Whitehead, 1988, 1994, 1996; Langer and Jackson, 1995). Less attention has been paid to the more subtle processes that, nevertheless, throw light on the forging of relations of colonial dependency and domination, such as exchange and commerce, the introduction of new technologies, cultivars or domesticated animals, and the process of commodification of native raw materials, services, produce, and labor. Likewise, more effort needs to be made to understand the various indigenous strategies designed to resist domination and yet, at the same time, exploit the advantages of access to imported goods – both for their own consumption and as articles for exchange down the line in the vast networks that connected the tropical lowlands.

In light of increasing interest in the role of material culture in processes of colonialism, we focus on one of the most effective means for enticement employed in the Orinoco: the promotion of sugar cane as a cultivar and its consumption both in the form of sugar and, particularly, as *aguardiente* (firewater). Within the framework of postcolonial globalization studies, *caña*, or *aguardiente*, is particularly amenable to the analysis of the nature and consequences of contact in the Orinoco, where changing consumption patterns illustrate the way local indigenous societies entered into larger relations of economic and political power and the nature of the transformations they experienced in the process.[1] In this essay, we discuss archaeological and historical evidence for the transformation of drinking practices among indigenous societies of the Orinoco, following European intervention. We argue that the Europeans used distilled spirits as a strategy to seduce the aboriginal inhabitants of the area and to create new needs in the form of highly potent alcoholic beverages. This led to transformations in the traditional symbolic role of drink and its place in the creation and maintenance of political and economic status; in Dietler's words, the transformations in the "social construction of thirst" (1998:302). Furthermore, the adoption of distilled spirits and other imported items led to increasing dependency on cash cropping and professional gathering in order to obtain money or goods to exchange for the new needs.

Recent archaeological investigations in the Orinoco dating to the colonial and early to middle republican period (1680–1920) have revealed a fascinating record of the mutual transformation of local and colonizing populations through time. On the basis of archaeological evidence from 13 pre-Hispanic, colonial, and republican sites, including indigenous settlements, missions, and forts, we have constructed a preliminary archaeological framework for the understanding of the historical transformations undergone by local indigenous societies as a result of colonial intervention (Figure 8.1).

We have organized the archaeological data into four different periods: late pre-Hispanic (1200–contact), early colonial (1680–1766), late colonial (1767–1830), and republican (1831–1920).[2] These periods encompass the foundation and subsequent development of the colonial mission frontier along the Villacoa River, where the Jesuits founded Nuestra Señora de Los Angeles de Pararuma in 1734, and the ensuing transformations following the War of Independence in the 19th century.

The sequence is characterized by significant changes in the indigenous material assemblages, as evidenced in the increasing incorporation of foreign manufactures such as metal knives, hooks and spear points, glazed ceramics, beads, and glass into the archaeological record. Significant quantities of glass and ceramic bottles were recovered from the mission site in Pararuma and neighboring indigenous settlements pertaining to the early colonial period (Figure 8.2).

Some of these jars and bottles may have contained perfumes, medicines, and other liquids; the largest portion, however, constitutes palpable testimony of the ready incorporation of alcoholic beverages into the exchange system that developed during the colonial period. The presence of salt-glazed ceramic Bartmann jugs (so-called Bellarmine jars), Spanish olive jars, and a variety of glass bottles clearly suggests that liquor was being imported and consumed in both the mission sites and in the outlying indigenous communities. It is particularly interesting to note that the square-based bottles and Bartmann jars are probably Dutch in origin (Jay Haviser, personal communication, November 1998), and could point to trade with the Dutch colonies of the Essequibo.[3]

Two types of glass bottles are identifiable for the early colonial period: square-bottomed bottles and squat broad-bottomed bottles (Figure 8.2). The square-bottomed bottles are presumed to have been used to import

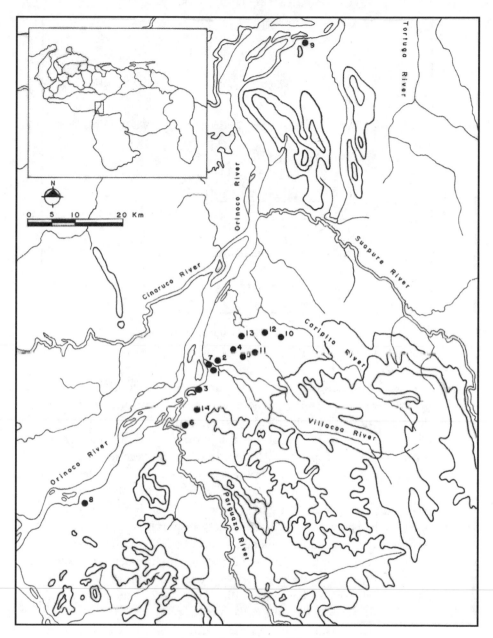

Fig. 8.1. Archaeological sites of the Orinoco

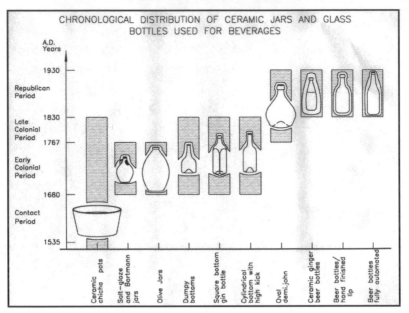

Fig. 8.2. Bottle types found in Orinoco

gin. According to Klein (1974), a new beverage distilled from malt and barley, known as *jeneverí* (gin) became popular during the latter half of the 17th century. The Netherlands was producing nearly 50 million liters of gin annually by the end of the 18th century and exporting it in the square bottles developed to pack easily in cases. The second type of bottle, the squat broad-bottomed bottle with a raised heart, was developed in England. During the latter half of the 17th century, these glass bottles came to replace the salt-glazed ceramic jars (such as the Bartmann jugs) that had prevailed up to this time to transport liquids. These bottles were used for wine, liquor, mineral water, and oil. This same type of bottle began to be manufactured in France, Belgium, the Netherlands, and Germany during the 18th century. Wine was stored in the bottles with a higher kick, which allowed the sediment to settle to the bottom with minimal contact with the wine (Klein 1974:34).

This initial demand for *aguardiente* documented in the early colonial period anticipates, on an even larger scale, the demand for drink that characterized late colonial and republican periods, when wine, bottled beer, and spirits became available through the market on a more regular basis. A dramatic increase in the frequency of glass containers is noted in the archaeological record for this period, where beer and wine bottles and large demi-johns constitute a major part of the archaeological remains (Figure 8.2). These are identified by local residents as bottles used to store rum or *aguardiente* brought by traders in the early decades of the 20th century. Wine bottles are easily identified by the high kick and the shape of the bottle. A wide variety of beer bottles, both glass and ceramic, are present. They are distinguished by different types of lips, which were developed to accommodate stoppers ranging from corks and levers to crown stoppers. The lettering on the body of the more recent bottles (early 20th century) indicates that beer was being brought in from many different parts of Venezuela and abroad.

It is, of course, one thing to infer the contents of the bottles from their distinctive forms. It is quite another to affirm that they were actually filled with their original contents at the time they were brought to the sites where we found them. Many of the bottles may have been reutilized over time as containers for water, pepper sauce, gunpowder, kerosene, or even locally distilled liquor. On occasion, even the glass itself appears to have been reshaped to make scrapers, bores, and spear points. It does, however, seem clear from the archaeological evidence that liquor bottles were present throughout the sequence and increased in variety and quantity over time.

Documentary evidence for the extent of the commerce in *aguardiente* is somewhat equivocal for the colonial period. The missionaries are silent about the use of alcoholic beverages as a means to enter into contact with indigenous groups and entice them to come to the missions. They do, however, ascribe this means of persuasion to other European traders in the area. Fray Ramón Bueno, Franciscan missionary in La Urbana (1795–1804), describes his encounter with Fernando Laya, a mulatto from the neighboring region of Cunaviche, who came to ask permission to sell *aguardiente* and sweets among the Indians. Bueno denied the license and threatened to punish Laya if it turned out that he had sold "even one drop" (see Bueno 1933:115–116).

The missionaries are much more communicative on the subject of the effects of drinking and "drunkenness" on the Indians they were proselytizing. The ubiquitous drinking party was the bane of the missionaries, who recorded the innumerable occasions on which the unrestrained consumption of alcoholic beverages lubricated the festivities to the point of brawling, "promiscuous" sexual behavior, vomiting, and eventual loss of consciousness on the part of the participants" (Bueno, 1933:134–135; Gilij 1987 2:130–134).

Drinking was observed to form a part of nearly every ritual occasion: initiation rites, funerals, exchange parties, dances, and the preparations for battle. Once the missionaries banned drinking in the missions, they complained that the Indians carried out their festivities in "the woods," out of sight of the fathers. "At certain times of the year, the nations referred to organize their feasts adorned by a large gathering of drunkards, for which they begin to prepare some fifteen or twenty days in advance with huge quantities of drink and food; all this is carried out in seclusion, and only rarely in the [mission] town" (Bueno 1933:93; our translation).

Gilij (1987), a Jesuit missionary who spent 17 years in the Orinoco, describes the various fermented drinks that the Indians prepared from roots, seeds, and fruits. He was amazed at the proclivity to drink on the part of the Indians and the preference they expressed for distilled liquor, when available. "Even more gratifying to the Orinocan people than any Indian beer [chicha] is liquor, be it wine or aguardiente from sugar cane. But its abuse is dissuaded due to the clear damage it produces to their souls. Not so ruinous is chicha, which only makes them lose their senses when drunk immoderately, as at the aforementioned dances" (2:133; our translation). At the same time, Gilij suggests that a certain tolerance regarding indigenous drinking practices was necessary in order to keep the Indians in the missions. "Forbid them to drink chicha or dictate that they drink only a small quantity, before they understand the beauty of virtue and the ugliness of vice. They will turn their backs on you disdainfully, and with no benefit to our religion or the state, return to their dens. . . . Only the amount of drink that can be consumed in a Christian manner during one day should be permitted. And only on a few occasions during the year" (2:134).

These obviously Eurocentric descriptions of indigenous drinking practices clearly point to a "social construction of thirst" that pervaded the symbolic order of the aboriginal world and, at the same time, actively contributed to the construction and reproduction of the social order.

A brief look at the ethnographic and ethnohistoric literature concerning this region would be enough to recognize that drinking practices played a crucial role in indigenous social life and involved a complex set of meanings and practices (see Gassón, in this volume). The descriptions of these practices indicate certain prescriptions regarding the roles of the hosts and the invited guests. Sharp divisions were drawn for male and female participation. Gilij describes how the women were in charge of the preparation and serving of fermented beverages, whereas the males were the actual drinkers. The women also calmed the men if fighting occurred, and carried the drunken men to their hammocks at the end of the feast. In the propitiatory ritual described by Bueno (1933:93–94), a woman was whipped because she had attended the last year's dance while menstruating. This coincides with the detailed descriptions of drinking among the Araweté, where it is the woman's role to convert the raw fruit or vegetable into a fermented (cooked) state, but it is the men who consume the beverage. The more highly fermented the drink is, the less it is a food, and vomiting is the desired end product of the drink (see Viveiros de Castro 1992).

The role of drink in the construction and reproduction of Orinocan society is revealed in many myths. For example, in the Watunna, the mythic cycle of the Ye'kuana, drinking forms part of the construction of memory and is thus a key component of Native historicity (see Medina, in this volume; Pérez, in this volume).

The men clear the *conuco*, like Marahuaka in the beginning. The women plant and harvest and prepare it.

Now they came carrying *wuwa* filled with yuca. Then the men worked again. They wove baskets, strainers, trays, presses. They carved graters and *kanawa*. Those are their jobs. The women harvest, carry, grate, press, cook the cassava. They make *iarake* [fermented beer] in the *kanawa* [canoe].

"That's good," said Semenia. Then he said: "Let's dance. Let's sing and eat and drink. Now we'll remember."

It was the first harvest festival. . . . Now they played the *momi* bark horns and Semenia sang. Wanadi and Wade sang too. They remembered everything. They didn't forget anything. . . . *Watunna*, that's what we call the memory of our beginning. (Civrieux 1980:136)

We have shown that the Europeans were very aware of the importance of drink in the indigenous world. That this knowledge played a role in their colonizing strategy is another matter. The nonmissionary sources are more open in their descriptions of the types of transactions carried on by the missionaries in their strategies to gain acolytes and monopolize the trade in the area (Alvarado in Rey Fajardo 1966; Humboldt 1985). Eugenio de Alvarado, a member of the Expedición de Límites (Boundary Expedition) sent by Spain to establish the limits between the Spanish and Portuguese domains, spent several years at the Jesuit mission of

Carichana, the administrative center for the Middle Orinoco missions, as well as time in the Capuchin missions on the Lower Orinoco. He had been commissioned to prepare a report on the Capuchin and Jesuit holdings and is quite explicit in his descriptions of economic activities as well as the practices used to attract indigenous groups to the missions (Alvarado in Rey Fajardo 1966; Alvarado in Lucena Giraldo 1991). After two hundred years of efforts, the Spanish were still unsuccessful in their attempts to establish permanent colonies in the Orinoco. The causes for this failure include the remoteness of the area, the multiplicity of indigenous groups and the lack of a lingua franca, the disastrous effects of epidemic diseases, and the armed resistance of the Cariban-speaking Kariña, who, in alliance with the Dutch, effectively dominated the slaving and commercial activities throughout Guiana and beyond, into the Llanos region of what is now Colombia and Venezuela (N. Morey 1975; R. Morey 1979; Whitehead 1988). In the early 18th century, the Jesuits renewed their efforts to colonize the region, with a strategy that shifted the emphasis from one of purely missionary efforts to one of combined missionary and secular colonization (Gumilla 1944; Lucena Giraldo 1991). The Spanish were upset by the news of the Dutch expansion into the Essequibo, where they had established forts and large sugar plantations and were distilling sugar cane into *aguardiente* to distribute, among other items, to the indigenous population in exchange for slaves (Lucena Giraldo 1991:157). Rum was frequently used as payment to the Indians for dyes, foodstuffs, boats, wood, and services rendered to the Dutch post holders in the Essequibo (Whitehead 1988:160). The English, on their part, had occupied lands in the Demerara and were also producing sugar cane and *aguardiente* to trade, in contraband, with the Spanish for cocoa and silver. This had led the missionaries in Suay and Carichana to establish their own sugar cane plantations and to produce *aguardiente*, which was distributed among the Indians in order to dissuade them from their allegiance to the Dutch and English and their Carib allies (Lucena Giraldo 1991:158).

Even more explicit descriptions are found in Alvarado's report on the Jesuit missions in the Middle Orinoco (Alvarado in Rey Fajardo 1966:244–245). Here, Alvarado describes the sugar plantation where the cane was processed into molasses and *aguardiente:*

> On the plantation we have referred to there is a large field of sugar cane, and in the Mission, in full view of the Father Procurator, a sugar mill that

is in use during half of the year, and from which is obtained all the molasses and plenty of *aguardiente* for the consumption of the Fathers, paying from their own earnings, as has been said. These items are lucrative for the Procurator, since the molasses is sold for six *reales* a bottle and the *aguardiente* for ten, and being so much the consumption of the latter, that not even thousands of bottles would be enough, and for that reason, the amount they produce is like mere drops of water in the Orinoco, and they need large quantities of imported drink due to the fact that the Indians, soldiers, and all the rationals [other Europeans or Christians] drink in abundance. And the Indians and the soldiers pay for it in money, because the first [the Indians] pay with their crops of *cazabe* [manioc cakes], maize, etc., and from their earnings, and the second [the soldiers] take it on credit to their salary from Santa Fé, as I will explain further on. (Alvarado in Rey Fajardo 1966:244; our translation)

Alvarado also describes the *modus operandi* of the Jesuits in their incursions to bring back new Indian recruits for the missions, in which they took along *aguardiente* and other *rescates* or items of enticement, such as beads, fish hooks, and machetes (Rey Fajardo 1966). It might be argued that Alvarado's report was tendentious and aimed at discrediting the missionaries. In this case, however, the archaeological evidence of large numbers of beverage containers clearly lends support to Alvarado's affirmations. This is a good example of the methodological advantage of using several types of evidence in studies of the past. Taken singly, it is often difficult to judge the validity of a document, be it a text or an artifact, but when it is possible to contrast different sources, stronger inferences are possible.

COMMENSALITY TO COMMODITY

Although beer and spirits crossed into different spheres of the colonial exchange system (conceived of as inclusive of the two previously independent spheres), the value accrued to these items did not necessarily accompany them as they changed hands. Indeed, depending on context, the beverages, either in the form of wine, beer, or harder liquor, assumed the role of value peculiar to each sphere, as icons of social reproduction in the indigenous value systems and as mediums of exchange value in the monetary-based European economy. Thus we find references to the incorporation of European goods into preexisting practices or even their embellishment. In the Watunna, the initial Ye'kuana involvement with the Europeans enhanced the traditional means to obtain power through the successful completion of trading expeditions. "Now Iahena Waitie went back to the *so'to* (Ye'kuana) with his canoes loaded down with goods [obtained from the Hurunko or Dutch]. He went to all the houses, to the Yekuhana, the Dekuhana, the Ihuruhana, the Kunuhana. They all came out to see the *arakusa* [arquebus or rifle] and the other treasures he'd brought from Amenadiña. They held huge feasts when he came back. That was the beginning of the feasts we have now when people come back from trading far away" (Civrieux 1980:171).

Through time, however, a regional economy arose that responded to the exigencies of each sphere, even while transforming each, as new dependencies and "needs" dictated modifications of the overall system. This is particularly evident in the transformations that took place in the productive system.

A preliminary analysis of the archaeological evidence in the Middle Orinoco area suggests that the imposition of the mission system led to radical changes in productive activity, consumption, and social organization. A major shift in productive activity can be inferred from the artifact assemblages from precontact and postcontact sites. In the former, the numerous manos and metates point to an emphasis on maize production.[4] The colonial period, however, is characterized by a strong emphasis on manioc products, evidence for which can be found in the indigenous material assemblages mainly characterized by manioc griddles, cooking pots, drinking bowls, and large pots probably used to ferment *chicha*. Despite the change in the primary cultigen, the evidence from the early colonial period seems to indicate the maintenance of traditional forms of consumption with the gradual incorporation of European products, including alcoholic beverages. A significant change in indigenous consumption occurred at the end of the colonial period when large *chicha* pots were no longer found associated with the habitation sites. Manioc production was maintained, and perhaps even increased, as attested by the large griddles and the substitution of stone graters by perforated sheet-metal graters during the late 19th and 20th centuries. This more recent process could be interpreted as an indication that Native technologies for the production of fermented beverages were replaced by imported drinks, even while manioc production was continued.

This evidence seems to indicate, then, the early incorporation of distilled liquor into Native systems of consumption and hospitality. The Native-brewed beverages, in the form of *chicha*, *cachiri*, or *iarake*, were produced by domestic units and used in feasts and other ritual contexts to display the productive power, generosity, and hospitality of the host. As a consequence, the prestige that accrued to the sponsor of the drinking party was restricted to those men who were able to mobilize – through their wives – the large amounts of beer required for these festivities. It is likely that the stronger, distilled spirits were incorporated into these displays, much as Pepsi or Coca-Cola are being used in many places of the world today, as prestige items that enhance the status of the host. As a consequence, however, once the consumption of imported beverages replaced the consumption of locally produced drinks, the hosts were obliged to obtain them through exchange with outside agents: "Since in the towns [missions] there are no other shops or taverns, the Procuraduría assumes these duties, and the Father in charge must sell small quantities of the goods and appease the desires of the Indian who comes to exchange his cake of *cazabe* for a drink of *aguardiente*, and in the same way with his honey, tobacco, and other produce" (Alvarado in Rey Fajardo 1966:246; our translation). As a result, the adoption of distilled spirits and other imported items led to increasing dependency on the cash cropping of manioc and "professional gathering" of items such as dyes, honey, quinine, and *sarrapia* (tonka beans), in order to obtain money or goods to exchange for the newly created needs. As in the case of the Procuraduría, the outlet for the sale of the desired items was often monopolized by European agents, who could charge the Indians arbitrary prices and entrap the consumers into relations of debt peonage (see Arvelo-Jiménez and Biord 1994:68). This cycle came to a climax during the period of *sarrapia* and rubber exploitation in the early 20th century.

In this essay we show how the Spanish colonizers created a strategy to entice the indigenous population into the mission regime. The Spanish, who feared the loss of the Guiana territory to the other European powers, were aware of the great advantage to be gained in breaking the monopoly on trade held by the Dutch/English/Carib alliance. At the same time, they were distressed by the impact of the slave trade on the indigenous groups of the Orinoco and Llanos region.[5] The Spanish missionary strategy was twofold: they offered the desired trade goods, including the *aguardiente* they produced with indigenous labor, to attract the Indians to the missions, and they provided military protection to the Indians who were being victimized by the slave trade.

These enticements to enter the mission system resulted in profound transformations in the traditional productive modes – both economic and symbolic. The missionaries offered as commodities items that hitherto had been produced through a domestic mode of production that relied on a division of labor in which women played a major role, especially in regard to agricultural activities.

Under the missionary rule, the division of labor was forcibly reversed – men were expected to labor in the fields, while women were constrained to domestic tasks. Polygamy was forbidden, and the access to surplus, with its concomitant symbolic capital achieved through the drinking parties, was therefore denied. Feasting, dancing, and other "pagan" activities were also suppressed. Political positions were assigned by missionaries – with little or no respect for traditional status roles.

Drinking continued, as it continues today, but alcohol became a commodity – a product that had to be bought, rather than produced. Manioc was now grown to be exchanged for the coveted trade goods, including liquor, rather than to be converted itself into *chicha* or *iarake* to drink. Alcohol continued to play a central role in social life, but no longer was its production a factor in the creation and maintenance of the social position of those who drank. Rather, drinking came to be a compensation for labor, a prize for the cultivation of surplus for the colonizer. In this process, profound changes occurred in the role of drink as a part of the reciprocal obligations that were essential to the creation of memory (history) and the very reproduction of society itself. It is tempting to suggest that these transformations in social reproduction and productive modes, in combination with other modes of "colonization of consciousness" (Comaroff and Comaroff 1991, 1992, 1997), contributed to the loss of indigenous identity on the part of most of the groups that had been proselytized in the Jesuit missions. Following the War of Independence (1810–1830), nearly all of the missionized groups, including the Tamanaco, Sáliva, Achagua, Otomaco, Guamo, and Pareca, "disappear" as distinctive ethnic identities, at the same time that the mestizo *llanero* has its genesis along with its own distinctive identity (see ethnogenesis of Maroons in Pérez, in this volume).

In this context, it is clearly evident that the adoption of imported items prefigured in the indigenous structure of consumption, such as alcoholic beverages, led to unsuspected consequences of dependency and exploitation. These relations, in turn, brought about radical transformations in the social construction of memory – through the eradication of traditional modes for obtaining status and creating remembrance through ceremonial exchange and feasting.

ACKNOWLEDGMENTS

This project was made possible in part by the contribution of the populations of the Orinoco who have recorded in their oral tradition passages and testimonies about the incorporation of alcoholic beverages into Native social life and its role in the transformation of these societies. We are particularly indebted to Capitán Simón Bastidas, José Reyes, Victor Cañas, and Damasio Caballero of the Palomo community for their guidance in the field. Elizabeth González, Richard Romero, Luramys Díaz, Daniela Rivera, Alicia Galarraga, Mariana Flores, Maura Falconi, Tatiana Jiménez, Bernardo Urbani, and Marcia López contributed hours of their time to the cataloguing of the archaeological glass and ceramic collection. Xiomara Escalona drafted Figure 2. We are most grateful to the organizers of the American Society for Ethnohistory and to the Universidad Central de Venezuela for providing funds to assist the meetings in London, Ontario. In the context of these meetings we received many helpful comments that have contributed to this expanded version of our original paper. We wish to thank Neil Whitehead and Manuela Carneiro da Cunha for the invitation to participate in this volume, and we give special recognition to Michael Dietler and Marshall Sahlins for their insights on the "multifarious" role of material culture in colonial situations.

NOTES

1. Caña is literally translated as "cane," as in sugar cane, but is commonly used to refer to alcoholic beverages in Venezuela even today.

2. Although we are aware that the date for the colonial period is a relatively late date compared to colonial occupations for other regions, the systematic colonization of the Middle Orinoco commenced with the establishment of the first Jesuit missions in 1680. For this reason we refer to the period as early colonial.

3. That alcoholic beverages were a frequently import item in the latter area can be inferred from the following list of the inventory of the Boxel plantation on the Upper Surinam River in 1820 (Klein 1974):

7 cases of Muscatel
2 cases of Noyeau
35 cases (23 bottles each) of sherry

5 jars and 5 bottles of black current whisky

50 cases (12 bottles each) of red wine

33 bottles of Muscatel

1 case of gin

9 bottles of anisette, 5 cases of champagne

24 bottles of Rhine wine

2 cases containing 83 bottles of Rhine wine

7 cases of arrack

1 case of cordial

14 jars of Cologne water

16 bottles of Ratafia

9 jars of castor oil

4. This is an inference upheld by starch analysis on stone implements from the Los Mangos site at Boca de Parguaza (Linda Perry, personal communication, May 2000).

5. See Whitehead (1988:chapters 7 and 8) for a detailed discussion of Dutch/ Spanish relations and the political manipulation of the Carib involvement in the slave trade.

9

Ceremonial Feasting in the Colombian and Venezuelan Llanos

Some Remarks on Its Sociopolitical and Historical Significance

RAFAEL GASSÓN

Ceremonial feasting has only recently received attention in archaeology and historical anthropology (Dietler 1990:359; Hayden 1996:127; Dietler and Hayden 2001). However, ceremonial feasting, including speeches, singing, dancing, and the public consumption of food and alcoholic beverages, was one of the most important aboriginal institutions in lowland South America. Special feasts for harvest, first fish catch, fertility, marriage, mourning, alliance, and war were once widely distributed among the indigenous groups of the area, constituting the most important (if not the only, in many cases) form of public ceremonialism and as well the main social arena in which different villages could meet in a peaceful fashion, thus having a critical role in the constitution of collective identities (Steward 1949:707; Viveiros de Castro 1996:190). Moreover, in some instances those ritual occasions were opportunities for public displays of wealth and political power, often having important evolutionary and sociopolitical consequences. As Lathrap once stated: "The crucial mechanism by which one tropical forest village could achieve or maintain a position that would impress its neighbors was to give a fiesta which lasted longer, expended more beer, and unleashed more drunken brawls than any other fiesta in memory" (Lathrap 1970:54).

Ethnographic examples to support those propositions are abundant. I mention only three from the northwestern Amazon: the Wanano, the Wakúenai, and the Yanomamö.

The Wanano of the Brazilian Amazon had a "sociotopographical" order in which concepts of geographical and mythical origins define differences among sibs. The highest-ranked sibs were located downriver, where natural resources were plentiful, and the lower ones were situated

179

upriver, where resources were scarce. This pattern was reflected in the organization of dance ceremonies: high-ranked sibs were said to be "succulent" and were expected to sponsor such ceremonies with abundant foods and drinks. Those dance ceremonies included special songs called Sib Litanies, specifically designed to commemorate ancestors and to promote diachronic exchange with them (Chernela 1993:5–6, 82).

The Wakuénai, a ranked society of the Venezuelan Amazon, have two different types of food-giving ceremonies related to different features of social organization based on seasonal variation and on resource availability. Like all other activities, these feasts are directly related and organized according to the sacred knowledge and organization of the hierarchical descent groups, in two cycles: mode 1, social-natural, and mode 2, ritual-hierarchical (Hill 1984, 1993:12–14). Among the Wakuénai, musical and poetic modes of speech (*málikai*) are important for the development of ritual power and historical consciousness (Hill 1993:201).

For the Yanomamö of the Brazilian-Venezuelan border region, feasts are, above all, political events created to form or maintain political alliances among villages. The main purpose of feasting is to consolidate and cultivate intervillage relations in the context of food consumption and gift giving – hence, creating a cycle of mutual feasting and deferred exchange to promote even closer partnership and to reduce the risk of warfare. Mourning rites, including the ritual drinking of cremated corpse ashes by relatives and friends in plantain soup, are a special form of funerary feasting (Chagnon 1992:115, 159–162).

In spite of the importance of the ceremonial feasting complex for contemporary societies, the ethnohistory and archaeology of ceremonial exchange has been studied very little in lowland South America. An important exception is Boomert's (2000) archaeological study of the Lower Orinoco Interaction Sphere. According to Boomert, exchange among the Barrancoid and Saladoid peoples of Trinidad, Tobago, and the Lower Orinoco frequently included ceremonial vessels, tobacco pipes, incense burners, and other shamanic paraphernalia that were highly appreciated because of their aesthetic and supernatural qualities. He proposes that this system of exchange included not material but verbal forms of art, including myths, tales, songs, dances, news, and esoteric knowledge, and suggests that the exchange of verbal art was one of the main purposes of this interaction sphere (394, 492).

Much less is known about the archaeology and ethnohistory of ceremonial feasting in northwest lowland South America. This essay partially fills this gap by discussing some aspects of ceremonial feasting in the lowland Llanos of Colombia and Venezuela, with emphasis on its importance to the complex societies of the area, and by describing archaeological data possibly related to those ceremonies recently found at the El Cedral region in Barinas, Venezuela.

THE LLANOS OF COLOMBIA AND VENEZUELA

In South America, the two main tropical savanna areas are the high, dry savannas of central Brazil (the Cerrado) and the low, wet savannas of the Orinoco Basin known as the Llanos, between Colombia and Venezuela. The Orinoco Llanos are located in a large geosyncline, limited by the Guiana shield to the south, the Andean Cordillera to the west, and the Caribbean Cordillera to the north (Medina 1980:297; Vila 1960:106–107). The savannas are ecosystems of the lowland tropics usually dominated by a herbaceous cover, with a clear seasonality and a period of low activity during the dry season (Sarmiento 1984; Solbrig 1993). However, vegetation types, altitude, soils, and fauna are diverse enough as to prohibit a uniform perception of savanna ecosystems. In addition, the seasons show unpredictable variations over the medium and long term. This feature of savanna environments deserves more attention than it has hitherto received, since the temporal rhythms of the different components of the environment impose particular problems and possibilities for human adaptation and political evolution (Harris 1980; Sarmiento 1984; Solbrig 1993; Moran 1993).

By the time of the European invasion, the Amerindian societies of the savannas of Colombia and Venezuela had developed a complex interaction network known as the System of Orinoco Regional Interdependence. The extension, complexity, and composition of this network is a matter of controversy (Arvelo-Jiménez and Biord 1994; Gassón 1996:153, 2000b:584–585; Gómez and Cavelier 1998:169; Morey and Morey 1975; Whitehead 1988:53). According to ethnohistorical studies, different forms of political organization existed, but tribal formations, often of considerable size, were predominant. This mutual dependence precluded social inequality, and peer-polity exchange and reciprocity was the norm (Morales 1990; Morales and Arvelo-Jiménez 1981; N. Morey 1975). However, the recognition of prehistoric social complexity and political inequality in the lowlands is one of the most important insights provided by new archaeological research in the Amazon and Orinoco lowlands

(Roosevelt 1987:153; 1993:259). In the Orinoco Llanos, complex societies of the chiefdom level developed hierarchical settlement patterns, regional networks of communication, long-distance exchange of primitive valuables, and interpolity war (Spencer 1998; Spencer and Redmond 1992). It is likely that ethnohistorians and archaeologists are not only using different approaches but are also examining different classes of data at different levels of analysis. Hence, it becomes important to identify and analyze social institutions that systematically linked peoples and cultures in different ways and at the same level of analysis, one that refers to specific communities, factions, and individuals. A deeper comprehension of the nature of social relations, the development of social complexity, and the rise of a historical consciousness among aboriginal groups of the Llanos of Colombia and Venezuela would be better reached through the examination of certain institutions with economic, sociopolitical, and ritual functions, such as ceremonial feasting.

CEREMONIAL FEASTING IN THE ETHNOHISTORICAL RECORD OF THE LLANOS

Ethnohistorical data indicate that ceremonial feasts were once widely distributed in the Llanos of northern South America. They made up the obligatory social etiquette in the majority of social encounters within and among aboriginal communities. The ethnohistorical record of the Llanos includes many narratives of activities of this kind. Those accounts describe the importance of ceremonial exchange, feasting, and other classes of public events as mechanisms for the development of a social arena in which trade and exchange, military alliances, religious ceremonies, and displays of wealth and power would be carried out. Within the community, marriage, initiations, burials, communal works, the designation of community leaders, transmission of historical and mythical information, and other critical forms of social relations were also public and highly ritualized.

According to ethnohistorical accounts from the Llanos, social encounters among the Amerindians were performed through a standard ceremony known as *mirray*. Those *mirrayes* were held throughout the area among different groups. In actuality, the data on ceremonial feasting described here came from the Caquetío, Achagua, Sáliva, Girara, and Guahibo-Chiricoa Indians. All those groups had different levels of social organization, settlement pattern, and subsistence activities, ranging from agricultural ranked societies to hunters and gatherers organized in bands (Morey and Morey 1975:536).

Mirray, from the Achagua verb *numerraidary* meaning "to talk," "to address" (Rivero 1956:430), consisted in a long, ceremonial speech that was sung or recited in a low, fast, and continuous tone. Singing and other forms of poetic performance were, and still are, extremely important and powerful forms of discourse. These verbal art forms have many political, historical, and ritual functions among the societies of northwestern Amazonia (Chernela 1993:82; Civrieux 1992:16–20; Hill 1993:16–17). During the *mirray* guests were addressed with kinship terms and abundantly provided with food and alcoholic beverages. All kinds of important matters, including community problems, news, myths, and historical information were discussed. *Mirrayes* were given in different languages, not always mutually intelligible (Rivero 1956:324). Father Rivero gave the most detailed account of an Achagua *mirray*:

> The seats and chairs were already in place. They were skillfully made, lined with lion, tiger, and otter skins. The guests began to take their seats. They were grave and silent, with their weapons in their hands. The chief made a gesture to his followers to greet the *cousins*, as they called them, even though there is no kin relationship. . . . Then they began to drink, sharing the gourds. The women brought many gourds, in such a fast way as if they were competing for bringing them as fast as possible. Then, the guest speaker sits down in a low seat, resting his elbows on his knees, with his weapon in his left hand and the right hand free or on his cheek, as he prefers. He has to be sitting with his head down, looking at the floor. Then he starts his *mirray*, singing in a low, fast, and continuous tone, almost mumbling the words. He keeps doing so for a long time. Everyone is silent until the guest speaker is done with the first part of the *mirray*, for it has several parts. When the first part is done, the final words sound like a lament. When the guest speaker has finished, the village chief, to whom the *mirray* is dedicated, starts singing in the same way for a long time. So they continue singing to each other for about an hour and a half. After that, they remain silent, without anything else to say.[1] (Rivero 1956:429–430)

Food and alcoholic beverage consumption, particularly *chicha*, was an important part of these rituals, and so both were served in great quantities. The rejection of the food or drink was considered a grave offense (Morey and Morey 1975:536; Rivero 1956:329; Gilij 1965, 2:244). Gilij specifically indicates that, in many cases, maize and bitter manioc were cultivated just for making alcoholic beverages (Gilij 1965, 2:133).[2] In addition, many beverages were made from wild fruits. The elaboration of the huge quantities of beverages to be employed on special occasions required more permanent and controlled resources, for feasts usually lasted many days (Rivero 1956:116). There were special vessels and containers for preparing and serving foods and drinks. For important occasions, *chicha* was prepared in big canoes, just as the Ye'kuana and other Venezuelan Amazon groups still do today (Civrieux 1992:16). *Embaques* and *múcuras* were big *ollas* for fish cooking and liquid storage in the Apure River region. Large containers up to six feet high called *chamacu* were used in the Orinoco River area for *chicha*. The Achagua had special vessels called *muríques* used for serving, similar to the Spanish *artesa*. In the Orinoco, *tutumas*, made of gourds, were the usual serving vessels (Carvajal 1985:124; Gilij 1965, 2:257; Rivero 1956:111). Sometimes ethnohistorical narratives give us references about the association of more elaborated material culture with public or ceremonial activities. For instance, in 1647 Friar Jacinto de Carvajal observed at the shores of the Apure River a big cache of maize and artifacts, including many ceramic vessels. He specifically indicated that those things were in reserve to be used in a forthcoming ceremony:

> They found many elaborately carved *macanas* [clubs] and also many ceramic vessels so well done that they could be compared to the best vessels from China. . . . These clubs and ceramics were stored for use at their feasts, *areitos*, and drinking parties, and the maize was saved to make *chichas* and *mazatos* and other drinks. (Carvajal 1985: 117–118).[3]

Mirray feasts were critical to the constitution of the society. Missionaries, well aware of this, devoted special attention to eradicate them, accusing the Indians of alcoholism and sexual excesses. It is not coincidental that Gilij was greatly concerned not only with describing many kinds of ordinary and extraordinary ceremonial dances among the groups of the Orinoco River but also with the most effective ways to eradicate those practices (Cassani 1967:144–147; Gilij 1965, 2:130–134, 227–242).

What matters were *mirrayes* more concerned with? All the questions that affected their livelihood were addressed, as stated above. However, the regulation of conflict was one of the most important functions of the *mirray*. It is important to emphasize that quite frequently the content of the *mirrayes* noted in the ethnohistorical record was related to wars and feuds. This information had a historical dimension. For instance, Chacuamare, a Chiricoa chief, accused the Achagua people of selling

Chiricoa slaves to the Carib. He gave a *mirray* to declare war against the Achagua (Rivero 1956:40–41). Later on, his son, whose mother was an Achagua, made every possible effort to convince Chacuamare to stop the war. He finally did so and gave another *mirray* in an Achagua town, where each party recalled the different past deaths and offenses. Offenses were often remembered up to the fourth and fifth generations (Rivero 1956:128). Those differences were usually resolved through elaborate feasts that included speeches, dancing, and club fighting.

Different authors explicitly say that offenses and differences were carefully endured and transmitted through generations "as an inheritance." Elders frequently remembered and retold the causes of war to younger generations (Cey 1994:102; Rivero 1956:333). Among the Giraras, ceremonial feasts lasted for as long as eight days and frequently ended in fighting. As in other groups, warriors used to attend those encounters with their weapons at hand: "When the Giraras start to drink, they always have their arms and clubs at hand, because while they are drinking they begin to remind each other about past offenses, about what their grandfathers and ancestors did to each other, and so one thing leads to another, and they end up fighting and wounding everyone" (Rivero 1956: 42–43).[4]

Another important function of *mirray* was the display of power and prestige, including the honoring of the death and diachronic exchange with the ancestors. Among the Caquetío, an aboriginal group widely distributed in western Venezuela, ceremonial feasts were one of the strategies used by chiefs and salient identities to consolidate their power. According to Morey (1976), Caquetío chiefs from the lowlands were described as holding their positions through their wealth and generosity (56). Among the Caquetío of the Barquisimeto region in northwestern Venezuela, where no chiefs were recognized, social prestige was based on gift-giving parties (Oliver 1989:288). The transmission of historical information related to war and feuds was another important function of the feasting among the Caquetío.

> They dance in circles, singing ancient tales learned from their parents and elders, left to them as an inheritance. Another way of dancing is embracing each other in a row, ten or twelve on one side and the same number on the other, coming back and forth. They call these dances *areitos*. It is dangerous to be among them when they are singing and dancing, because even the shyest Indian, remembering the bad things done to them by the Christians, can kill anyone by just saying "let's kill this one." (Cey 1994:102–103).[5]

So important were these feasting activities to Caquetío society that paramount chiefs, minor chiefs, and salient identities were ritually consumed after their death by the community in communal meals involving ceremonial speeches and songs. According to Oliver (1989:283), the treatment of the corpses and the mortuary ceremonies varied accordingly to the social prestige of the deceased. The mourning ceremony was described by Fernández de Oviedo for the Caquetío of the Coro region, in the north coast of Venezuela, in the following manner:

> When a cacique or principal dies, the Indians from the province of Venezuela, particularly the *çaquitíos*, get together in the town where the deceased used to live. His friends from neighboring villages come and cry, singing at night and saying in their songs what he did during his life. The next day, they gather a lot of dry wood and burn the body in such a way that the flesh disappears. They put the bones aside before they become ash, and when the bones are very dry, they grind them with two stones and make a beverage called *mazato*. . . . They add and stir the ground bones into it, and all drink, having it as an excellent beverage. This is the greatest honor and solemnity in obsequies that can be offered to the dead among them.[6] (Fernández de Oviedo 1944, 2:37–38)

Similar rites were held among other groups in the lowland savannas. Father Jacinto de Carvajal describes elaborate funeral ceremonies among some groups of the Orinoco Llanos, including the Caribs and other lesser known tribes, such as the Chaguanas, Chucuayas, and Auiuries (which may have been tribal subdivisions or local partialities). This suggests that those funeral rites were also widely distributed in the lowland area. In those ceremonies, the corpses were first desiccated and buried for a whole year. After that period, many people from different groups gathered to eat the ashes of the dead and, as among the Caquetío, to remember his or her deeds:

> After one year, the people from all over the region gather together again at the deceased person's house with large quantities of food and drink, and again they get drunk. The Indians are all in mourning, painted with charcoal and turpentine and without weapons. When men and women see the funerary poles that are at each road, they start to cry out loudly. The different nations [tribes] arrive at the deceased's house and mourn in turns. They cry once in the morning and once in the afternoon during a period of eight days, and each day they would get drunk, and in silence. On the last day they make the biggest celebration, and they drink the deceased's ashes.[7] (Carvajal 1956:250)

Here again, we can notice the great amount of time invested in those ceremonies, the use of special wardrobes and ornaments, the consumption of important quantities of food and alcoholic beverages, and particular modes of speech employed on such occasions. It is worthwhile to note that, according to Carvajal, the complexity and duration of the mourning ceremonies were also proportional to the social importance of the deceased.

What does this say about the nature of ceremonial feasting, social relationships, and history among the aboriginal groups of the Llanos? I believe that three inferences can be made. First, ceremonial feasting was a key feature in the political economy and the sociopolitical exchange among the groups of the Llanos area. Social relationships among different groups were in a delicate state of balance between war and peace, in a natural environment characterized by fluctuation and unpredictability, and in a social environment singled out by war as an endemic condition. Ceremonial feasts were aimed not only to redistribute sources but also to regulate social relations among different factions and groups. The dual character of relations among and within the different factions and societies of the Llanos helps to explain why in a *mirray* the guests were armed, and why they frequently finished in discussions and fights (Rivero 1956:112; Gilij 1965:132).[8] It clarifies observations such as Federmann's report of the societies of the Venezuelan savannas, where different groups were social partners and enemies at the same time (Federmann 1958:67–68).[9]

Second, although local and simple, the transmission of information through generations about feuds, enemies, and also treaties and peace agreements was the transmission of *historical information* aimed at creating a sense of belonging to specific groups and factions; the stories of particular individuals and specific feuds constitute a genuine source of historical consciousness, though concrete and limited in scope (Turner 1988, Lederman 1986). The development of a historical consciousness occurred not only among the more complex societies but also in simpler ones as a result of warfare and exchange (Turner 1998: 247).

Finally, the ritual consumption of the ashes of chiefly bodies through special beverages in funeral ceremonies was probably of importance in the construction of a collective identity. As stated by Sahlins and others (Sahlins 1978:53, 1988:92; Sanday 1987:48; Strathern 1982:127) this form of endo-cannibalism should be understood in terms of a symbolic gesture related to both the ingestion of substances necessary to the reproduction of future generations and to the maintenance of diachronic exchange with the ancestors. The consumption of an individual belonging to an important clan or family made the participants share a part of that important "house" (in the sense given by Levi-Strauss 1987a:149), or chiefly in a genealogy sense, it thus was the ultimate expression of commonality. In a sense, then, the participants in the mourning ceremonies of the Caquetío, the Carib, and other groups of the Llanos were drinking their own history.

CEREMONIAL FEASTING IN THE ARCHAEOLOGICAL RECORD OF THE LLANOS

If ceremonial feasting was critical to the chiefly political economy and to the promotion of collective identities, hence it should be an ancient institution in the Llanos of Colombia and Venezuela. The examination of the archaeological record of the western Llanos of Venezuela (see Figure 9.1) suggests that this is indeed the case.

At the Gaván region in Barinas, Charles Spencer and Elsa Redmond addressed the problem of social change and intersocietal relationships in the high Llanos and the Andean piedmont from a neo-evolutionary perspective. In that region, they traced the development of chiefdoms nearly one thousand years before the arrival of the Europeans. Regional analysis suggested that the productive potential of drained fields located near the primary regional center of El Gaván exceeded the basic needs of the associated local community. Since these authors found no evidence for demographic pressure, they suggested that the main purpose of the agricultural fields was to facilitate the production of surplus, in order to fund and reinforce the chiefly economy (Spencer 1998; Spencer and Redmond 1992; Spencer et al. 1994:33). Research on the political economy of those chiefdoms has continued with the archaeological project currently underway at the El Cedral region (Gassón 1998, 2000a; Koerner and Gassón 2001; Redmond et al. 1999).[10]

The El Cedral region is located in a long and narrow valley between the Ticoporo, Acequia, and Anaro Rivers. It comprises more than 200 square kilometers in what is now the state of Barinas, Venezuela. In contrast with many other lowland savanna regions, characterized by a rather monotonous landscape, the El Cedral region is extremely varied and diverse. The El Cedral is at the intersection of three different types of landscape: to the north, there is an area of dry savanna; to the southeast, there

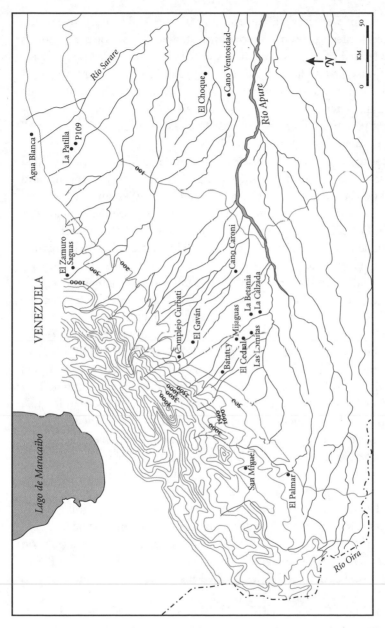

Fig. 9.1. The western Llanos of Venezuela, showing the location
of the most important archaeological sites in the Barinas area
(after Gassón 1998:49)

is an area of wet savanna; and running from the southwest toward the northeast, there is a semi-seasonal forest. The climate of the region is characterized by high temperatures (24–28§C) and high levels of precipitation (with an annual mean of 2,542 millimeters at the Canaguá weather station) during seven to nine months a year. The local climate can be characterized as cyclical and unpredictable, for seasons show important variations from year to year (Aguilar et al. 1986; Gravina et al. 1989; Sarmiento et al. 1971).

Since 1995, archaeological fieldwork in the region has been preceded by several stages, such as an intensive pedestrian survey, mapping, and excavations at the site of El Cedral, as well as in other smaller sites that were arranged in a hierarchical settlement pattern (see Figure 9.2). The site C1, El Cedral, occupies the first level of the regional hierarchy. This site can be described as being enclosed by a big causeway, with more than 139 earthen structures inside, ranging from small house mounds to civic-ceremonial mounds more than 12 meters tall and with an open space that may have been a public space or *plaza*. The second level of the local hierarchy was occupied by at least one site (site C18, Cerrito Conchero o Cerro Mijaguas), which is connected to El Cedral by means of a causeway. The site had public architecture and covered a smaller area than El Cedral. Finally, the third level of the regional hierarchy was occupied by eight sites with no recognizable public architecture and estimated areas of 0.5 to 1 hectare. Those sites might represent hamlets or individual dwellings, although more research at this level is badly needed.

The site of El Cedral shows a concentric distribution of earthen structures, open spaces, drained fields, and forests (see Figure 9.3). Almost all the mounds are located at the center, which is also the area of maximum artifact concentration in black soils with well-developed soil horizons. The open spaces around those mounds show brown soils, scanty artifacts, and poorly developed soil horizons, which may be taken as evidence of the presence of gardens and orchards in past times (Gassón 2000a:5–9). A large-scale network of causeways spreads out from El Cedral into the agricultural fields located just aside the settlement and to other parts of the region.

Drained fields were constructed in the areas between the large causeways that connect different sites, covering an estimated area of at least 416 hectares. Smaller causeways and streams that collect and channel water into the ditches between the fields further subdivide the fields. Therefore, it is likely that, during the time of the El Cedral occupation (dated

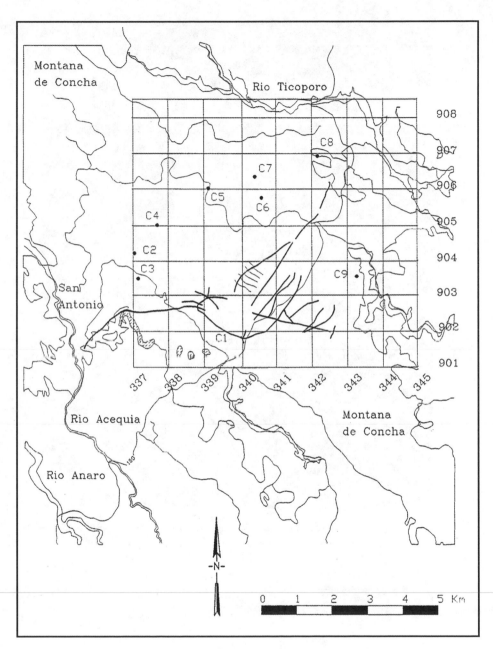

Fig. 9.2. El Cedral's immediate hinterland, with the location of
the regional center (C1), agricultural fields, and eight village sites recorded
within the area of intensive survey (after Gassón 1998:88)

Fig. 9.3. Aerial picture of El Cedral regional center and agricultural fields
(Instituto Geográfico de Venezuela "Simón Bolívar"; Misión 050391;
scale approx. 1:25,000)

around A.D. 660–690), different forms of cultivation were practiced in a series of concentric rings within and extending outward from the site, with gardens and orchards within El Cedral and permanent raised fields and areas for slash-and-burn agriculture surrounding it (Gassón 2000a; Koerner and Gassón 2001:201; Redmond et al. 1999:123). I analyzed the potential productivity of the area where the El Cedral site and associated communities were located. Calculations done under different assumptions do not support the idea that the area was experiencing population pressure. In comparison to the potential of production available, the El Cedral site seems to hold a relatively low number of people. Labor likely limited agricultural production more than land did. The productive potential of the drained fields alone indicates they could have supported the entire population of the site. Thus we must consider that the ancient inhabitants of El Cedral region had the capacity for producing moderate to important quantities of agricultural surpluses that might have been used to finance chiefly activities. Furthermore, it is significant that the drained fields were closely associated with the central place, for it suggests direct control of production and probably a bigger effort by the inhabitants of El Cedral to produce locally, rather than rely on surplus mobilization from other sites. In addition, where warfare is endemic, it is advantageous to use land close to nucleated and fortified settlements (Gassón 1998:78–80; Redmond et al. 1999:122).

The study of the ceramics found in the region had the purpose of examining the role of food production, distribution, and consumption in the chiefly political economy. The purpose of the analysis was to explore the proportions of vessel types in the ceramic assemblages from the different sites of the El Cedral regional hierarchy. The proposition underpinning this analysis is that the activities carried out at the different sites affected the characteristics and proportions of the vessel types of the ceramic assemblage at each site, and differences in vessel shape, size, and decoration should then reflect these activities (Blitz 1993:84). The ceramic analysis indicated differences in the proportions of vessel forms, size, and decoration among the different levels of the regional hierarchy. The analysis also indicated that, at the central place of the region, there was a major concern with serving and drinking activities, rather than with cooking or storage. Serving vessels were more abundant, smaller, and somewhat more decorated there, whereas cooking or storage vessels were more abundant, larger, and somewhat less decorated at the second-level sites. Third-level sites tended to have more and larger cooking or storage vessels of certain types, but decoration was not common. These observations have implications for some degree of centrally organized production and consumption, since they indicate that part of the surplus generated by agricultural activities could have been used in the regional center for public encounters where foods or drinks were served (Gassón 1998:124–125).

As stated, a remarkable feature of the primary regional centers of El Cedral and El Gaván is that they were surrounded by causewayed enclosures (see Figure 9.4). They have been described mostly as defensive facilities. In fact, there is abundant evidence that war was an endemic condition in the Llanos (Redmond et al. 1999). However, the identification of feasting activities at El Cedral opens new possibilities of interpretation in relation to the functions and meaning of such enclosures. Besides their known functions as military facilities and elite residences, such enclosures may have served as places for ceremonial feasting that probably included diachronic exchange with ancestors and supernatural beings. Associations of social and ecological practices with the ancestors and deities may have been metaphorically objectified by the monumentality of the sites themselves and of the large-scale structures surrounding them; the concentric circles of gardens, orchards, raised fields, and other agricultural facilities; and the location of the centers at the intersection of different types of landscape (Koerner and Gassón 2001:202).

This particular disposition is by no means unique to the Cedral region. It has been noted by a number of authors that there are important regularities in the settlement system and spatial organization of agricultural sedentary communities of lowland South America. In many South American groups architecture tends to favor circular to semicircular patterns with open areas or plazas at the center of the village. Those patterns have sacred and cosmological implications that act as organizing principles to many lowland cultures (Siegel 1996:315–317). In the Xingúarea of central Brazil, Heckenberger has identified vast archaeological sites surrounded by semicircular ditches. The sites were strategically located so as to provide access to different ecological zones. Although defense was almost certainly an important function of the ditches, those features also had important symbolic and aesthetic functions. Heckenberger concludes that sedentary life and the distribution of features in those pre-Columbian settlements promoted intra- and intervillage ceremonialism and reflect the same underlying concentric mode of spatial organization typical of contemporary Kuikuru settlements (Heckenberger 1998:635–638). Hornborg observes that, although a number of ethnographers have noted formal resemblances respecting conceptions of social space among different lowland groups, only Lathrap has thus far suggested a useful framework for interpreting those resemblances (Hornborg 1990). Drawing upon Lathrap's work, Hornborg observes that several cultures in South America express in their architecture a mental template by which space is organized in terms of an absolute center, located on the *axis mundi*, surrounded by a circular perimeter yielding a radial distribution of social and cosmological categories. Recurrent features reported for contemporary societies also include a mirror-image asymmetry, produced by the projection of a hierarchical dimension parallel to the central axis, and a conflation of space and time, so that the perimeter is imbued with calendrical significance (Hornborg 1990:84). These observations give further support to our impression concerning the possible cosmological and sociopolitical significance of the spatial arrangement of El Cedral and its environment (Koerner and Gassón 2001).

Finally, a closer look at other aspects of the material culture of the El Cedral region gives us a further glimpse at the ideological and political-economic world of those communities. There is a wealth of objects that may have participated in such ritual occasions. For instance, we have found human figurines of various sizes and shapes. Some of them represent seated males holding cups or animals. Similar figurines were rather common in the Venezuelan Andes, where they have been interpreted as shamans or leaders (Clarac de Briceño 1996:30). The symbolism of female figurines could have been very different. Female figurines are much more abundant, representing adult females with their sexual attributes clearly indicated, including pregnant and twin women. What could be the meaning of such figurines? In the pre-Hispanic world women did most of the agricultural work, thus being extremely important for the reproduction of the society in every sense. Females are universal symbols of fertility, and twins are frequently related to climatic phenomena around the world (Levi-Strauss 1987a:47–55). When Father Jose Gumilla asked about the reason for this, the Indians replied: "Because women know how to give birth, and since they know how to give birth to the seed, so let them sow, for we do not know as much about it as they do" (Gumilla 1944, 2:210). Women were extremely important to the political economy for they were an important part of the labor force. It has been proposed that one of the dynamics of chiefly warfare in the Llanos was a scarcity

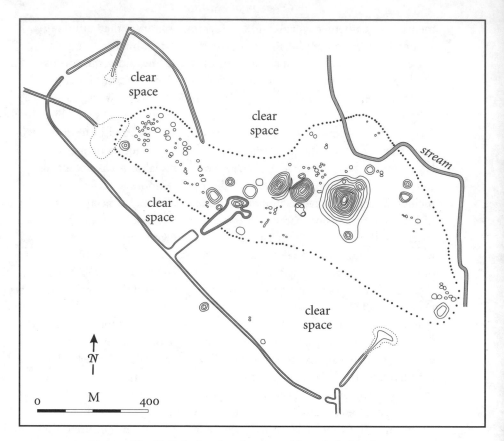

Fig. 9.4. The El Cedral regional center, with main habitation area
delimited by dotted line (after Gassón 1998:89)

of labor. In fact, drained and raised fields may have been the means to increase output in an environmental context where available labor was a major factor limiting production (Drennan 1995:321; Gassón 1998:165; Spencer et al. 1994:137). Ethnohistorical accounts strongly support those arguments. Gumilla noted that, in the Orinoco, war was oriented to the capture of women, children, and occasional booty (Gumilla 1944, 2:85).

Other figurines represent more subtle hierophanies. A "green stone" pendant found at El Cedral seems to represent a small amphibian or reptile. In lowland South American cosmologies, animals such as green lizards and frogs have climatic, sexual, and underworld connotations, being related to female-oriented cults (Boomert 1987:38, Roe 1982:152–153; Whitehead 1993:296). According to Eliade (1981:164), the rain-frog-woman-fertility combination has lunar connotations that refer to fertility and immortality, that is, the supernatural basis for agricultural production. These kinds of objects seem to be particularly abundant at the regional centers, and their detailed study will open important avenues for the understanding of the cosmological realm of those societies.

In summary, a number of archaeological indicators such as the existence of enclosures with causeways, surplus production, differences in ceramic assemblages such as those described above, and other aspects of the material culture suggest the use of ritual feasting for political purposes in the El Cedral region. Hence, this research gives support for the idea that ritual feasting was a critical sociopolitical institution for the aboriginal societies of the Llanos, with deep roots in the pre-Columbian past.

There is abundant ethnohistorical and archaeological data that support the notion that ceremonial feasting involving certain forms of verbal art was a critical mechanism to the political economy, to interpolity relationships, and for the transmission of historical information among the societies of the neo-tropical savannas and tropical forests of northern South America. In the Llanos area, ritual feasting was one of the main mechanisms employed by elites and salient identities to enhance their power and prestige and to have diachronic exchange with the ancestors. To the commoners, ritual feasting created a public arena where conflict could be mediated and social ties developed within and among communities, by means of commensality and the transmission of historical knowledge. I suggest that, in the Llanos, ceremonial feasting could be properly understood as a total social fact (Boomert 2000:417), for it seems to have permeated and shaped in important ways almost all the economic, social, and supernatural aspects of the life of the aboriginal societies that once populated that area.

It is important to note that this statement is supported by the joint examination of ethnohistorical and archaeological data. It would have been rather difficult to reach such a conclusion by using only one data set. As stated by Drennan and Uribe (1987:vii), one of the ways in which ethnohistorical information can be most useful is when linked to archaeological information. There are, however, important differences between the complex pre-Columbian polities of the Llanos studied by archaeologists and the apparently simpler societies described by ethnohistorians in the same area during the contact period. Although great progress is being made in the understanding of colonial transformations in aboriginal institutions such as feasting at the Middle Orinoco (see Scaramelli and Tarble, in this volume), much less is known for the Llanos area. One of the most important and exciting avenues for future research in the Llanos is the archaeology of political transformation of aboriginal societies and their institutions during the contact period, the end of the sequence for many complex polities but also the "flashpoint" of some post-Columbian chieftaincies and chiefdoms.

ACKNOWLEDGMENTS

Thanks are due to Marshall Sahlins, Manuela da Cunha, and Neil Whitehead for inviting me to participate in the special panel titled "Amazon Histories and Historicities" at the 2000 annual meeting of the American Society for Ethnohistory. The Wenner-Gren Foundation for Anthropological Research gave generous funding to my work in Barinas (grant number 5781) and to cover my expenses in London, Ontario. Neil Whitehead rightly pointed out to me the importance of "eating" chiefly bodies for the ancient inhabitants of the Llanos. Paul Hurtado made the manuscript much more readable and elegant. Ana Maria Gómez and Juan Carlos Rey helped me with the final details of the paper. All translations in this article are my own.

NOTES

1. "Ya estaban prevenidos los asientos y algunas sillas de respaldo, que las fabrican muy curiosas y las aforran con pieles de leones, tigres o lobos de agua;

fuéronse sentando por su turno los huéspedes, muy callados y graves, con sus armas en la mano; hizo seña el cacique entonces a los suyos para que saludaran a los *primos*, que así se llaman en tales casos aunque nunca los sean . . . luego se siguió a la bebida, como lo principal de todo; empezó desde el primero a recorrer la totuma, luego pasó al segundo, y así prosiguieron corriendo multitud de vasijas, que se atropellaban unas a otras e iban trayendo las mujeres como quien va de apuesta. . . . Siéntase, pues, el orador, en un asiento bajo o en cuclillas, pone sobre las rodillas los codos, y en la mano izquierda las armas: la derecha ha de estar ociosa totalmente o puesta sobre la mejilla, si le parecíese mejor; ha de estar cabizbajo mientras ora, y con los ojos en el suelo; empieza luego su *mirray* en tono de oración de ciego, medio entre dientes, y con velocidad suma como estudiada; así se está recitando largo tiempo, callando todos hasta concluir la primera parte de su sermón, que tiene muchas; al acabarse esta, remata con tono de lamentación, o como se acaba de cantar una epistola, levantando un poco la voz y dejándola caer de golpe; apenas acaba este, cuando responde el que hace cabeza, a quien se dedica el *mirray* y habla de la misma suerte por largo tiempo, rematando del mismo modo; luego prosigue sus puntos el primero, y asi se estan sermoneando cerca de hora y media, y ya uno, y ya el otro, como si rezaran a coros; quedándose después muy serenos, sin otros parabienes al predicador, ni mas aplausos, que levantarse cada cual de su asiento a salirse a digerir la bebida por el pueblo para beber mas" (Rivero 1956:429–430).

2. Lathrap clearly indicated that reason for cultivating the two plants: "Bitter manioc is raised only where there is a reason to build up an economic surplus. Where maize is grown extensively, it typically replaces bitter manioc in this function, since maize can be prepared for long-term storage with a far smaller expenditure of labor" (1970:53).

3. "Hallóse cantidad de macanas labradas con curiosidad grande, y entre otros trastes, muchedumbre de loza curiosísima, y vidriada la pequeña con perfección tanta que pudiera aprender de sus lindezas la que se labra en la China, como de las múcuras, embaques, cazuelas y otras vasijas la que se obra en Estremoz, no suponiendo con éstas lo terso y sazonado de las alcarrazas de Sevilla. Tienen reservada esta loza para la celebración de sus asiduos convites y borracheras, como las guirnaldas y macanas para sus bailes, aretos y fiestas, si el maíz para sus ordinarias chichas y mazatos y otras bebidas de que usan" (Carvajal 1985:117–118).

4. "En poniéndose a beber tienen siempre estos Giraras las armas y macanas en las manos, porque de allí resultan sus pendencias, haciéndose recordación unos a otros, entre el calor de la bebida, de los agravios que se han hecho en otros tiempos, de los que se hicieron sus abuelos y antepasados, y de una y otra comienza a arder el furor, y para en macanazos y heridas toda la fiesta" (Rivero 1956:42–43).

5. Su bailar es un baile circular, donde uno canta y los otros responden, cantando antiguedades aprendidas de los padres y abuelos y de sus mayores, como dejadas en herencia. Otro modo de bailar tienen, abrazándose juntos en una fila, 10 o 12 de una parte y otros tantos de la otra, yendo al encuentro abrazados cantando, alejándose y acercándose; a todos estos bailes llaman areitos. Es peligroso andar entre ellos en ese perìodo porque hasta el màs apocado indio que esté allí, que comience a cantar y decir el mal que los cristianos les han hecho, con decir 'matemos a este' la sentencia està dada" (Cey 1994:102–103).

6. "En la provinçia de Veneçuela los indios naturales della, en espeçial los de generaçión que llaman çaquitíos, tienen por costumbre, cuando muere algún señor o caçique ó indio prinçipal juntarse todos en aquel pueblo donde el difunto vivía, y los amigos de las comarcas, llóranle de noche en tono alto y cantando, y diçiendo en aquel cantar lo que hizo mientras vivió. El otro dia siguiente allegan mucha leña seca. Y queman el cuerpo de tal arte, que como la carne se va consumiendo por el fuego, apartan los huesos antes de que se hagan çeniça, y muy quemados y secos los muelen entre dos piedras, y haçen cierto brevaje quellos llaman maçato, . . . y tiénenlo por muy exçelente brevaje, y echan en ello los huesos del difunto molidos, y revuélvenlo mucho y bébenlo todos. Esta es la mayor honra y solemidad de obsequias que entrellos se puede haçer" (Fernández de Oviedo 1944, 6:37–38).

7. "Acabado el año se junta la comarca toda y buelue a la cassa donde estava el muerto con grandes prevençiones de beuidas y comidas, hallando en ellas las mismas, porque todos le estan contribuyendo desde que queman al cadaver para esta occasion, y llegada bueluen a la junta y borrachera tropas de yndios como hormigas y todos enlutados con el carbon molido y trementina y sin armas, y en llegando a la uara guarneçida que esta en cada camino levantan el llanto con aullidos desacompassados y griterias notables, assi hombre como mujeres, y llegando los unos y los otros a la cassa de el defuncto haçen por su orden las naçiones todas sus alaridos y lamentos, los quales haçen por las mañanas y las tardes por espaçio y tiempo de ocho dias, y cada dia de aquestos passan en borracheras y con mucho silençio, si puede averlo en ocasiones tales: al ultimo dia de los ocho se çelebra la borracherra mayor, y en esta de dan los poluos de el cuerpo o huessos de el muerto, que án mesclado con el jugo que despedia el cadauer suyo al quemarle: estos van repartiendo en las totumas de cada uno, y quien lo va repartiendo es una vieja muy enlutada con la mezcla de el carbon y la trementina" (Carvajal 1956:250).

8. There are reports about factional competition within the same group. For instance, Father Rivero reported: "The Achagua nation, which was divided in various partialities, was in continuous wars; they were lessening, because they were killing themselves, one way a secret one using poison and the other openly in fierce battles. They had many chieftains and were well populated, but the

wars were annihilating them so they were then afraid of being captured by the Caribes, for they were very brave, had firearms and were more numerous." Original: "La nación Achagua, que estaba dividida en varias parcialidades que se hacian contínuas guerras, fue menoscabándose, porque se mataban unos á otros, ya ocultamente con veneno, ya descubiertamente en batalla campal. Eran muchas las capitanías al principio y bien populosas, pero reducidas con el tiempo a corto número, entraron en bien fundados temores de que subiendo los caribes los cautivarían á todos, por ser tan aventajados éstos así en el valor y las armas como en el exceso de la gente" (Rivero 1956:396).

9. "They [the Caquetío] are enemies with the three nations that surround them and with some Xagua villages. Although they are confederated with some of these villages with which they trade with salt, they are also, as I stated, their enemies." Original: "Pues son enemigos de las tres naciones que los rodean y de algunos pueblos o aldeas de los Xaguas, de los que también son enemigos. Pues aunque estan confederados con algunos de estos pueblos y otros vecinos con quienes comercian con sal, son, sin embargo, como he dicho, también sus enemigos" (Federmann 1958:67–68).

10. In this essay, *chiefdom* refers to societies that are "based on hierarchical principles of sociopolitical organization and comprehend more than a single local group and yet lack the organized bureaucracies of states" (Drennan 1992:57). This broad conceptualization has the advantage of avoiding classificatory schemes, since gradations on scale of social hierarchy are more important than the type of hierarchy (Brown 1981:28).

Bibliography

Aguilar, Luis, Violeta Rondón, and Ricardo Ponte. 1986. La agresividad climática en la reserva forestal de Ticoporo. *Revista Geográfica Venezolana* 27:5–33.

Albert, Bruce. 1994. Gold Miners and Yanomami Indians in the Brazilian Amazon: The Hashimu Massacre. In *Who Pays the Price? The Socio-cultural Context of Environmental Crisis.* B. R. Johnston, ed. Pp. 47–55. Washington DC: Island Press.

———. 2002. Introdução. In *Pacificando o Branco: Cosmologias do contato no norte amazônico.* B. Albert and A. Ramos, eds. Pp. 9–21. São Paulo: Edunesp/ Imprensa Oficial de São Paulo/Institut de recherche pour le développement.

Amerindian Peoples Association (APA). 1998. *A Plain English Guide to the Amerindian Act.* Electronic document. http://www.sdnp.org.gy/apa/topic7.htm, accessed April 18, 2002.

Appadurai, Arjun. 1986. Introduction: Commodities and the Politics of Value. In *The Social Life of Things: Commodities in Cultural Perspective.* Cambridge: Cambridge University Press.

———. 1997. *Modernity at Large: Cultural Dimensions of Globalization.* Minneapolis MN: University of Minnesota Press.

Arvelo-Jiménez, Nelly. 1973. *The Dynamics of the Ye'cuana Political System: Stability and Crises.* Copenhagen: IWGIA.

———. 1974. *Relaciones Políticas en una Sociedad Tribal: Estudio de los Ye'cuna, indigenas del Amazonas Venezolano.* Ediciones Especiales: 68. Mexico D.F.: Instituto Indigenista Interamericano.

———. 1980. Autogestión y Concientización. In *Indigenismo y Autogestión.* Andrés Serbín and Omar González Ñáñez, eds. Pp. 225–237. Caracas: Monte Avila.

———. 1981. Recursos Humanos o el Juego de Fuerzas en la Región Amazónica. In *El Universo Amazónico y la Integración Latinoamericana.* Pp. 103–115. Caracas: Fundación Bicentenario de Simón Bolívar y Impresos Urbina.

———. 1982. The Political Struggle of the Guayana Region's Indigenous Peoples. *Journal of International Affairs* 36:43–54.

———. 1989. Organización social, control social, y resolución de conflictos: Bases para la formulacion y codificacion del derecho consuetudinario ye'kuana. *América Indígena* 49(2):323–343.

————. 2000. Three Crises in the History of Ye'kuana Cultural Continuity. *Ethnohistory* 47:731–746.

————. 2001. Movimiento Etnopolíticos Contemporáneos y sus Raices Organizacionales en el Sistema de Independencia Regional del Orinoco. *Serie Antropología.* Pp. 2–24. Brasil: Departamento de Antropología, Universidade de Brasília.

Arvelo-Jiménez, Nelly, and Horacio Biord Castillo. 1994. The Impact of Conquest on Contemporary Indigenous People of the Guayana Shield: The System of Orinoco Regional Interdependence. In *Amazonian Indians from Prehistory to the Present: Anthropological Perspectives.* Anna Roosevelt, ed. Pp. 55–78. Tucson: University of Arizona Press.

Arvelo-Jiménez, Nelly, and K. Conn. 1995. The Ye'kuana Self-Demarcation Process. *Cultural Survival Quarterly* 18(4):40–42.

Arvelo-Jiménez, Nelly, F. Morales Méndez, and Horacio Biord Castillo. 1989. Repensando la Historia del Orinoco. *Revista de Antropologia* 5(1–2): 155–174.

Arvelo-Jiménez, Nelly, and Juan V. Scorza. 1974. El integracionismo y sus modalidades de acción en el indigenismo venezolano. Paper presented at the 41st Congress of Americanists, Mexico City.

Bailey, R. C., and N. R. Peacock. 1988. Efe Pygmies of Northeast Zaïre. In *Coping with Uncertainty in the Food Supply.* I. de Garine and G. Harrison, eds. Pp. 88–117. Oxford: Clarendon Press.

Bailey, Robert C., Genevieve Head, Mark Jenike, Bruce Own, Robert Rechtman, and Elizbieta Zechenter. 1989. Hunting and Gathering in the Tropical Rain Forest: Is It Possible? *American Anthropologist* 91:59–82.

Balée, William. 1988. Indigenous Adaptation to Amazonian Palm Forests. *Principes* 32:47–54.

————. 1994a. The Destruction of Pre-Amazonia: Governmental Negligence versus Indigenous Peoples in Eastern Brazilian Amazonia. Prepared statement read on May 10 before the Subcommittee on Western Hemisphere Affairs, Committee on Foreign Affairs, U.S. House of Representatives.

————. 1994b. *Footprints of the Forest: Ka'apor Ethnobotany – The Historical Ecology of Plant Utilization by an Amazonian People.* New York: Columbia University Press.

————. 1998. *Advances in Historical Ecology.* W. Balée, ed. New York: Columbia University Press.

————. 1999. Mode of Production and Ethnobotanical Vocabulary: A Controlled Comparison of Guajá and Ka'apor (Eastern Amazonian Brazil.) In *Ethnoecology: Knowledge, Resources and Rights.* T. L. Gragson and B. Blount, eds. Pp. 24–40. Athens GA: University of Georgia Press.

————. 2000. The Antiquity of Traditional Ethnobiological Knowledge in Amazonia: The Tupí-Guaraní Family and Time. *Ethnohistory* 47(2):399–422.

Bibliography

Barandiaran, D. de. 1986. Introducción a la Cosmovisión de los Indios Ye'kuana-Makiritare. *Revista Montalban* 9:737–841.

Bartra, R. 1994. *Wild Men in the Looking Glass: The Mythic Origin of European Otherness.* Ann Arbor: University of Michigan Press.

Basso, Ellen B. 1995. *The Last Cannibals: A South American Oral History.* Austin: University of Texas Press.

Beghin, François-Xavier. 1951. Les Guajá. *Revista do Museu Paulista,* n.s. 5:137–139.

———. 1957. Relation du premier contact avec les Indiens Guajá. *Journal de la Société des Américanistes,* n.s. 46:197–204.

Bello, Luis. 2000. Los derechos de los pueblos indígenas en la nueva constitución. *Asuntos Indígenas* 1:32–35.

Bender, B. 1999. Subverting the Western Gaze: Mapping Alternative Worlds. In *The Archaeology and Anthropology of Landscape.* P. Ucko and R. Layton, eds. London: Routledge.

Bierhorst, John. 1988. *The Mythology of South America.* New York: William Morrow.

Bilby, Kenneth. 1997. Swearing by the Past, Swearing to the Future: Sacred Oaths, Alliances, and Treaties among the Guianese and Jamaican Maroons. *Ethnohistory* 44:655–689.

Blitz, Jeffrey. 1993. Big Pots for Big Shots: Feasting and Storage in a Mississipian Community. *American Antiquity* 58:80–96.

Bonfil Batalla, G. 1989. La teoría del control cultural en el estudio de procesos étnicos. *Arinsana* 5:5–36.

Boomert, Arie. 1987. Gifts of the Amazons: "Green Stone" Pendants and Beads as Items of Ceremonial Exchange in Amazonia and the Caribbean. *Antropologica* 67:33–54.

———. 2000. *Trinidad, Tobago and the Lower Orinoco Interaction Sphere.* Alkmaar, Netherlands: Cairi.

Bourdieu, P. 1984. *Distinction: A Social Critique of the Judgement of Taste.* Cambridge: Harvard University Press.

Boyarin, Jonathan. 1994. Space, Time, and the Politics of Memory. In *Remapping Memory: The Politics of TimeSpace.* Jonathan Boyarin, ed. Pp. 1–37. Minneapolis: University of Minnesota Press.

Bradley, C. P. 1961. The Party System in British Guiana and the General Election of 1961. *Caribbean Studies* 1(3):1–26.

Brett, Rev. W. H. 1868. *The Indian Tribes of Guiana: Their Condition and Habits.* London: Bell and Daldy.

Bridges, John, S.J. 1985. *Rupununi Mission: The Story of Cuthbert Cary-Elwes, S.J., Among the Indians of Guiana, 1909–1923.* London: Jesuit Missions.

Bibliography

Brightman, R. 1993. *Grateful Prey: Rock Cree Human-Animal Relationships.* Berkeley: University California Press.

Bros, R., A. Chamanare, S. Jimenez, S. Lopez, M. Martinez, L. Milano, and M. E. Villalon. N.d. *Aprendiendo la cultura Ye'kwana.* Caracas: Comision de la Union Europea; MARNR; Direccion de Asuntos Indigenas, ME.

Brown, James. 1981. The search for rank in prehistoric burials. In *The Archaeology of Death.* R. Chapman, I. Kinnes, and K. Ransberg, eds. Pp. 25–37. Cambridge: Cambridge University Press.

Bueno, Fray Ramón, O.F.M. 1933. *Apuntes Sobre la Provincia Misionera de Orinoco e Indígenas de su Territorio con algunas otras particularidades.* Caracas: Tipografía Americana.

Burnett, D. G. 2000. *Masters of All They Surveyed: Exploration, Geography, and a British El Dorado.* Chicago: University of Chicago Press.

Butt-Colson, Audrey J. 1973. Inter-tribal trade in the Guiana Highlands. *Antropológica* 34:5–70.

Caballero, Manuel. 1995. *Ni Dios, Ni Federación.* Caracas: Editorial Planeta.

Carneiro da Cunha, M. 1978. *Os mortos e os outros.* São Paulo, Hucitec.

————. 1992. *Historia dos Indios no Brasil.* São Paulo: Editora Schwarz.

Carvajal, Jacinto de. 1956. *Relación del Descubrimiento del Rio Apure hasta su ingreso en el Orinoco.* Caracas: Ediciones Edime.

————. 1985. *Descubrimiento del río Apure.* Madrid: Historia 16, Colección Crónicas de América.

Carvalho, João Evangelista. 1992. Relatório de Contato com um Grupo Guajá /Maio/Junho 1992. Ministério da Justiça, Fundação Nacional do Índio.

Cassani, Joseph. 1967. *Historia de la Provincia de la Compañia de Jesus del Nuevo Reyno de Granada en la America.* Caracas: Academia Nacional de la Historia.

Cey, Galeotto. 1994. *Viaje y descripción de las Indias 1539–1553.* Caracas: Fundación Banco Venezolano de Crédito. Colección V Centenario del Encuentro Entre Dos Mundos.

Chagnon, Napoleon A. 1992. *Yanomamö.* New York: Harcourt Brace Jovanovich.

————. 1997. *Yanomamö.* New York: Holt, Rinehart and Winston.

Chernela, Janet M. 1993. *The Wanano Indians of the Brazilian Amazon.* Austin: University of Texas Press.

————. 2001. Guesting, Feasting, and Warfare in the Northwest Amazon. Paper presented at Indigenous Amazonia at the Millennium: Politics and Religion, New Orleans, January 11–14.

Chirif Tirado, A., P. Garcia Hierro, and R. Chase Smith. 1991. *El Indígena y su territorio son uno solo. Estrategias para la defensa de los pueblos y territorios indígenas en la cuenca amazónica.* Lima, Peru: OXFAM América; COICA.

Civrieux, Marc de. 1957. Un Mapa Indígena de la Cuenca del Alto Orinoco. *Memoria de la Sociedad de Ciencias Naturales La Salle* 17:73–84.

————. 1959. Datos Antropológicos de los Indios Kunuhana. *Antropológica* 8:85–145.

————. 1980. *Watunna: An Orinoco Creation Cycle*. David M. Guss, ed. and trans. San Francisco: North Point Press.

————. 1992. *Watunna: Un ciclo de creación en el Orinoco*. Caracas: Monte Avila Editores.

Clarac de Briceño, Jacqueline. 1996. Las antíguas etnias de Mérida. In *Mérida a través del tiempo: Los antíguos habitantes y su eco cultural*. Jacqueline Clarac de Briceño, comp. Pp. 23–51. Mérida, Venezuela: Universidad de los Andes.

Clementi, C. 1919. Report on the Condition of the Colony of British Guiana during the Great Europe War and on the Chief Local Problems Awaiting Solution. *British Guiana Combined Court, First Special Session*. Georgetown, Demerara, Government Printers.

Clifford, James, and George E. Marcus, eds. 1986. *Writing Culture: The Poetics and Politics of Ethnography*. Berkeley: University of California Press.

Codazzi, Agustín. 1940. *Atlas Físico y Político de la República de Venezuela*. Paris: Imprenta H. Fournier y Cia.

Colchester, Marcus. 1997. Ecología Social de los Sanema. *Scientia Guaianae: Ecologia de la Cuenca del Rio Caura, Venezuela*, Estudios Especiales 2(7):111–140.

Comaroff, Jean. 1985. *Body of Power, Spirit of Resistance: The Culture and History of a South African People*. Chicago: University of Chicago Press.

Comaroff, Jean, and John L. Comaroff. 1991. *Of Revelation and Revolution: Christianity, Colonialism, and Consciousness in South Africa*. Chicago: University of Chicago Press.

Comaroff, John L. 1996. Ethnicity, Nationalism, and the Politics of Difference in an Age of Revolution. In *The Politics of Difference: Ethnic Premises in a World of Power*. Edwin N. Wilmsen and Patrick McAllister, eds. Pp. 162–205. Chicago: University of Chicago Press.

Comaroff, John L., and Jean Comaroff. 1992. *Ethnography and the Historical Imagination*. Boulder CO: Westview Press.

————. 1993. Introduction. In *Modernity and Its Malcontents: Ritual and Power in Postcolonial Africa*. Jean Comaroff and John Comaroff, eds. Pp. xi–xxxvii. Chicago: University of Chicago Press.

————. 1997. *Of Revelation and Revolution: The Dialectics of Modernity on a South African Frontier*. Chicago: University of Chicago Press.

————. 1998. *Occult Economies and the Violence of Abstraction: Notes from the South African Postcolony*. Chicago: American Bar Foundation.

Comissáo pe la Criacao do Parque Yanomami (CCPY). 1993. Masacre expoe vulnerabilidad do territorio Yanomamai. Pp. 1–3. Sao Paulo: *Comissao pe la Criacao do Parque Yanomami*.

Coppens, W. 1981. *Del canalete al motor fuera de borda: Misión en Jiwitina y otras áreas de aculturación en tres pueblos Ye'kuana del Caura-Paragua.* Caracas: Fundación La Salle, Instituto Caribe de Antropología y Sociología.

Cormier, Loretta. 1999. Ritualized Remembering and Genealogical Amnesia. *Southern Anthropologist* 26:31–41.

———. 2000a. Ethnoprimatology of the Guajá Indians of Maranhão, Brazil. Ph.D. dissertation, Tulane University. Ann Arbor: Microfilms International.

———. 2000b. Monkey Ethnobotany: Preserving Biocultural Diversity in Amazonia. Paper presented at the meeting of the International Society of Ethnobiology, Athens GA, October.

Coronil, Fernando. 1996. Beyond Occidentalism: Toward Nonimperial Geohistorical Categories. *Cultural Anthropology* 11(1):51–87.

Coudreau, H. 1887–88. Voyage au Rio Branco, aux Montagnes de la Lune, au Haut Trombetta. *Bulletin de la Societé Normande de Géographie*, 1887, 9:189–211, 261–311, 325–358; 1888, 10:63–89.

Cousins, Andrew. 1991. La Frontera Étnica Pemon y el Impacto Socio-Económico de la Minería de Oro. Master's thesis, Instituto Venezolano de Investigaciones Científicas, Caracas.

Crumley, C. 1994. *Historical Ecology: Cultural Knowledge and Changing Landscapes.* Santa Fe: School of American Research Press.

Csikszentmihalyi, Mihaly. 1995. Toward an Evolutionary Hermeneutics: The Case of Wisdom. In *Rethinking Knowledge: Reflections across the Disciplines.* Robert F. Goodman and Walter R. Fisher, eds. Pp. 123–146. SUNY series in the Philosophy of the Social Sciences. Albany: State University of New York Press.

d'Abbeville, Claude. 1614. *Histoire de la mission des Pères Capucins en l'Isle de Maragnan et terres circinfines. . . .* Paris.

d'Acuña, Cristobal. 1859. A New Discovery of the Great River of the Amazons. In *Expeditions into the Valley of the Amazons.* C. R. Markham, ed. Pp. 44–142. London: Hakluyt Society.

Denevan, William. 1992a. The Aboriginal Population of Amazonia. In *The Native Population of the Americas in 1492.* William Denevan, ed. Pp. 205–235. Madison: University of Wisconsin Press.

———. 1992b. The Pristine Myth: The Landscape of the Americas in 1492. *Annals of the Association of American Geographers* 82:369–385.

———. 1992c. Stone vs. Metal Axes: The Ambiguity of Shifting Cultivation in Prehistoric Amazonia. *Journal of the Steward Anthropological Society* 20:153–165.

Descola, P. 1995. *In the Society of Nature: A Native Ecology in Amazonia.* Cambridge: Cambridge University Press.

Bibliography

Descola P., and G. Pálsson. 1996. *Nature and Society: Anthropological Perspectives*. New York: Routledge.

Dietler, Michael. 1990. Driven by Drink: The Role of Drinking in the Political Economy and the Case of Early Iron Age France. *Journal of Anthropological Archaeology* 9:352–406.

———. 1995. The Cup of Gyptis: Rethinking the Colonial Encounter in Early-Iron-Age Western Europe and the Relevance of World-Systems Models. *Journal of European Archaeology* 3(2):89–111.

———. 1998. Consumption, Agency, and Cultural Entanglement: Theoretical Implications of a Mediterranean Colonial Encounter. In *Studies in Culture Contact: Interaction, Culture Change, and Archaeology*. J. G. Cusick, ed. Center for Archaeological Investigations Research Paper series, 25. Carbondale: Southern Illinois University.

Dietler, Michael, and Bryan Hayden. 2001. Digesting the Feast: Good to Eat, Good to Drink, Good to Think. In *Feasts: Archaeological and Ethnographic Perspectives on Food, Politics and Power*. Michael Dietler and Bryan Hayden, eds. Pp. 1–20. Washington DC: Smithsonian Institution Press.

Dodt, Gustavo. 1939[1873]. *Descripção dos Rios Parnahyba e Gurupy*. Coleção Brasiliana, 138. São Paulo: Companhia Editora Nacional.

Drennan, Robert. 1992. What Is the Archaeology of Chiefdoms About? In *Metaarchaeology*. Lester Embree, ed. Pp. 53–74. Dordrecht, Netherlands: Kluwer Academic.

———. 1995. Chiefdoms in Northern South America. *Journal of World Prehistory* 9(3):301–340.

Drennan, Robert, and Carlos Augusto Uribe. 1987. Introduction. In *Chiefdoms in the Americas*. Robert Drennan and Carlos Augusto Uribe, eds. Pp. vii–xii. Lanham MD: University Press of America.

Eliade, Mircea. 1981. *Tratado de historia de las religiones*. México: Editorial Era.

Engels, F. 1972. The Bakuninists at Work: An Account of the Spanish Revolt in the Summer of 1873. In *Marx, Engels, Lenin: Anarchism and Anarcho-Syndicalism*. Pp. 128–146. New York: International Publishers.

Erickson, C. L. 1994. Archaeological Methods for the Study of Ancient Landscapes of the Llanos de Mojos in the Bolivian Amazon. In *Archaeology in the Lowland American Tropics*. P. Stahl, ed. Pp. 42–95. Cambridge: Cambridge University Press.

Espinosa Arango, M., and F. Andoque. 1999. Managing the World: Territorial Negotiations among the Andoque People of the Colombian Amazon. In *The Archaeology and Anthropology of Landscape*. P. Ucko and R. Layton, eds. London: Routledge.

Fabian, J. 1983. *Time and the Other: How Anthropology Makes Its Object*. New York: Columbia University Press.

Farage, N. 1991. As muralhas dos sertões: Os povos indígenas no rio Branco e a colonização. Rio de Janeiro: Paz e Terra/ANPOCS.

———. 1997. As flores da fala: Práticas retóricas entre os Wapishana. Ph.D. thesis, Universidade de São Paulo.

———. 2002. Instruções para o presente: Os brancos em práticas retóricas Wapishana. In Pacificando o Branco: Cosmologias do contato no norte amazônico. B. Albert and A. Ramos, eds. Pp. 507–31. São Paulo: Edunesp/Imprensa Oficial do Estado de São Paulo/Institut de recherche pour le développement.

Federmann, Nicolás. 1958. *Historia Indiana.* Madrid: ARO Artes Graficas.

Feld, S., and K. Basso. 1997. *Senses of Place.* Santa Fe: School of American Research Press.

Ferguson, R. B., and N. L. Whitehead, eds. 1999[1992]. *War in the Tribal Zone: Expanding States and Indigenous Warfare.* 2nd ed. Santa Fe: School of American Research Press.

Fernández de Oviedo, Gonzálo. 1944. *Historia general y natural de Las Indias,* vols. 1–7. Asunción del Paraguay, Editorial Guarania, Biblioteca de Historiadores de Indias.

Fisher, W. 1994. Megadevelopment, Environmentalism, and Resistance: The Institutional Context of Kayapó Indigenous Politics in Central Brazil. *Human Organization* 53:220–232.

Forte, J. 1990. The Populations of Guyanese Amerindian Settlements in the 1980s. Occasional Publications of the Amerindian Research Unit. Georgetown: University of Guyana.

Fortier, Anne-Marie. 1999. Historicity and Communality: Narratives about the Origins of the Italian "Community" in Britain. In *Identity and Affect: Experiences of Identity in a Globalising World.* John R. Campbell and Alan Rew, eds. Pp. 199–223. Anthropology, Culture and Society series. London: Pluto Press.

Foster, Nancy Fried. 1990. Contexts of Guianan Amerindian Identity. Ph.D. dissertation, Columbia University.

Fritz, S. 1922. *Journal of the Travels and Labours of Father Samuel Fritz in the River of the Amazons between 1686 and 1723.* G. Edmundson, ed. London: Hakluyt Society.

Fuentes-Figueroa Rodriguez, J. N.d. *Historia de Venezuela: Los Aborígenes, el Descubrimiento, La Conquista y la Colonia.* Vol. 1. Caracas: Impresos Tiuna.

Gassón, Rafael. 1996. La evolución del intercambio a larga distancia en el nororiente de Suramérica: Bienes de intercambio y poder político en una perspectiva diacrónica. In *Caciques, Intercambio y Poder: Interacción regional en el Area Intermedia de las Américas.* Carl H. Langebaek and Felipe Cárdenas Arroyo, eds. Pp: 133–154. Bogotá: Departamento de Antropología, Universidad de Los Andes.

———. 1998. Prehispanic Intensive Agriculture, Settlement Pattern and Political Economy in the Western Venezuelan Llanos. Ph.D. dissertation, University of Pittsburgh.

————. 2000a. Cultivation Systems of a Prehispanic Chiefdom of Barinas, Western Venezuelan Llanos. Paper presented at the 65th Annual Meeting of the Society for American Archaeology, Philadelphia, April 5–9.

————. 2000b. Quiripas and Mostacillas: The Evolution of Shell Beads as a Medium of Exchange in Northern South America. *Ethnohistory* 47(3–4):581–609.

Geertz, C. 1963. *Agricultural Involution.* Berkeley: University of California Press.

Geschiere, P. 1997. *The Modernity of Witchcraft: Politics and the Occult in Postcolonial Africa.* Charlottesville: University Press of Virginia.

Gheerbrant, Alain. 1952. *La expedición Orinoco-Amazonas, 1948–1950.* Buenos Aires: Libería Hachette S.A.

Gilij, F. S. 1965. *Ensayo de Historia Americana.* Vols. 1–3. Caracas: Academia Nacional de la Historia.

————. 1987. *Ensayo de Historia Americana: Fuentes para la Historia Colonial de Venezuela.* 2nd ed. Vols. 71, 72, and 73. Caracas: Biblioteca de la Academia Nacional de la Historia.

Global Law Association, Forest Peoples Programme, Amerindian Peoples Association of Guyana, and Upper Mazaruni Amerindian District Council. 2000. *Indigenous Peoples, Land Rights and Mining in the Upper Mazaruni.* Nijmegen, Netherlands: Global Law Association, 2000.

Gomes, Mércio Pereira. 1985. *Relatório Antropológico sobre a Área Indígena Guajá (Awá-Gurupi).* Setembro. Ministério da Justiça, Fundação Nacional do Índio.

————. 1988. *O Povo Guajá e as Condiçoes Reais para à sua Sobrevivencia: Reflexões e Propostas.* Ministério da Justiça, Fundação Nacional do Índio.

————. 1996. Os Índios Guajá: Demografia, Terras, Perspectivas de Futuro: Relatório de Pesquisas Realizadas em Fevereiro de 1996. Unpublished manuscript.

Gómez, Augusto, and Inés Cavelier. 1998. Las sociedades indígenas de los Llanos: Sistemas socieconómicos y carácterísticas socioculturales. In *Colombia Orinoco.* Camilo Domínguez, ed. Pp. 167–185. Bogotá: Fondo FEN Colombia.

Gómez-Picón, Rafael. 1953. *Orinoco, Río de la Libertad.* Madrid: Afrodisio Aguado, S.A.

Gonzalez del Campo, M. 1984. *Guayana y el Gobernador Centurion, 1766–1776.* Caracas: Academia Nacional de la Historia.

Gow, Peter. 1990. Aprendiendo a defenderse: La historia oral y el parentesco en las comunidades nativas del bajo Urubamba. *Amazonia Indigena* 16:10–16.

————. 1991. *Of Mixed Blood: Kinship and History in Peruvian Amazonia.* Oxford: Clarendon Press.

Bibliography

————. 1995. Land, People and Paper in Western Amazonia. In *The Anthropology of Landscape: Perspectives on Space and Place*. Erich Hirsch and Michael O'Hanlon, eds. Pp. 43–62. Oxford: Clarendon Press.

————. 2001. *An Amazonian Myth and Its History*. Oxford: Oxford University Press.

Graham, Laura R. 1995. *Performing Dreams: Discourses of Immortality among the Xavante of Central Brazil*. Austin: University of Texas Press.

Granada Television Ltd. 1969. The Trail of the Vanishing Voters. Transcripts on "World in Action" on Guyana Elections, 1968. Unpublished manuscript. Institute of Commonwealth Studies, London.

Gravina, Guido Ochoa, Carlos Alvarado, Yajaira Oballos, Jorge Pereyra, and Franklin Vargas. 1989. *Caracterizacion de Suelos de la Reserva Forestal de Ticoporo, Barinas*. Merida: Universidad de Los Andes.

Gregor, Thomas A. 1974. Publicity, Privacy, and Marriage. *Ethnology* 13:333–349.

Gumilla, José. 1944. *El Orinoco Ilustrado y Defendido*. Vols. 1–2. Bogotá: Biblioteca Popular de Cultura Colombiana, Editorial ABC.

Gupta, Akhil, and James Ferguson. 1997. Culture, Power, Place: Ethnography at the End of an Era. In *Culture, Power, Place: Explorations in Critical Anthropology*. A. Gupta and J. Ferguson, eds. Pp. 1–29. Durham NC: Duke University Press.

Guss, D. 1986. Keeping It Oral: A Yekuana Ethnology. *American Ethnologist* 13:413–429.

————. 1989. *To Weave and Sing: Art, Symbol, and Narrative in the South American Rain Forest*. Berkeley: University of California Press.

Harris, David. 1980. Tropical Savanna Environments: Definition, Distribution, Diversity and Development. In *Human Ecology in Savanna Environments.*, David Harris, ed. Pp. 3–27. New York: Academic Press.

Hart, Terese B., and John A. Hart. 1986. The Ecological Basis of Hunter-Gatherer Subsistence in African Rain Forests: The Mbuti of Eastern Zaire. *Human Ecology* 14:29–56.

Hayden, Brian. 1996. Feasting in Prehistoric and Traditional Societies. In *Food and the Status Quest: An Interdisciplinary Perspective*. Polly Wiessner and Wulf Schiefenhövel, eds. Pp. 87–125. Providence RI: Berghan Books.

Headland, Thomas N. 1987. The Wild Yam Question: How Well Could Independent Hunter-Gatherers Live in a Tropical Rain Forest Ecosystem? *Human Ecology* 15:463–491.

Heckenberger, Michael. 1996. War and Peace in the Shadow of Empire: Sociopolitical Change in the Upper Xingu of Southeastern Amazonia, AD 1400–2000. Ph.D. dissertation, University of Pittsburgh. Ann Arbor MI: University Microfilms.

————. 1998. Manioc Agriculture and Sedentism in Amazonia: The Upper Xingu Example. *Antiquity* 72:633–648.

Hendricks, Janet W. 1993. *To Drink of Death: The Narrative of a Shuar Warrior.* Tucson: University of Arizona Press.

Henfrey, Colin. 1965. *Through Indian Eyes: A Journey among the Indian Tribes of Guiana.* New York: Holt, Rinehart and Winston.

Henríquez, Manuel. 1994. *Amazonas: Apuntes y Crónicas.* Caracas: Ediciones de la Presidencia de la República.

Hilhouse, William. 1978[1825]. *Indian Notices; or, Sketches of the Habits, Characters, Languages, Superstitions, Soil, and Climate of the Several Nations.* New ed., with introduction and notes by Mary Noël Menezes. Georgetown, Guyana: National Commission for Research Materials on Guyana.

Hill, Jonathan D. 1984. Social Equality and Ritual Hierarchy: The Arawakan Wakuenay of Venezuela. *American Ethnologist* 11:528–544.

————. 1987. Wakuénai Ceremonial Exchange in the Venezuelan Northwest Amazon. *Journal of Latin American Lore* 13:183–224.

————. 1988. Introduction: Myth and History. In *Rethinking History and Myth: Indigenous South American Perspectives on the Past.* Jonathan D. Hill, ed. Pp. 1–18. Urbana: University of Illinois Press.

————. 1993. *Keepers of the Sacred Chants.* Tucson: University of Arizona Press.

————. 1996. Ethnogenesis in the Northwest Amazon: An Emerging Regional Picture. In *Power and Identity: Ethnogenesis in the Americas, 1492–1992.* Jonathan D. Hill, ed. Pp. 142–160. Iowa City: University of Iowa Press.

Hill, Jonathan D., and Robin M. Wright. 1988. Time, Narrative, and Ritual: Historical Interpretations from an Amazonian Society. In *Rethinking History and Myth: Indigenous South American Perspectives on the Past.* Jonathan D. Hill, ed. Pp. 78–105. Urbana: University of Illinois Press.

Hobsbawm, E. J. 1970. *Rebeldes Primitivos: Estudos sobre formas arcaicas de movimentos sociais nos séculos XIX e XX.* Rio de Janeiro: Zahar Editores.

————. 1976. *Bandidos.* Rio de Janeiro: Editora Forense-Universitária.

Holmberg, Allan R. 1985[1950]. *Nomads of the Long Bow: The Siriono of Eastern Bolivia.* Rev. ed. Prospect Heights IL: Waveland Press.

Hornborg, Alf. 1990. Highland and Lowland Conceptions of Social Space in South America: Some Ethnoarchaeological Affinities. *Folk* 32:61–92.

Howard, C. V. 2001. Wrought Identities: The Waiwai Expeditions in Search of the "Unseen Tribes" of Northern Amazonia. Ph.D. dissertation, Department of Anthropology, University of Chicago.

Hugh-Jones, C. 1979. *From the Milk River: Spatial and Temporal Processes in Northwest Amazonia.* Cambridge: Cambridge University Press.

Humboldt, A. 1985. *Viaje a las regiones equinocciales del Nuevo Continente.* Caracas: Monte Avila Editores.

Bibliography

Im Thurn, Everard F. 1883. *Among the Indians of Guiana*. London: Kegan Paul, Trench.

Instituto Nacional de Parques (INPARQUES). 1993. *Anteproyecto del Plan de Ordenamiento y Reglamento de Uso del Parque Nacional Duida-Marahuaka*.

Iribertegui, Ramón. 1987. *Amazonas, el Hombre y el Caucho*. Caracas: Vicariato Apostólico de Puerto Ayacucho.

Jackson, Jean E. 1994. Becoming Indians: The Politics of Tukanoan Ethnicity. In *Amazonian Indians from Prehistory to the Present: Anthropological Perspectives*. Anna C. Roosevelt, ed. Pp. 383–406. Tucson: University of Arizona Press.

Jagan, C. 1969. What Future Holds for Guyana. *Thunder: Quarterly Theoretical and Discussion Journal of the People's Progressive Party* (Georgetown, Guyana) 1(1):37–59.

Jimenez, Simeon. 1974. Algunas reflexiones sobre la lucha del Indígena Americano. *Uno y Multiple* 1:35–37.

———. 1995. Foreword. In *Indigenous Peoples and the Future of Amazonia: An Ecological Anthropology of an Endangered World*. L. E. Sponsel, ed. Arizona Studies in Human Ecology. Tucson: University of Arizona Press.

Jimenez, Simeon, and Abel Perozo, eds. 1994. *Esperando a Kuyujani: Tierras, Leyes y Autodemarcación. Encuentro de comunidades Ye'kuanas del Alto Orinoco*. Caracas: Asociacion Otro Futuro; Gaia; Insituto Venezolano de Investigaciones Científicas (IVIC).

Johnston, B. R., ed. 1994. *Who Pays the Price? The Socio-cultural Context of Environmental Crisis*. Washington DC: Island Press.

Keymis, Lawrence. 1596. *A Relation of a Second Voyage to Guiana*. London: Thomas Dawson.

Klein, W. H. A. 1974. *Antique Bottles in Surinam*. 2nd ed., number 13. Mededelingen: Stichting Surinaams Museum.

Koerner, Stephanie, and Rafael Gassón. 2001. Historical Archaeology and New Directions in Environmental Archaeology: Examples from Neolithic Scandinavia and Venezuela (AD 400–1400). In *Environmental Archaeology: Meaning and Purpose*. Alberella Umberto, ed. Pp. 177–210. Dordrecht, Netherlands: Kubler Academic.

Kuppe, R. 1997. The Indigenous People of Venezuela between Agrarian Law and Environmental Law. *Law and Anthropology* 9:244–257.

Langer, E., and R. Jackson, eds. 1995. *The New Latin American Mission History*. Lincoln: University of Nebraska Press.

LaRose, Jean, and Fergus MacKay. 1999. Our Land, Our Life, Our Culture: The Indigenous Movement in Guyana. *Cultural Survival Quarterly* 23(4):29–34.

Lathrap, Donald. 1970. *The Upper Amazon*. New York: Thames and Hudson.

Lederman, Rena. 1986. Changing Times in Mendi: Notes toward Writing Highland New Guinea History. *Ethnohistory* 33(1):1–30.

Lévi-Strauss, Claude. 1987a. *Mito y Significado*. Madrid: Alianza Editorial.

———. 1987b. *La Vía de las Máscaras*. México City: Siglo XXI Editores.

López-Borreguero, Ramón. 1886. *Los Indios Caribes*. Madrid: Imprenta de T. Fortanet.

Lucena Giraldo, M. 1991. *Laboratorio Tropical: La Expedición de Límites al Orinoco, 1750–1767*. Caracas: Monte Avila.

Luzardo, A. 1988. *Amazonas: El negocio de este mundo: Investigación Indigenista*. Caracas: Ediciones Centauro.

Magaña, Edmundo. 1983–84. La palabra, el silencio y la escritura: Notas sobre algunas tribus de la Guayana. *Revista Chilena de Antropología*, no. 12. Electronic document, http://www.uchile.cl/facultades/csociales/antropo/rch12–8.htm, accessed November 5, 2000.

Mandle, J. 1973. *The Plantation Economy: Population and Change in Guyana (1838–1960)*. Philadelphia: Temple University Press.

Mansutti, Alexander. 1993. Una Mirada al Futuro de los Indígenas de Guayana. *Boletin Antropológico* 29:16–31.

Marcus, George E., and Michael J. Fischer. 1986. *Anthropology as Cultural Critique: An Experimental Moment in the Human Sciences*. Chicago: University of Chicago Press.

Marx, K. 1964[1852]. *The Eighteenth Brumaire of Louis Bonaparte*. New York: International.

Matos dos Santos, Renildo. 1997. *Projecção de Orcamento do Serviço de Apoio de Santa Inês, para o Perído de Julho a Dezembro de 1997*. Ministério da Justiça, Fundação Nacional do Índio.

McCann, T., ed. 1972. *The Rupununi Development Company Limited: The Early History by Harry Everard Turner, O.B.E.* Georgetown.

Medina, Ernesto. 1980. Ecology of Tropical American Savannas: An Ecophysiological Approach. In *Human Ecology in Savanna Environments*. David Harris, ed. Pp. 297–319. New York: Academic Press.

Meggers, B. 1977. *Amazonia Man and Culture in a Counterfeit Paradise*. Chicago: Aldine.

Meirelles, Jose Carlos dos Reis, Jr. 1973. *Contato com os Guajás do Alto Rio Turiaçu*. Ministério da Justiça, Fundação Nacional do Índio.

Mignolo, Walter. 1995. *The Darker Side of Renaissance: Literacy, Territoriality, and Colonization*. Ann Arbor: University of Michigan Press.

Mintz, S. 1985. *Sweetness and Power: The Place of Sugar in Modern History*. New York: Penguin Books.

Morales Méndez, Filadelfo. 1979. Reconstrucción etnohistórica de los Kari'ña de los siglos XVI y XVII. Master's thesis, Caracas, Centro de Estudios Avanzados (CEA), Instituto Venezolano de Investígaciones Científicas IVIC.

———. 1990. *Los Hombres del Onoto y la Macana*. Caracas: Tropykos.

Morales Méndez, Filadelfo, and Nelly Arvelo-Jimenez. 1981. Hacia un Modelo de Estructura Social Caribe. *América Indígena* 41:603–626.

Moran, Emilio F. 1993. *Through Amazonian Eyes: The Human Ecology of Amazonian Populations*. Iowa City: University of Iowa Press.

Moreno, Maria del Carmen. 2001. Contrasting Lives and Shared Vision: William Brett and John Peter Bennet among the Lokono of Guyana. Paper presented at Indigenous Amazonia at the Millennium: Politics and Religion, New Orleans, January 11–14.

Morey, Nancy. 1975. *Ethnohistory of the Columbian and Venezuelan Llanos*. Salt Lake City: University of Utah, Department of Anthropology.

———. 1976. Ethnohistorical Evidence for Cultural Complexity in the Western Llanos of Venezuela and the Eastern Llanos of Colombia. *Antropologica* 45:41–69.

Morey, R. V. 1979. A Joyful Harvest of Souls: Disease and the Destruction of the Llanos Indians. *Antropológica* 52:77–108.

Morey, Robert, and Nancy Morey. 1975. Relaciones comerciales en el pasado en los llanos de Colombia y Venezuela. *Montalban* 4:533–563.

Moron, Guillarmo. 1970. *Historia de Venezuela*. 5th ed. Caracas: Italgráfica, S.R.L.

Mundy, Barbara E. 1996. *The Mapping of New Spain: Indigenous Cartography and the Maps of the Relaciones Geográficas*. Chicago: University of Chicago Press.

Murphy, Robert F. 1956. Matrilocality and Patrilineality in MundurucúSociety. *American Anthropologist* 56:414–434.

Neto, Carlos de Araújo Moreira. 1988. *Indios da Amazônia: De maioria a minoria (1750–1850)*. Petrópolis: Vozes.

Nimuendajú, Curt. 1948. The Guajá. In *The Handbook of South American Indians*, vol. 3. Julian Steward, ed. Pp. 135–136. Bureau of American Ethnology Bulletin, 143. Washington DC: Smithsonian Institution.

Nobre de Madeiro, Roberto Amãncio. 1988. *Relatório de Viagem*. Guajá: Ministério da Justiça, Fundação Nacional do Índio.

Nugent, Daniel. 1994. The Center at the Periphery: Civilization and Barbarism on the Northern Mexican Frontier. *Identities* 1(2–3):151–172.

Oakdale, S. 2001. History and Forgetting in an Indigenous Amazonian Community. *Ethnohistory* 48(3):381–402.

Obeyesekere, G. 1992. *The Apotheosis of Captain Cook: European Myth-making in the Pacific*. Princeton: Princeton University Press.

Oficina Central de Estadística e Informática (OCEI). 1994. *Censo Indígena de Venezuela 1992: Nomenclador de Asentamientos*, vol. 2. Caracas: Oficina Central de Estadística e Informática.

Oliver, José. 1989. The Archaeological, Linguistic and Ethnohistorical Evidence

Bibliography

for the Expansion of Arawakan into Northwestern Venezuela and Northeastern Colombia. Ph.D. dissertation, University of Illinois at Urbana-Champaign.

Painter, M., and W. H. Durham, eds. 1995. *The Social Causes of Environmental Destruction in Latin America: Linking Levels of Analysis.* Ann Arbor: University of Michigan Press.

Papadakis, Yiannis. 1998. Greek Cypriot Narratives of History and Collective Identity: Nationalism as a Contest Process. *American Ethnologist* 25(2):149–165.

Parise, Fiorello. 1987. Plano de Ação para Reestruturação da Frente de Atração Guajá e Programa Awa. February. Ministério da Justiça, Fundação Nacional do Índio.

Parise, Valeria. 1973a. *Exposição da Motivos.* Ministério da Justiça, Fundação Nacional do Índio.

————. 1973b. *Relatorio da Viagem ao Alto Rio Caru e Igarape da Fome para Verificar a Presença de Indios Guajá.* Ministério da Justiça, Fundação Nacional do Índio.

————. 1988. *Relatório Histórico dos Grupos Guajá Contatados e Sua Situação Atual.* Ministério da Justiça, Fundação Nacional do Índio.

Perera, M. A. 1995. El Desarrollo Sustentable. Base de Nuevos Males o Posibilidad Real de Crecimiento Etnoeconómico? In *Amazonas Modernidad en Tradición: Contribuciones al Desarrollo Sustentable en el Estado Amazonas.* A. Carrillo and M. A. Perera, eds. Pp. 9–42. Caracas: CAIAH-SADAAMAZONAS, GZT.

Pérez, Berta E. 1995. Versions and Images of Historical Landscape in Aripao, a Maroon Descendant Community in Southern Venezuela. *America Negra* 10:129–148.

————. 1997. Pantera Negra: An Ancestral Figure of the Aripaeños, Maroon Descendants in Southern Venezuela. *History and Anthropology* 10:219–240.

————. 1998. Pantera Negra: A Messianic Figure of Historical Resistance and Cultural Survival among Maroon Descendants in Southern Venezuela. In *Blackness in Latin America and the Caribbean: Social Dynamics and Cultural Transformations,* vol. 1. Norman E. Whitten Jr. and Arlene Torres, eds. Pp. 223–243. Bloomington: Indiana University Press.

————. 2000a. Introduction: Rethinking Venezuelan Anthropology. *Ethnohistory* 47:513–533.

————. 2000b. The Journey to Freedom: Maroon Forebears in Southern Venezuela. *Ethnohistory* 47:611–633.

Pérez, Berta E., and Perozo, Abel. 2000a. *Aripao y el Ethos Cimarron: La Hermeneutica Cultural del Mestizaje en Venezuela.* Unpublished manuscript.

————. 2000b. *Fictitious and Real Venezuelan Society: Prospects for Mestizaje and Pluricultural Democracy.* Unpublished manuscript.

Pratt, M. L. 1992. *Imperial Eyes: Travel Writing and Transculturation.* London: Routledge.

Price, Richard. 1973. Introduction. In *Maroon Societes.* New York: Anchor.

————. 1983. *First-Time: The Historical Vision of an Afro-American People.* Baltimore: John Hopkins University Press.

Ralegh, Walter. 1997. *The Discoverie of the Large, Rich and Bewtiful Empire of Guiana by Sir Walter Ralegh.* Neil Whitehead, ed. Exploring Travel series, 1. Manchester: Manchester University Press. American Exploration and Travel series, 71. Norman: University of Oklahoma Press.

Ramos, Alcida Rita. 1998. *Indigenism: Ethnic Politics in Brazil.* Madison: University of Wisconsin Press.

Rappaport, Roy A. 1984. *Pigs for the Ancestors: Ritual in the Ecology of a New Guinea People.* New Haven: Yale University Press.

Redmond, Elsa, Rafael Gassón, and Charles Spencer. 1999. A Macroregional View of Cycling Chiefdoms in the Western Venezuelan Llanos. In *Complex Polities in the Ancient Tropical World.* Elisabeth Bacus and Lisa Lucero, eds. Pp. 109–129. Archaeological Papers of the American Anthropological Association, 9. Arlington VA: American Anthropological Association.

Reichel-Dolmatoff, G. 1985. Cosmology as Ecological Analysis. *Man* 11:307–318.

Reiss, Arthur Cesar Ferreira. 1974. Economic History of the Brazilian Amazon. In *Man in the Amazon.* Charles Wigley, ed. Pp. 33–44. Gainesville: University Presses of Florida.

Rey Fajardo, José del, ed. 1966. *Documentos Jesuíticos Relativos a la Historia de la Compañía de Jesús en Venezuela.* Fuentes para la Historia Colonial de Venezuela. Caracas: Biblioteca de la Academia Nacional de la Historia.

————. 1971. *Aportes Jesuíticos a la Filologia Colonial Venezolana.* Caracas: Ministerio de Publicaciones, Departamento de Publicaciones.

————. 1974a. *Bibliografía de los Jesuitas en la Venezuela Colonial.* Caracas: Instituto de Investigaciones Históricas, Universidad Católica Andrés Bello.

————. 1974b. *Documentos Jesuíticos relativos a la Historia de la Compañía de Jesús en Venezuela II.* Caracas: Biblioteca de la Academia Nacional de la Historia.

————. 1988. Fuentes para el Estudio de las Misiones jesuíticas en Venezuela, 1625–1767. *Paramillo* 7:173–349.

Ridgewell, W. M. 1972. *The Forgotten Tribes of Guyana.* London: Tom Stacey.

Rival, L. 1998. *The Social Life of Trees.* Anthropological Perspectives on Tree Symbolism. Oxford: Berg.

Rivière, P. 1972. *The Forgotten Frontier: Ranchers of North Brazil.* New York: Holt, Rinehart and Winston.

————. 1995. *Absent-Minded Imperialism: Britain and the Expansion of Empire in Nineteenth-Century Brazil.* London: I.B. Tauris.

Rivero, Juan. 1956[1883]. *Historia de las Misiones de los Llanos de Casanare y los rios Orinoco y Meta.* Bogota: Editorial Argra.

Roe, Peter. 1982. *The Cosmic Zigote: Cosmology in the Amazon Basin.* New Brunswick, NJ: Rutgers University Press.

Rojas, Filintro Antonio. 1994. La Ciencia Kurripako: Origen del Miyaka o Principio [The Kurripako Indian science: The Miyaka or beginnings]. Unpublished manuscript.

Roosevelt, Anna C. 1987. Chiefdoms of the Amazon and Orinoco. In *Chiefdoms in the Americas.* Robert Drennan and Carlos A. Uribe, eds. Pp. 153–185. Lanham, MD: University Press of America.

————. 1991. *Moundbuilders of the Amazon: Geophysical Archaeology on Marajo Island, Brazil.* New York: Academic Press.

————. 1992. *The Excavations at Corozal: Stratigraphy and Ceramic Seriation.* New Haven: Yale University Press.

————. 1993. The Rise and Fall of the Amazon Chiefdoms. *L'Homme* 126(8): 255–284.

————, ed. 1994. *Amazonian Indians from Prehistory to the Present: Anthropological Perspectives.* Tucson: University of Arizona Press.

Roosevelt, A. C., M. Imazio, S. Maranca, and R. Johnson, R. 1991. Eight Millennium Pottery from a Prehistoric Shell Midden in the Brazilian Amazon. *Science* 254:1621–1624.

Roosevelt, A. C., M. Lima da Costa, C. Lopes Machado, et al. 1996. Paleoindian Cave Dwellers in the Amazon: The Peopling of the Americas. *Science* 272:373–384.

Sahlins, Marshall. 1978. Culture as Protein and Profit. *New York Review of Books* 25(18):45–53.

————. 1981. *Historical Metaphors and Mythical Realities: Structure in the Early History of the Sandwich Islands Kingdom.* Ann Arbor: University of Michigan Press.

————. 1985. *Islands of History.* Chicago: University of Chicago Press.

————. 1988. Cosmologies of Capitalism: The Trans-Pacific Sector of the World System. *Proceedings of the British Academy* 74:1–51.

————. 1992. The Economics of Develop-Man in the Pacific. *Anthropology and Aesthetics RES* 21(spring):12–25.

————. 1993. Goodbye to Tristes Tropes: Ethnography in the Context of Modern World History. *Journal of Modern History* 65:1–25.

————. 1995. *How Natives Think: About Captain Cook for Example.* Chicago: University of Chicago Press.

————. 1999. What Is Anthropological Enlightenment? Some Lessons of the Twentieth Century. *Annual Reviews of Anthropology* 28:i–xxiii.

————. 2000. *Culture in Practice: Selected Essays.* New York: Zone Books.

Saint Augustine. 1988. *Confessions,* vol. 2, book 10. William Watts, trans. Cambridge MA: Harvard University Press.

Sanday, Peggy Reeves. 1987. *El canibalismo como sistema cultural.* Barcelona: Editorial Lerna.

Sanders, A. 1972. Amerindians in Guyana: A Minority Group in a Multi-ethnic Society. *Caribbean Studies* 12(2):31–51.

Santos-Granero, Fernando. 1998. Writing History into the Landscape: Space, Myth, and Ritual in Contemporary Amazonia. *American Ethnologist* 25(2): 132–143.

Sarmiento, Guillermo. 1984. *The Ecology of Neotropical Savannas.* Cambridge: Harvard University Press.

Sarmiento, Guillermo, M. Monasterio, and J. Silva. 1971. Reconocimiento Ecologico de los Llanos Occidentales, part 1: Las Unidades Ecologicas Regionales. *Acta Cientifica Venezolana* 22:52–60.

Schomburgk, Richard. 1922–23. *Travels in British Guiana, 1840–1844,* vols. 1 and 2. Walter Edmund Roth, trans. Georgetown, British Guiana: Daily Chronicle Office.

Schomburgk, Robert H. 1903. Reports (1836–1839) to the Royal Geographical Society. In *Questions de la frontière entre la Guyane Britannique et le Brésil: Annexes au mémoire présenté par le gouvernement de sa Majesté Britannique,* vol. 3. London.

————. 1941. Journey from Fort San Joaquin, on the Río Branco, to Roraima, and thence by the Rivers Parima and Merevari to Esmeralda, on the Orinoco in 1938–39. *Royal Geographical Society Journal* 10:191–247.

Schwerin, K. H. 1966. *Oil and Steel: Process of Karinya Cultural Change in Response to Industrial Development.* Los Angeles: University of California, Latin American Center.

Seeger, Anthony. 1981. *Nature and Society in Central Brazil: The Suya Indians of Mato Grosso.* Cambridge: Harvard University Press.

Shapiro, Michael J. 1997. *Violent Cartographies: Mapping Cultures of War.* Minneapolis: University of Minnesota Press.

Siegel, Peter. 1996. Ideology and Culture Change in Prehistoric Puerto Rico: A View from the Community. *Journal of Field Archaeology* 23:313–333.

Silva Monterrey, Nalúa. 1997. La Percepción Ye'kwana del Entorno Natural. *Scientia Guaianae: Ecología de la Cuenca del Río Caura, Venezuela.* Estudios Especiales 2(7):65–84.

Smith, C., H. Burke, and G. K. Ward. 2000. Globalization and Indigenous Peoples: Threat or Empowerment? In *Indigenous Cultures in an Intercon-*

nected World. C. Smith and G. K. Ward, eds. Vancouver: University of British Columbia Press.

Solbrig, O. T. 1993. Ecological Constraints to Savanna Land Use. In *The World's Savannas: Economic Driving Forces, Ecological Constraints and Policy Options for Sustainable Land Use.* M. D. Young and O. T. Solbrig, eds. Pp. 21–47. UNESCO, Man and the Biosphere series. London: Butler and Tanner.

Spencer, Charles. 1998. Investigating the Development of Venezuelan Chiefdoms. In *Chiefdoms and Chieftaincy in the Americas.* Elsa Redmond, ed. Pp. 104–137. Gainesville: University Press of Florida.

Spencer, Charles, and Elsa Redmond. 1992. Prehispanic Chiefdoms of the Western Venezuelan Llanos. *World Archaeology* 24(1):134–157.

Spencer, Charles, Elsa Redmond, and M. Rinaldi. 1994. Drained Fields at La Tigra, Venezuelan Llanos: A Regional Perspective. *Latin American Antiquity.* 5(2):119–143.

Steward, Julian. 1949. South American Cultures: An Interpretative Summary. In *Handbook of South American Indians*, vol. 5. Julian Steward, ed. Pp. 669–772. Bureau of American Ethnology Bulletin, 149. Washington DC: Smithsonian Institution.

Strathern, Andrew. 1982. Witchcraft, Greed, Cannibalism and Death. In *Death and the Regeneration of Life.* Maurice Bloch and Jonathan Parry, eds. Pp. 111–133. Cambridge: Cambridge University Press.

Tarble, Kay. 1985. Un nuevo modelo de expansión Caribe para la época prehispánica. *Antropológica* 64–65: 45–81.

Tate, C. H., and C. B. Hitchcock. 1930. The Cerro Duida Region of Venezuela. *American Geographical Review* 20(1):31–52.

Taussig, Michael. 1987. *Shamanism, Colonialism and the Wild Man: A Study in Terror and Healing.* Chicago: University of Chicago Press.

———. 1997. *The Magic of the State.* New York: Routledge.

Tavera Acosta, B. 1954. *Anales de Guayana.* Caracas: Gráficas Armitano, C.A.

Taylor, Anne Christine. 1993. Remembering to Forget: Identity, Mourning and Memory among the Jivaro. *Man:* 28:653–678.

Thomas, D. J. 1972. The Indigenous Trade System of Southeast Estado Bolivar, Venezuela. *Antropológica* 33:3–37.

———. 1973. Pemon Demography, Kinship and Trade. Ph.D dissertation, University of Michigan. Ann Arbor MI: University Microfilms.

Thomas, Keith. 1983. *Man and the Natural World: Changing Attitudes in England, 1500–1800.* Harmondsworth UK: Penguin Books.

Thomas, N. 1991. *Entangled Objects: Exchange, Material Culture, and Colonialism in the Pacific.* Cambridge: Harvard University Press.

Turner, Terence. 1977. Cosmetics: The Language of Bodily Adornment. In

Conformity and Conflict: Readings in Cultural Anthropology. J. P. Spradley and D. W. McCurdy, eds. Pp. 162–171. Boston: Little, Brown.

———. 1984. Dual Opposition, Hierarchy and Value: Moiety Structure and Symbolic Polarity in Central Brazil and Elsewhere. In *Differences, valeurs, hiérarchie: Textes offertes à Louis Dumont et reunis par Jean-Claude Galey.* J. C. Galey, ed. Pp. 335–370. París: Editions de l'Ecole des Hautes Etudes en Sciences Sociales.

———. 1987. From Cosmology to Ideology: Resistance, Adaptation and Social Consciousness among the Kayapó. Paper presented at the Symposium Pesquisas Recentes em Etnologia e Historia Indigena da Amazonia, Belem do Para, Brazil.

———. 1988. History, Myth, and Social Consciousness among the Kayapó of Central Brazil. In *Rethinking History and Myth: Indigenous South American Perspectives on the Past.* Jonathan Hill, ed. Pp. 195–213. Urbana: University of Illinois Press.

———. 1991. Representing, Resisting, Rethinking. Historical Transformations of Kayapó Culture and Anthropological Consciousness. In *Colonial Situations: Essays on the Contextualization of Ethnographic Knowledge.* J. G. W. Stocking, ed. Pp. 285–313. Madison: University of Wisconsin Press.

———. 1995. An Indigenous People's Struggle for Socially Equitable and Ecologically Sustainable Production: The Kayapó Revolt against Extractivism. *Journal of Latin American Anthropology* 1(1):98–120.

———. In press. The Sacred as Alienated Social Consciousness: Ritual and Cosmology among the Kayapo. In *Treatise on the Anthropology of the Sacred,* vol. 6: *Le Religioni Indigine Delle Americhe.* L. E. Sullivan, ed. Milan: Editoriale Jaca.

———. N.d. Social Complexity and Recursive Hierarchy in Indigenous South American Societies. *Time and Cosmology in the Andes.* G. Urton and D. Poole, eds. Unpublished manuscript.

Urban, Greg. 1996. *Metaphysical Community: The Interplay of the Senses and the Intellect.* Austin: University of Texas Press.

Urbina, Luis. 1984. Some Aspects of the Pemon System of Social Relationships. *Antropológica* 59–62: 183–198.

Urbina, Luis, and Heinen Dieter. 1982. Ecología, organización social y distribución especial: Estudio de caso de dos poblaciones indígenas: Pemón y Warao. *Antropológica* 57:25–54.

Vall de la Ville, Keila. 1998. El Caño San Miguel: El recuerdo de los comienzos. Undergraduate thesis, Caracas, Escuela de Antropología-FACES, Universidad Central de Venezuela.

Vidal, Silvia M. 1987. El proceso migratorio prehispánico de los Piapoco. Hipótesis y evidencias. Master's thesis, Caracas, Centro de Estudios Avanzados (CEA), Instituto Venezolano de Investigaciones Científicas (IVIC).

———. 1993. Reconstrucción de los procesos de etnogénesis y de reproducción social entre los Baré de Río Negro (Siglos XVI–XVIII). Ph.D. dissertation, Caracas, CEA, IVIC.

———. 1999. Amerindian Groups of Northwestern Amazonia: Their Regional System of Political Religious Hierarchies. *Anthropos* 94(2): 515–528.

———. 2000a. Kuwé Duwákalumi: The Arawak Sacred Routes of Migration, Trade, and Resistance. *Ethnohistory* 47(3):221–280.

———. 2000b. Secret Religious Cults and Political Leadership: Multiethnic Confederacies from Northwestern Amazonia. Paper presented at the Wenner-Gren Foundation and Smithsonian Tropical Research Institute Conference, Arawakan Histories: Rethinking Culture Area and Language Family in Amazonia, Panama City, May.

Vidal, Silvia, and Edilto Bernabé. 1996. Informe Confidencial sobre la Minería Ilegal en el Río Guainía, estado Amazonas. Confidential information for the Venezuelan authorities. Unpublished manuscript.

Vidal, Silvia, and Neil L. Whitehead. In press. Dark Shamans and the Shamanic State: Sorcery and Witchcraft as Political Process in Guyana and the Venezuelan Amazon. In *Darkness and Secrecy: The Anthropology of Assault Sorcery and Witchcraft in Amazonia.* Neil L. Whitehead and Robin Wright, eds. Durham NC: Duke University Press.

Vidal, Silvia M., and Alberta Zucchi. 2000. Los Caminos del Kúwai: Evidencias del Conocimiento Geopolítico, de las Expansiones y Migraciones de los grupos Arawacos. In *Caminos Precolombinos: Las vías, los ingenieros y los viajeros.* Leonor Herrera and Marianne Cardale de Schrimpf, eds. Bogotá: Instituto Colombiano de Antropología.

Vila, Pablo. 1960. *Geografía de Venezuela.* Caracas: Ministerio de Educación.

Viveiros de Castro, Eduardo. 1992. *From the Enemy's Point of View: Humanity and Divinity in Amazonian Society.* Catherine V. Howard, trans. Chicago: University of Chicago Press.

———. 1996. Images of Nature and Society in Amazonian Ethnology. *Annual Review of Anthropology* 25:179–200.

———. 1998. Cosmological Deixis and Amerindian Perspectivism. *Journal of the Royal Anthropological Institute* 43:469–488.

Waterton, Charles. 1984[1825]. *Wanderings in South America, the North-West of the United States and the Antilles, in the years 1812, 1816, 1820 & 1824.* London: Century.

Waugh, Evelyn. 1987[19]. *Ninety-Two Days: A Journey in Guiana and Brazil.* Harmondsworth UK: Penguin Books.

Wearing, I. 1972. Guyana: Present Political Situation. In *Guyana: A Composite*

Monograph. B. Irving, ed. Pp. 32–39. Hato Rey, Puerto Rico: Interamerican University Press.

Weinstein, Barbara. 1983. *The Amazon Rubber Boom, 1850–1920.* Stanford: Stanford University Press.

Whitehead, Neil L. 1988. *Lords of the Tiger Spirit: A History of the Caribs in Colonial Venezuela and Guyana, 1498–1820.* Providence RI: Foris.

———. 1993. Ethnic Transformations and Historical Discontinuity in Native Amazonia and Guyana, 1500–1900. *L'Homme* 33(2–4):285–305.

———. 1994. The Ancient Amerindian Polities of the Amazon, the Orinoco, and the Atlantic Coast: A Preliminary Analysis of Their Passage from Antiquity to Extinction. In *Amazonian Indians from Prehistory to the Present.* Anna C. Roosevelt, ed. Pp. 33–53. Tucson: University of Arizona Press.

———. 1995. The Historical Anthropology of Text: The Interpretation of Ralegh's Discoverie of Guiana. *Current Anthropology* 36:53–74.

———. 1996. Ethnogenesis and Ethnocide in the European Occupation of Native Surinam, 1499–1681. *History, Power, and Identity: Ethnogenesis in the Americas, 1492–1992.* Jonathan D. Hill, ed. Pp. 20–35. Iowa City: University of Iowa Press.

———. 1997. Introduction. In *The Discoverie of the Large, Rich and Bewtiful Empyre of Guiana by Sir Walter Ralegh.* Neil Whitehead, ed. Pp. 1–117. Exploring Travel series, 1. Manchester: Manchester University Press. American Exploration and Travel series, 71, Norman: Oklahoma University Press.

———. 1998. Indigenous Cartography in Lowland South America and the Caribbean. In *The History of Cartography: Cartography in the Traditional African, American, Arctic, Australian, and Pacific Societies*, vol. 2. D. Woodward and G. M. Lewis, eds. Pp. 301–326. Chicago: University of Chicago Press.

———. 2000. Hans Staden and the Cultural Politics of Cannibalism. *Hispanic American Historical Review* 80(4):41–71.

———. 2001. Kanaimà: Shamanism and Ritual Death in the Pakaraima Mountains, Guyana. In *Beyond the Visible and the Material.* L. Rival and N. L. Whitehead, eds. Oxford: Oxford University Press.

———. 2002. *Dark Shamans: Kanaimà and the Poetics of Violent Death.* Durham NC: Duke University Press.

Whitten, Norman E., Jr., and Rachel Corr. 1996. Las Imágenes de lo Negro en Mitos, Discursos y Rituales Indigenas. Paper presented at the 49th Congreso Internacional de Americanistas, Pontificia Universidad Católica del Ecuador, Quito, Ecuador, July 7–11.

Wickham, Henry, and Jules Crevaux. 1988. *El Orinoco en dos direcciones.* Caracas: Fundación Cultural Orinoco.

Wilbert, Johannes. 1972. *Survivors of Eldorado: Four Indian Cultures of South America.* New York: Praeger.

Bibliography

————. 1981. Warao Cosmology and Yekuana Roundhouse Symbolism. *Journal of Latin American Lore* 7:37–72.

Wolf, E. R. 1982. *Europe and the People without History.* Berkeley: University of California Press.

Wright, Robin M. 1993. Pursuing the Spirit: Semantic Construction in Hohodene Karidzamai Chants for Initiation. *Amerindia* 18:1–40.

————. 1998. *For Those Unborn: Cosmos, Self, and History in Baniwa Religion.* Austin: University of Texas Press.

Wright, Robin M., and Jonathan D. Hill. 1986. History, Ritual, and Myth: Nineteenth Century Millenarian Movements in Northwest Amazonia. *Ethnohistory* 33:31–54.

Zucchi, Alberta. 2000. The Expansion of Northern Arawakan Groups: Old Models and New Evidences. Paper presented at the Wenner-Gren Foundation and Smithsonian Tropical Research Institute Conference, Arawakan Histories: Rethinking Culture Area and Language Family in Amazonia, Panama City, May.

Contributors

Loretta Cormier received her Ph.D. from Tulane University in 2000 and is Assistant Professor of Anthropology at the University of Alabama at Birmingham. Her research interests and activities are primarily in the area of ecological anthropology. She is currently completing a manuscript on the role of monkeys in the culture of the Guajá of eastern Amazonia.

Nádia Farage is Lecturer in the Department of Anthropology at the University of Campinas, Brazil. She is author of *As Muralhas dos Sertões: Os povos indígenas no rio Branco e a colonização* and other articles on Wapishana history and ethnography.

Rafael Angel Gassón Pacheco is a research associate at the Departamento de Antropología, Instituto Venezolano de Investigaciones Científicas (IVIC), Caracas. From 1995 to 1998 he was Curator of Archaeology at the Museo de Ciencias, Caracas. He obtained the title of Anthropologist (magna cum laude) from the Universidad Central de Venezuela in 1988 and obtained his Ph.D. degree from the University of Pittsburgh in 1998. His research interests include lowland South American archaeology and cultural ecology and the history of archaeology in Latin America. His recent works include articles in *Ethnohistory*, *Antropológica*, and the publications series of the American Anthropological Association.

Domingo A. Medina is a project and research assistant for Otro Futuro, a Venezuelan NGO supporting the De'kuana of the Alto Orinoco in their initiatives for land demarcation, economic development, and biodiversity conservation. He has a background in natural resource management, community development, and tourism impacts, with extensive fieldwork experience among the Pemon and De'kuana of Venezuelan Guayana. His research interests are population dynamics of indigenous peoples and environmental change specifically as it relates to the impacts of market integration (e.g., tourism and mining) on the household ecology and its environmental consequences. Recently he coordinated the De'kuana Atlas and Archive Project and contributed to the mapping of the De'kuana territory and the writing of a De'kuana atlas.

Berta Elena Pérez received her bachelor's degree in Anthropology and Art History in 1980 from Hamline University in St. Paul, Minnesota, and her M.A.

(1982) and Ph.D. (1990) in Anthropology from the University of Minnesota in Minneapolis. She has taught at Hamline University and the Minneapolis College of Art and Design. She has been working in the Departamento de Antropologia at the Instituto Venezolano de Investigaciones Científicas since 1992 and is currently chair. Her research interests include processes of ethnogenesis and sociocultural reproduction, interethnic relations, resistance, and historico-cultural landscapes among Afro-Venezuelan communities. She has published extensively on these topics in both national and international journals and in edited volumes.

Mary Riley is Assistant Professor and Director of the Urban Studies Program at Calumet College of St. Joseph in Whiting, Indiana. Currently she is working on a monograph of the Makushi Amerindians of the North Rupununi Savannahs, Guyana, based on her dissertation research.

Franz Scaramelli is a Ph.D. candidate in the Department of Anthropology, University of Chicago, and is currently working on his dissertation on the exchange of foreign manufactures among the indigenous population of the Middle Orinoco in Venezuela. His publications and research interests include the archaeology, history, and ethnography of northern South America, with emphasis on the tropical lowlands of the Orinoco, where he has a particular interest in the late precontact, colonial, and republican periods. Broader research concerns include the archaeology and historical anthropology of colonialism, the role of material culture in contact situations, global capitalism, heritage and nationalism, ethnic movements, representations of the past, material culture and memories of the past, and the comparative analysis of colonialism, consumption, and identity.

Kay Tarble is a Ph.D. candidate in the Department of Anthropology, University of Chicago, and has taught in the Escuela de Antropología, Universidad Central de Venezuela, Caracas, since 1985. Her current research and publications center on postcontact transformations in the indigenous societies of the Orinoco as manifested in the ceramic record. Research interests include contextual analysis of material culture, stylistic analysis of ceramics and rock art, time-space relations, and the construction of cultural space.

Silvia Margarita Vidal Ontivero did her undergraduate studies in Anthropology at the Universidad Central de Venezuela (1971–76), and her M.A. (1987) and doctoral (1994) studies at the Instituto Venezolano de Investigaciones Científicas. She has been doing fieldwork among the Arawak-speaking groups of Venezuela, Brazil, and Colombia since 1973, focusing her research on the sociocultural, political, economic, religious, symbolic, and historical characteristics of the Arawakan peoples, as well as their past and present migratory patterns, sociopolitical formations and identities, oral traditions, and intercultural-bilingual education projects.

Neil L. Whitehead is Professor of Anthropology at the University of Wisconsin-Madison and Editor of the journal *Ethnohistory*. He is author of numerous works on the native peoples of South America, and his most recent publications include a coedited volume on the anthropology of Amazonia, *Beyond the Visible and the Material*, and an ethnography of assault sorcery among the Patamuna, *Dark Shamans: Kanaimà and the Poetics of Violent Death*.

Index